The
Race
Within

The Race Within

Passion, Courage, and Sacrifice at the Ultraman Triathlon

Jim Gourley

TRIUMPH
B O O K S

This book is available in quantity at special discounts for your group or organization. For further information, contact:

Triumph Books LLC
814 North Franklin Street
Chicago, Illinois 60610
(312) 337-0747
www.triumphbooks.com

Printed in U.S.A.
ISBN: 978-1-62937-021-7
Design by Patricia Frey
Photos courtesy of the author unless otherwise indicated

Contents

Foreword

I don't think one can race Ultraman and not emerge a changed person. Taking place in the home of the most historic Ironman event, Ultraman is at once a throwback to the golden days of Ironman and a new frontier in terms of pushing the limits of the human body through an ultra-distance triathlon stage race. It was for both of these reasons that I was drawn to this three-day, 320-mile challenge, and for these and more that I fell in love with the experience.

During my rookie year in 2010, there were moments—no, hours—during which I was reduced to a state I had never before encountered in competition. Never before had I faced the challenge of hours of racing ahead of me when I was too tired to even extend my arm to grab the hydration and fuel on offer. Never before had I been expected to start a 52.4-mile foot race after a night when my body hurt so badly just to lie on a mattress that sleeping was out of the question. Yet somehow I made it through—I got to the finish line and even rose to the challenge when the race turned into a 10k "sprint finish." I left having learned that I could push far past where I had previously been, both mentally and physically, yet hungry to return with a more bulletproof arsenal.

While triathlon is usually an individual sport, I learned during my first go in 2010 that one of the most unique benefits of the Ultraman experience is the team or family element—*ohana*, they call it. I think because Ultraman is a no-frills, 320-mile test against oneself, it attracts a very special group of people; we go to Kona and meet others like ourselves when we may not encounter these kind of people very often in our daily lives.

I once heard a saying about what motivates endurance triathlon athletes: "If you have to ask *why*, you will never know." In Kona we find 35 others who would never ask us *why*—people like Mike Rouse, who celebrates every birthday by running his age in miles (this year is 62), and others like Gary

Wang, for whom his annual pilgrimage to Kona is his "time to meditate." They get it. We have an instant bond that intensifies with each day of shared suffering during the race.

What I did not anticipate was what an incredible bond the experience would create between my crew and me. It is a strange and somewhat uncomfortable feeling to be able to essentially call out orders and have a team of people there to meet them for more than three straight days—but in Ultraman this team, the crew, becomes one's lifeline. I am now incredibly proud and honored to say that I have an Ultraman World Championship title to my name, but am well aware that without my amazing crew, this would not have been possible. And what I have now that is actually even more valuable that any trophy is the incomparable bond with my Ultraman ohana: Amy, Michael, Maik, Ian, Dave, and Marilyn. Every time I travel those island roads now, I think of these people and how grateful I am for their friendship. I am still overwhelmed by their team effort in helping make my dream a reality.

—Hillary Biscay

Hillary Biscay is an Ultraman World Champion and the most prolific Iron-distance competitor on the professional women's racing circuit, having completed more than 60 Ironman triathlons.

Introduction

"Ambition leads me not only farther than any other man has been before me, but as far as I think it possible for man to go."

—Captain James Cook

THERE ARE ALL KINDS OF ENDURANCE RACES. There are marathons, duathlons, biathlons, triathlons, aquathlons, and adventure races. You can swim, bike, run, snowshoe, crawl through mud pits, and even flee from people dressed as zombies. There are 5k runs, traditional 51.5 km Olympic triathlons, the famous 140.6-mile Ironman, and cycling races such as the Tour de France that span thousands of miles. Just to complete many of these races is considered an accomplishment earned through months or even years of dedicated training.

Athletes at the elite level establish the ceiling of human performance. The fruits of their labors range from the private and intrinsic to a relative amount of fame and fortune. Yet the inordinate amount of time and suffering spent in training makes one wonder if the gain is indeed worth the pain. From first-time marathoners to Ironman World Champions, the question comes up over and again: *Why do you do this?* What goals compel these people to suffer so mightily, and what does it satisfy within them once they've reached it? We view a moth's attraction to flame as an evolutionary defect. But in a music video built around an against-all-odds sports story, country singer Garth Brooks insisted that "life is not tried, it is merely survived / if you're standing outside the fire." Self-destructive as the journey may be, the destination is somehow worth the risk.

Reaching the summit fails to quell the stirring within. Every two-time champion is another testament to the notion that once just isn't enough. Finish lines may be the greatest snipe hunt in human history; no matter how many some athletes cross, they can never truly feel that they're finished. There can be no end to the running if the running is an end unto itself. Expressing wanderlust through the pursuit of arbitrarily placed gateways is simply part of who we are. Maybe that's why we refer to ourselves as the human *race*.

There is no better place to see these principles in motion than in a category of events known as ultra endurance. In the last decade these races have grown in popularity among entrants and captured the imagination of the greater public. Our interest is driven by an assumption that the athletes' astonishing physical accomplishments must be equaled either by some profound philosophy or insanity. Beyond their extraordinary endurance, they have the discipline to train for countless hours and the determination to push their bodies far beyond what is natural, sometimes to the point of permanently damaging themselves. So if a 5k or an Ironman just isn't enough, what waits for them at the end of a 100-mile run or a 3,000-mile nonstop bike race? What do they know that we don't? What are they getting out of life that we're missing?

It's not money. More often than not there are no prizes for the winners. The conventional wisdom, developed from centuries of participation in professional leagues and Olympic competition, says that money isn't just the fuel that kindles interest in a sport, it's the essential nutrient for survival. Without it, leagues can't resource events and athletes can't dedicate the necessary time to hone their skills to a higher level. Potential that goes untapped for too long grows stagnant. The fans get bored, the stadiums go empty, the competitors fade away, and the sport dies on the vine. Yet ultra endurance sports defy that convention. With very little material compensation for their efforts, the athletes keep getting faster and go to ever-greater distances. Likewise, organizers have kept the races alive and growing on very narrow margins, often operating in the red.

Nor is it fame. Before Dean Karnazes penned his autobiographical account *Ultramarathon Man*, there was no such thing as an "ultra endurance celebrity," and the most prominent ultra races didn't always fill up with entrants. Today, even the most prolific ultra endurance competitors are largely anonymous and the races remain small. Very few people get to compete on a level that pays the bills, and they readily admit it has more to do with luck than skill or success. Therein lies the foundation of ultra's mystique: just about everyone who does it trains as hard as a professional athlete, despite there being virtually no prospect of doing it on a professional basis. It's a huge investment with no tangible return. This aspect leads to a unique purity in ultra racing. More than any other sport in the world, the ultra endurance crowd is seeking something beyond popular comprehension—and they are literally going further than anyone else to find it.

Still, what "it" is remains elusive. Many race to test themselves against the courses. A few play to win. Some do it to quiet the voices in their heads, others to obey them. Everyone has their own set of reasons for going to these races, but the one reason they all have in common is to strive toward that finish line together. Though they can't articulate it, they have an unmistakable sense that there is a goodness in these events that you can't get anywhere else.

Outside efforts to explain it are as comically lacking in context as Andy Griffith describing a football game. The problem is one of perspective. Our basis of comparison is the lowest common denominator of mainstream sports with neatly groomed ballfields and oval tracks designed by computers. They're marketed to the masses and prepackaged by your cable provider for easy digestion in high-definition. They're familiar to all, easy to comprehend, and accessible by a 15-minute commute to a well-worn field or park. To play or watch them doesn't require much effort or imagination—the things sports are supposed to be all about.

Every ultra-distance athlete has played those sports. And they've found them lacking nothing. The irony is that sometimes a little nothing is exactly what one needs. Austerity and solitude offer a unique kind of freedom. There is a cleansing virtue to be found in suffering. You're not going to find those things at a gym that has its own smoothie bar. Just like professional baseball and football, the traditional endurance races have been taken over by corporations. They're franchised like fast-food joints and operated like circuses. So those who crave the unmolested authenticity of pure racing do what they've always done: move further out to the fringe. Is the Boston Marathon too crowded for you? Try the Badwater Ultramarathon. Tired of seeing people use drugs in your local amateur cycling league? Sign up for the Race Across America. Does Ironman just feel like a bunch of yuppies trying to get a badge they can stick over their midlife crisis? Maybe you're looking for the Ultraman triathlon.

Ultraman is much more than a demonstration of human endurance. It is a demonstration of human being. Seeing the event and the people who put it on is a shining example of what sport should be. It's about what really matters in sport, and how it relates to what really matters in life. Ultraman answers that essential question of why people do this. Remarkably, the people who best demonstrate it aren't the athletes but the people who put in an equal number of miles and hours to make the event happen.

Ultraman and other races of its ilk have survived more than three decades without live television coverage, major sponsorships, or any of the other things contemporary society deems necessary for the success of sport. Instead, they've flourished thanks to the organizers and volunteers who dedicate an inordinate amount of their personal time and money to organizing events that they neither profit from nor participate in. They do it simply because it's their passion.

It's a strong indicator that what society has learned about sport is wrong. Perhaps that's why, after surviving on the fringe for so long, ultra races are experiencing an exponential surge in participation and media attention. More and more athletes grow weary of the cookie-cutter race experience and begin looking for a flame hot and bright enough to reignite that instinctual, mothlike attraction to sports. Some dance around the flame; others get too close and are consumed by the fire. But each path and its outcome explains something about their relationship with ultra endurance and, by association, humanity's relationship with sports.

That is the truly important message of this story, and it is especially relevant today. Sports journalists and commentators frequently question the value of sports in the wake of each scandal. They opine that sports are teaching our children that winning is the only thing that matters and that cheating is an acceptable way of getting what you want. Of course there's no *I* in "team"— because *I come first*, many think. But if that is what sports have become, and to play is to be human, then the condition of sports is nothing more than a reflection of the human condition. If our sports fail us, it can only be because we have failed them. If society has learned the wrong lessons about what makes a sport successful, the right ones are to be found in Ultraman.

chapter one

Wisdom, Like Car Keys

"Even when I'm old and grey, I won't be able to play it, but I'll still love the game."

—Michael Jordan

DECEMBER 1, 2013. When it was over, the first thing he did was call his mom and kids. Even in defeat, he looked every bit as invincible as he had a year earlier. The crystal blue eyes still had that sparkle. The easy, confident smile hadn't dimmed in the slightest. Lean, bronze, handsome—he looked every bit the sports legend. The only place he wasn't a champion was on paper. And sitting there in his presence, paper didn't seem to count for anything.

This was the journey's end for him. He'd said as much before he started this time. There'd be no comeback, but it was hard to imagine this place without him. It was just as difficult to imagine him without this place. For 11 years he'd raced here. The people who made this happen were like family to him. Like few other things in life, it was obvious that he loved being here. What would it be like for him this time next year, when everyone would be here and he wouldn't? Could he be happy? The look on his face said yes. I had to know. So I asked him straight out: "What's the secret to happiness?"

What he told me sounded like something off one of overpriced daily Zen books on the counter at Starbucks. But it was as genuine as you could get—an absolute truth distilled to its fundamental essence over years in the lava fields of Hawaii. It was so pure and potent that it brought clarity to everything all at once. After thousands of miles and scores of interviews, the answer had been here all along. I could have saved myself the trouble if only

I'd started under this picnic shelter beside the parking lot at the end of the world.

And then I realized that, no, that wasn't the case at all. Like your car keys, the truth is always found in the last place you look. It waits for you until you're ready to find it. And invariably you're never ready to look there until you've gone everywhere else first. It wasn't that fate chose this man, in this time and place, to reveal the truth to me. Those thousands of miles and scores of people weren't a search for truth. They were a journey to a place, both literally and figuratively, where I could finally let the truth find me. Maybe that's what it had been for him, too.

Maybe that's what sports are for all of us.

chapter two

The Parking Lot at the End of the World

"It is not up to me whether I win or lose. Ultimately this might not be my day. And it is that philosophy toward sports, something that I really truly live by. I am emotional. I want to win. I am hungry. I am a competitor. I have that fire. But deep down, I truly enjoy the art of competing so much more than the result."

—Apollo Ohno

NOVEMBER 25, 2012. It doesn't even look like anyone is supposed to be here. Right after you pass the aquatic center and the neatly manicured soccer fields along the Kuakini Highway, there's a chain-link fence topped with barbed wire, a mobile home with graffiti on it being used for some sort of construction business, and some storage sheds with heavy-duty pickup trucks parked in front of them. Keep going straight past the small orange cones warning you not to enter, and the asphalt eventually dissipates into gravel and brush. Turn right and it puts you on Makala Boulevard back to the Queen K Highway. Turn left and it looks like you've found free parking at the end of the world.

A relatively new two-lane swath of asphalt has been laid over the cracked, graying layer sprawling endlessly toward the horizon like a freshly dried flow of *pahoehoe* over the ancient lava fields. But up ahead on the left is a tiny stretch of black sand beach with neatly spaced palm trees surrounding the covered picnic areas and public showers of the Old Kona Airport State Recreation Area. You'd never find it unless you had come looking for it, and once you get there it's not much to look at. Truth be told, this must be the

3

most unscenic place in all of Hawaii: a discarded manmade construct amid a paradise of natural wonders. But now, in the heat of the afternoon, there are 30 people who are in fact seeking this exact spot. They've spent three days and an extraordinary amount of effort getting here. In their eyes, there's little difference between this site and the pearly gates. Their patron saint is even here waiting on them.

The tables at one of the sheltered picnic sites are filled with giant platters of food, tended by a catering service. People are milling between it and a 20' x 20' canopy tent with speakers underneath blaring a mix of rock and '80s dance beats. Yet on the whole it's a quiet setting. You'd almost mistake it for a family reunion—and more than one person there would tell you that it sort of is—except for the length of AstroTurf flanked by international flags and a metal archway at the end with a giant banner overhead reading ULTRAMAN WORLD CHAMPIONSHIPS.

Here, in the parking lot at the end of the world, one of the most phenomenal athletes on the planet is about to win one of the most extreme endurance competitions ever created. There's no prize money. There's not even a trophy for first place. There are no television cameras. No newspaper reporters. There is no stadium filled with adoring fans. Coming here and competing cost him at least $10,000. After swimming 6.2 miles, cycling 261.4 miles, and running 52.4 miles, he gets a Hawaiian lei and a finisher's plaque that looks exactly the same as the one they'll give to the last-place finisher. Right now, before it all starts, what he's thinking about is making it to that finish line so he can get a hug. The kind only a patron saint can give you.

After seven hours of running through the stifling heat and jarring winds, he makes that last, lonely turn, onto the runway to nowhere. His lean bronze figure glides over the surface of the earth, his feet buoyed by the shimmering convection currents roiling along the ground. Striding confidently across the wide, paved area, Alexandre Ribeiro makes the final push to the finish line. Followed by the two men who have supported his efforts during the last 72 hours, he carries the Brazilian flag through the archway and meets Jane Bockus. She drapes a lei around his neck and then gives him his hug as the crowd cheers.

The legs that had only moments before looked invincible against the length of concrete finally surrender to the pain he's ignored the last three days. His knees begin to wobble and his steps resemble those of a newborn foal. He staggers about the crowd, sharing more hugs and taking photos, then collapses into a lawn chair on the beach right in front of the finish line. His race is over, but there are still 29 people out there struggling. He'll stay and honor as many of them as he can before fatigue overwhelms him. That's how families work.

Ribeiro doesn't have to wait long. Miro Kregar of Slovenia arrives just 13 minutes later, receiving the same finisher's lei and hug from Jane before embracing Ribeiro. The separation is deceptive. Though they started this day at the same time, Ribeiro's cumulative margin of victory is more than an hour. Not that it's all that important. They are both simply elated to be in this place, sharing this experience together.

The third finisher brings all kinds of surprises. It is a woman, Yasuko Miyazaki of Japan. She gets more than just a lei and a hug, though. She and her support crew barely cross the finish line before her boyfriend, Atsusha, suddenly goes to one knee, a small box in his hand. The pair met eight months prior, when Miyazaki put in an online request for a training partner to help her achieve her Ultraman dream by first qualifying at Ultraman United Kingdom and then coming to Hawaii. A cycling enthusiast, Atsusha responded and they soon began riding bikes together. It only took him four months to decide she was the one. He made the silver band inside the box by hand.

She says yes. The crowd cheers. This is Miyazaki's first time running in the Ultraman World Championships, and her cumulative performance will put her third overall. She won Ultraman United Kingdom earlier this year. For a woman who only got into ultra-distance events a year ago, it might be the promising start to a stellar career. But actually this is the swan song. There's a wedding to plan and children to prepare for; she's eager to start a family. After all of the long days and miles spent training, she's going to give it all up. Or maybe it's that she had to come all this way to get what she really wanted.

Juan Craveri and Chris Draper come next, followed by Kevin Becker. Kathy Winkler is the second woman to finish the run, but she's actually ahead of Miyazaki in the overall race standings, and possibly the winner. Her body is in severe caloric debt. She's suffering from extreme cramps and has begun to urinate blood. Only at the finish line does she finally let the tears come forth. Kathy's written a huge check in an attempt to buy herself a 34-minute lead over the woman chasing her. It's pushed her body into overdraft. But if she's beaten that margin, she'll be the new Ultraman Women's World Champion.

The other woman comes into view just six minutes later. Accompanied by her father on one side and her husband of only a few months on the other, Amber Monforte crosses the line to meet Jane and the others. As much torture as Kathy has put herself through, Amber appears more battered. A better cyclist than a runner, Amber knew that preventing Kathy from opening up too large a gap would take her beyond her limits. Her gait has been reduced to a shuffle by shin splints. It's a familiar place for the two-time defending Ultraman women's world champion and course record holder. Her previous victories challenged her to overcome injury and some of the fiercest competition ever seen in the event's history. This time, the exertion has taken her beyond a point she didn't know existed. She'll remember this race as the most painful, and for that reason it may be her last. Yet there are other memories that will make the pain all worthwhile. The trip has helped Amber and her father, David, reconnect and even add new bonds to their relationship. It's also the beginning of her honeymoon with Ryan. Maybe that will be encouragement enough to do this again. Or, like Miyazaki, maybe this race will be a turning point. This isn't the only ultra race in the world, after all. And Hawaii isn't the only exotic land to explore. Yet there's something special about it, something that draws you back. Only time will tell if its magnetism will work its magic on her again.

More familiar faces arrive. Three minutes behind Amber, Gary Wang finishes his 12th Ultraman, tying for third-most finishes in the race's history books. For Peter Mueller behind him it's finish number six. Tony O'Keefe completes his fifth race behind them. Though his run is almost 90 minutes slower than Ribeiro, O'Keefe's cycling performance from the previous two days was fast enough for him to finish fourth overall. Maybe this shouldn't be a surprise, considering O'Keefe finished fourth place in the 2010 Race Across America, a nonstop bicycle race from California to Maryland. Or maybe it's one of the biggest surprises of the entire event. He was hit by a car while riding his bike the previous year. After he went through the car's windshield, the gearshift drove through his leg close to the knee. Considering this, his comeback is nothing short of miraculous. His meeting with his wife,

support crew, and Jane at the finish line is a doubly profoun
living life on the edge and coming back from the brink of d

Mark Ford and Roberto Parseghian arrive next. Then
Alan Macpherson. Eleven others come in to round out the official finishers.
Every name carries with it an incredible story. Just as incredible, three
others cross the finish line and receive a "DNF"—*did not finish*—for the
race. Trung Lively, Suzy Degazon, and Amy Palmeiro-Winters all met with
some misfortune in the previous two days and failed to make the finish line
before the cutoff. They knew even before they took their first steps this
morning that their run would not change that classification. But they are
here to experience, not conquer. For them, today is just a great opportunity
to go for a long run and maybe learn something about themselves. They
don't run to win or finish. They run because they love to run.

Suzy bounds down the runway looking like a girl playing hopscotch.
She's so carefree that it almost fools you into thinking she's the champion. In
a way, she is. She's competed in the race 15 times and scored official finishes
in 12 of them, tying for third with Gary Wang on the all-time finishers list.
She beams as she crosses the line with her family, moving toward Jane. Suzy
began the weekend crying as she started the swim on the first day. Now she's
all smiles, as bittersweet tears streak faces among those at the finish line.
Suzy and many of the people here knew what this one meant to her before
she even began. At 48, it's not so much age catching up with her as it is
injuries. After 15 years, this is Suzy's last Ultraman.

For continuing onward, Suzy, Trung and Amy will receive a participant's
plaque, acknowledging that they stuck with it even when things didn't go
their way. Five other athletes are not so lucky. Josef Ajram of Spain was
heading for an official finish this morning when a leg injury simply became
too painful, forcing him to stop entirely. Not all of the other non-finishers
are injured. Stephen Johnson did not feel well enough to continue after
the swim on the first day. Instead of continuing around the course for an
unofficial finish, he decided to abandon his race effort completely and spend
the trip as a vacation with his children. For a man who has finished the Deca
Ironman—an event in which people run 10 consecutive Ironman races in
as many days—there isn't as much pressure to show he's tough enough to
keep going. Some people march to the beat of a different drummer. Johnson

arches to accordions, or talk radio, or whatever else he hasn't marched to yet. His finish lines aren't found on maps.

The hours go by and the arrivals come less frequently. The athletes surrender to their hunger and the allure of the catered meal under the picnic shelter on the beach just a few yards from the finish line. They eat slowly. Exhaustion diminishes their stomachs' tolerance and their sense of hunger is dulled by its relative constancy over the last few days. They don't gorge like survivors rescued from a deserted island, but this obscures the massive amounts they consume. They graze constantly throughout the rest of the afternoon. Their metabolisms are working at such a high rate that they will most likely lose two pounds during the night as they sleep. Once their hunger is sated for the time being, they amble to the next picnic shelter, where volunteer massage therapists have set up for the last time. The athletes strip down as much as possible on the beach, get on the tables, and receive much-needed treatment.

Floodlights on the finish line arch turn on as the sun sets. Trung Lively is the last one home, crossing the line just before the 12-hour cutoff. His wife, Consuela, joined him for the final 10 miles. She spent most of the weekend by Jane's side, watching how the event is put on so that she and Trung can organize the new Ultraman race in Florida next year. She asked Jane if she could go in the waning hours. "Something doesn't feel right," she said. "I can't explain it, but Trung needs me." When she reached him, he was thinking about quitting. They cross the line together.

The celebration goes on for a while afterward. The last of the finishers congratulate each other and give the thanks to their crews that they haven't been able to express in the last few days. But eventually the food is gone and the hours take their final toll on weary organizers, athletes, and spectators alike. By 8:00 volunteers begin pulling down the tents and the archway. The lights and sound system go down. Water coolers are rinsed out and stacked. In short order, it's all packed into a single moving truck. The truck's back door comes down with a deafening thud and suddenly all the magic disappears. What's left is the feeling that something was here, and now there's a vacuum that can't be filled. There are no bleachers or souvenir stands. You can't even hear the waves washing up on the beach. It's just nighttime at the parking lot at the end of the world.

It happens this way every year. With no fanfare or awards podium at the end, some of the world's most compelling athletes take part in an incredible three-day pilgrimage that pushes them to the edge of their being and forces them to reach deep within their souls. They do it for no clear reason. They receive no tangible reward. The motives behind their accomplishment are elusive and incomprehensible. Though a significant number of past Ultraman finishers have struggled with mental illness or addiction issues, they are not all crazy or exercise fanatics. While Alexandre Ribeiro and Amber Monforte occupy the stratosphere of human performance, there are plenty of "average Joes" for whom winning is just to finish. Some of them come to find Jesus, others Buddha. Some don't come looking for anything but find it by accident. Many of them affiliate with the church that is specific to this tiny congregation. Their suffering is their own kind of offering. The lava fields here serve as the altar of the Ultraman spirit, and according to the faithful it is generous in its blessings.

On the other hand, there are the nonbelievers who return to the yearly worship service again and again. So it's not even some unifying creed that binds them all. This year's participants came from 12 different countries and disparate walks of life. There are pro athletes as well as those who have only recently turned their life around from terrible eating and exercise habits and even substance abuse. They are prison guards, serial entrepreneurs, professors, and vagabonds. There are first-timers, last-timers, and bucket-listers. Some do this race and move on to the next thing. For others, this is the *only* thing.

This is the only thing they have in common, but for some reason it's the only thing that matters. The enigmatic unifying power of Ultraman is its single underlying principle. Ironically, the greatest example of that ethic isn't an athlete at all. It's the grandmother at the finish line giving out the hugs. Jane Bockus never competed in Ultraman, but she's the one who has kept it going for the last 20 years. Jane spent more of her own time and money keeping Ultraman alive than anyone will ever know and never asked for a thing in return. That's why she's the event's patron saint. She provides a much clearer understanding of Ultraman from behind the scenes than those on the course. The things she and her small group of followers do during a year on the Ultraman calendar are the purest expression of the reasons. They do it because they love it. They do it for the stories.

chapter three

Story Time

"Sports is human life in microcosm."

—Howard Cosell

NOVEMBER 26, 2012. The day after the race is over, a small group gathers on a quiet section of the grounds outside the Kona Sheraton hotel on Keauhou Bay. Among the athletes and volunteers is Jane Bockus. So are the three other members of the board of directors of Ohana Loa, LLC—the company that owns the Ultraman series of races. Sheryl Cobb is Jane's right-hand woman, considered virtually interchangeable with her husband and board member, David Cobb. The fourth member is Steve Brown, who is also the director and organizer of Ultraman Canada.

They're here to witness the renewal of wedding vows between Kevin and Katherine Becker, both of whom raced this weekend. Kevin and Kat raced Ultraman Canada together in 2011 and in 2012. This is their first time in Hawaii, but they feel at home here among the dedicated Ultraman family. The master of ceremonies is Steve King, renowned endurance event commentator and the official announcer of Ultraman. He has fulfilled announcing duties in Hawaii for the last four years, each time missing his own wedding anniversary. After his introductions, he turns to Kevin and Katherine in turn and asks them to recite their vows.

Lots of couples meet at a game, in the gym, or in a local recreation league. Recreation becomes the foundation for their affection. The Beckers discovered triathlons through each other. Kevin took them up as a way of getting back in shape after they were married. Katherine followed him into them both out of curiosity and to support him, and found she loved competing just as much. What started with local events no longer than 20 miles eventually turned them into Ultraman and -wife. They tailored their vows to reflect the importance of ultra endurance in their life:

"I, Kevin, take you, Katherine, to be my renewed lawfully wedded wife and chief triathlon and running partner, for richer, for poorer, for faster, for slower, for better or worse overall placing, in sickness and in fitness, for when we compete and complete, and the very, very rare occasion when we DNF. I promise to love, honor, and cherish you, to service your bike, massage your feet, share my nutrition, and be the best Killer B I can be. This I vow to you."

Kat follows: "I, Katherine, take you, Kevin, to be my well-tanned and well-trained husband, to have and to continue to hold from this day forward, for better or for worse, for richer, for poorer, for even poorer when I've been sending off entry forms, in sickness and in health, to love and to cherish, from this day forward until Death Valley us do venture and we do run from rim to rim to rim, from sea to shining sea and TRI to the end of love. *Dictum meum pactum*, my word is my bond."

An hour after the Beckers reaffirm their love for one another and their sport, the entire cast of the weekend's adventure reconvenes at the Keauhou's grand convention hall for dinner and the event's closing ceremony. At most races, this would be the awards banquet. It would focus on the presentation of oversized checks and short victory speeches given by the top three finishers. Typically, the amateur athletes skip it. They've already boarded their flights home or are out playing tourist in the host city. Not here. There are no big checks. No special stage for the winners. No sponsor logos emblazoned on the tablecloths or the podium. Every athlete, regardless of their time or even if they finished, gets a turn at the microphone. This is the time to celebrate what everyone came for. It isn't the glory or the achievement; it's about being a part of the journey. It's story time.

First come those who didn't finish. Lori Beers abandoned the swim with a shoulder injury. She says that she'll try harder next year. No one doubts her. This was the fourth Ultraman for the Hawaii native who works as a lifeguard.

Next is Cory Foulk. He also ended his race in the water. After fighting off cancer earlier in the year, he simply couldn't find the energy to get himself through the swim. He tried continuing on for an unofficial finish on the bike, but he kept running out of steam on the first and second days. He didn't even attempt the run. He's able to take it in stride, and even finds a way to make a little humor out of the legacy he's carved for himself in this event.

"As most everyone knows, I have the record for most Ultraman finishes and DNFs," he tells the crowd. "So the trouble I have every year is deciding which record I'm going to defend. This year I picked DNF." The crowd bursts into laughter before he even finishes the punch line. His reputation for trickery is legendary in the triathlon world, and his mischievous smile lends him a Johnny Carson quality for inspiring laughter. He finishes by proclaiming his gratitude to the people who volunteered to crew for him and apologizing that he couldn't provide them with a longer and more fulfilling experience. He hopes that he can make it up to them next year.

Suzy Degazon's tale is the most emotional of the evening. It's obvious why everyone will miss her just from the way she tells her story. She wears a grin so big and goofy as she approaches the podium that you wonder if she's had one too many drinks. "Well, things don't always go right, but you have to keep going with the plan," she begins. She speaks with manic ebullience, at a pace so quick that it's difficult to understand her. She talks about the horrendous pushback from the current and getting stung by bees on the bike on the first day, and of keeping in mind how pretty the volcano looked on her way up. That was nothing compared to her luck on the second day. Working as her support crew, her husband, Al, and her two daughters drove ahead of her on the road to get food right as she got a flat tire on her bike. A race volunteer picked her up and they stopped at a Taco Bell. While she was eating, Al and the girls got back on the road and became frantic when they couldn't find her. By the time they caught up with her their nerves were a little frayed. "It's okay," she remarks. "It's Ultraman. That's how it goes."

The laughter that comes in response is of a knowing variety. Even Al chuckles a little as he looks down and shakes his head. It's evident he's thinking of a dozen other fiascoes from their years of coming here. She ends with the official announcement that this was her last race. The room goes quiet and fills with longing gazes to the stage. Suzy has been a presence on the island for half the event's history.

Amy Palmeiro-Winters is next. She is visibly shaken as she approaches the stage. After a motorcycle accident severely damaged her leg in 1994,

Amy spent three years in rehab before finally deciding that a below-the-knee amputation was her best hope for regaining enough mobility to run again. In the 15 years since, she's become a renowned ultra-distance runner, placing near the top or winning many events she entered. Her achievements and advocacy for the physically challenged garnered her an ESPY Award in 2010.

Heretofore, she's met every challenge in her life with the focus and energy of a bullet train, blowing right through every obstacle by sheer force of will. The velocity of her success magnifies the crushing impact of this setback. This is her second failed attempt to complete the race, her first being in 2011. The insult is made crueler by the fact that she has only chance and honest mistakes to blame. She was on her way to an official finish before human error—not her own—intervened. Cycling on pace to make the day two cutoff with time to spare, her crew lost sight of her before a critical intersection. She went the wrong way and rode miles off course. Wearing a prosthetic specially designed for cycling made it nearly impossible for her to get off the bike. As darkness set in, search crews were dispatched and local law enforcement was called. She was finally found 10 miles past the turn she missed.

On top of her frustration lies the residual fear from the ordeal. She barely begins her story before she chokes back tears. She talks about the night spent in terror, wondering if she'd ever see her children again, and how she wanted to quit seven miles into the run the next day, just so she could hold them again. The greatest challenges of Amy's race existed within her. Not the waves, the volcano, or even the lava fields compare to the darkness that possessed her heart. As she is overwhelmed by the memory, her young son leaps from his chair and rushes up onto the stage to hug her. She picks him up, and he lifts her spirits.

No one questions whether Amy is exaggerating or overreacting. The carbon-titanium prosthetic that begins above her left knee is a stark reminder of how far she's come just to get here. It makes her account of being lost and powerless disturbingly palpable. Through her description of those desperate, terrifying hours, everyone becomes a little more attuned to his or her own mortality. Among the super-athletes there's a shared epiphany of how misguided we are in our assumptions of invincibility. The mechanisms our society creates to keep us indulging in our fantasies of control and safety are increasingly sophisticated. Amy's experience cuts through the stilts of our pretenses, bringing everyone in the room eye level with the frailty of life. Sometimes these athletes can get a little saccharine in their proclamations about how grateful they are to be alive, or to ride a bike, or for something so trivial as good Kona coffee and a plate of vegetables. But when your reference point is the pain and privation of what they've just been through, maybe everything is just a little sweeter than the rest of us realize.

As if fate intended to reinforce the point, Vito Rubino comes next. He speaks only a few words, but they strike at something potent in ultra endurance sports. "I did not plan to do Ultraman at first, but when the slot opened I said 'Why not?'" Even for a man who regularly engages in 50-mile running races, the commitment necessary to adequately prepare this event was all-consuming. "This is very personal. It can be lonely."

On an evening of celebration and togetherness, Rubino underscores the reason why the attendees cling so strongly to the race and each other. Each of their life stories is an extraordinary chronicle of achievement. The basis of their camaraderie is a form of enlightenment few others share. But it comes with a price, and they have all paid it. Being among the greatest and most unique endurance athletes in the world also means being a member of a rare species whose members are isolated around the globe. Their passion for this sport is not conducive to companionship. How they account for the cost and what it has purchased them is a proposition athletes have worked through since time immemorial. It transcends endurance sports, and perhaps all of sport entirely. It speaks to the dilemma of greatness—the daily sacrifice required to underwrite a lifelong gamble.

Considering that Ingrid Hillhouse only got into triathlon four years earlier and failed to finish her first race because of an overwhelming fear of the water, her race record is monumental. She already finished Ultraman Canada in 2011 and again this year before coming to Hawaii. She's finished several Ironman and Half Ironman triathlons, as well as multiple other long distance runs and bike races. On paper she looks like the prototypical overachieving Ironman athlete, and indeed for a long time she has been a person overwhelmingly fascinated with metrics. But not anymore. All that was washed away before she even finished the swim on the first day. Along her way around the island, she found a new perspective and direction.

She thanks Steve King, telling him that without his words she wouldn't have made it through the swim. "I kept thinking of what you said: 'There can be no toxicity with gratitude.' And I am so grateful for you." She also thanks fellow athletes Rusty Carter, Mike Brown, and Mike Deichtman. Without their encouragement and help from their crews, she wouldn't have made it, she says. She thanks her friends and crew, Heather Herrick and Jeff McMahan, for coming along and sharing this journey. She then pays an emotional tribute to her mother—also a crewmember—who went out on the support canoe during the swim in order to be there for her from start to finish.

Just as with Amber and her father, their bond has been enriched by the epic proportions of their journey. There is no better expression of that than in how she describes her impression of the last three days. "This race has been a quest for me. Rarely do we have a chance to participate in a dream. Thank you all so much for giving me that opportunity."

Michael Brown follows Ingrid. If you only knew he was an athlete, you'd guess he was perhaps a heavyweight boxer or football player. Indeed, in a past life, he almost grabbed a spot on the Canadian World Cup rugby squad. Men his size often compete in a special weight-defined class known as "Clydesdale" (the women's analog goes by the more polite name of "Athena"). He was reminded of this several times the first day.

"I was up on the volcano, and the first guy passed me and said 'Come on, fatso!' And a while later somebody else passed me and said 'Come on, big guy!' And I must have heard it a dozen times that day. 'Let's go, big guy! Keep on trucking!'" He pauses to laugh along with the crowd, then reflects. "My father used to own a horse-racing track. I'd go down all the time and watch. One day, they brought a huge horse to the track. I'd never seen one so large. But instead of saddling it, they hooked it up to a big wagon. I asked my father, 'Dad, why doesn't that horse race?' He told me, 'Oh no, Mike. It's not why that horse doesn't race, it's why the other horses don't pull the wagon. Their hearts couldn't handle working so hard to pull that. You see, son, the bigger the horse, the bigger the heart.'" That's Michael's whole speech. Just a few things he heard on the road the first day and a childhood memory—a small story with big meaning.

Eventually, it's time for the final two athletes: the overall winners, Alexandre and Amber. Their speeches are relatively humble and unassuming.

It's somewhat expected. Adjusting the scale of pain and difficulty to the individual, their races were no more trying than anyone else's. Things went according to plan. In no way does that diminish their extraordinary athleticism. It's just that Ultraman is about more than being an athlete or winning. The champions are decided by the cumulative time it takes to reach the finish line. Math makes predictions possible on day two and reduces the final outcome to certainty long before the first person crosses the finish line. But who has the most profound race? That's determined by an athlete's path intersecting with fate. No one can predict when or how that will happen. Everyone here admires what Alexandre and Amber accomplished, but the reason they came is to share what people like Amy and Ingrid experienced.

Overall, the stories range from the eloquent to the crass, from simple retellings of their race to esoteric koans that explore the essence of what draws them to this place every year. Whoever they are, whatever they do, it is added to the greater story of Ultraman. Holding the patchwork tapestry together is the thread of one woman's story, nearly as long as that of Ultraman itself and so entwined that the two are almost indistinguishable from each other. She has been there since the beginning. She's Jane Bockus, the woman with the sparkling blue eyes and the indefatigable smile at the finish line giving out the hugs. And for all she's invested in it, she will be the first to say that Ultraman is not her story. She will not—cannot—take credit for that. It was never meant to be something that could be taken, only given. And that's the secret to her legacy. Hers is a special kind of endurance, fueled by a passion even some athletes cannot understand and unmatched by even her most faithful supporters. It is the endurance of the most selfless love imaginable.

It is one of the most gripping dramas on earth to watch these athletes swim, bike, and run a total of 320 miles. Yet it's even more compelling to witness Jane and the other Ultraman volunteers pouring so much compassion and kindness into every moment. Whether a competitor or a supporter, you can't make it through this event if you don't have the heart for it. For the athletes, it's a long way to race. For Jane and her group, it's a long weekend of caring for people who keep breaking themselves. For all of them, Ultraman is a long way to love.

The journey doesn't stop here for any of them. The end of the 2012 race marks the beginning of the 2013 cycle of events and possibly a new era in the sport's history. Jane and the Ohana Loa board members must immediately begin preparing for the 2013 race season. The athletes and their crews have less than a year to train and plan for the next race. Qualification and registration for Hawaii will become more difficult as new athletes attempt to enter. One of the most contentious races ever seen will take place in Canada. There will be unprecedented growth in what is slowly becoming a series of Ultraman events as a new pair of race directors, having just received Jane's blessing this weekend, begin work on a new Ultraman race in Florida. Interrupting that relative prosperity will also be an unexpected upheaval and loss that will cause everyone to wonder if they're doing what's necessary to guard the principles at the heart of the race. Their concessions over the last 30 years have been few and far between, but this year will test their resolve and find out whether Ultraman can resist the forces that have gripped every other sport at some point. There are two connotations to the phrase "run a race": it can either mean to compete in it or to organize and direct it. There's the race everyone knows, and then there's the race within.

At the end of the 2012 race season, Ultraman stands on the brink of monumental changes. How it got there is a unique story of the lives and efforts of several people who merged together like tributaries flowing into a great river. Some people have floated in and out. Others seem bound and determined to ride the current all the way to its end. But only a few have seen the headwaters. Ultraman didn't appear out of thin air. It had an inspiration, a catalyst, and even a prototype. The origin of Ultraman is the untold history of Ironman.

chapter four

The Iron Lady

"The second edition will, I fear, be the last. It has died of its success, of the blind passions that it unleashed, the abuse and the dirty suspicions."

—Henri Desgrange, Founder of the Tour de France

IT ALL STARTED IN 1978 at the Primo Beer Fun Run in Honolulu, on the island of Oahu. John Collins, an officer in the United States Navy, had just finished the race and was enjoying a beer with friends. A debate sprang up about who the best endurance athletes were: swimmers, cyclists, or runners. Parties took up different sides based on their sport of choice, tossing up statistics about such athletes as Mark Spitz and the famous cyclist Eddie Merckx.

By odd turns and after a few more beers, they decided to settle the argument in the least reasonable way possible. Someone had heard of a sport called triathlon and proposed combining the courses of three local events into a single race. The contestants would follow the 2.4-mile course of the Waikiki Rough Water Swim, then pedal the 112 miles of the Around Oahu Bike Race (a two-day event), and cap it off by running the Honolulu Marathon course. At 140.6 miles, it sounded absolutely insane. That's what made it irresistible to the group of endurance sports nuts, surfers, and Navy SEALs. These were not the type of guys who waited to be double-dared to do something. Vows were made and a date was set. In the decades since, the rest of the story has been gradually whittled down in the oral tradition's haste to "…and the rest is history." What's been forgotten by the masses is just how messy the rest of the story is.

Fifteen men entered the water on February 18, 1978. Three contestants didn't finish. Navy SEAL John Dunbar led throughout most of the race until late in the run, when his support crew ran out of water. They gave him beer instead, at which point he began weaving all over the road and nearly collapsed. A navy communications specialist named Gordon Haller passed Dunbar shortly before the finish line. For winning, everyone called Haller "the Ironman," the title Collins invented half-jokingly just before the race. The name stuck, and eventually became the official title for the event itself. Collins made a set of Ironman trophies for the first 12 finishers. They featured a crudely fashioned sculpture of a man made out of bits of pipe, with a large hex nut for a head, standing on a plain piece of plywood. If the original debate about the best athlete was settled, the decision was never published.

To Collins' surprise, he was asked to put the event on the next year. More than 50 contestants showed up to the 1979 race, including the first female participant. Unfortunately, bad weather and safety concerns forced Collins to delay the race by a day. Because some athletes anticipated taking 24 hours to complete the race and many had to be at work the following Monday, only 15 actually took the starting line. Barry McDermott, a journalist for *Sports Illustrated*, heard about the event and decided to come see it for himself. He wound up writing a 10-page feature story about it. Beyond the astounding nature of what the Ironman demanded from those who attempted it, McDermott's prose conveyed the awe he felt bearing witness to their suffering. That admiration was magnified by the everyman nature of the athletes. The first people who raced Ironman were not professional athletes—or even very practiced ones. Winner Tom Warren described himself as being in "mediocre shape." He was bothered greatly by the onset of a limp late in the run due to a childhood leg injury. McDermott was fascinated by the contestants' myriad origins and reasons for being there:

Among the Iron Man entries was an individual with a master's degree in exercise physiology, another with a degree in accounting, a fellow applying to law school, a research aneothesiologist, the treasurer of a San Francisco leasing company and Haller with his physics degree. Disparate as their backgrounds were, they shared a common bond. Henry Forrest, a Marine stationed in Jacksonville, N.C., had hitched rides on military transport planes to get to Honolulu. Until the 1978 Iron Man Triathlon, he had not ridden a bike since the fourth grade and had become lost during the race. He hoped to improve on his performance this year. People thought his name was Forrester, because when introduced he said rapidly, "Henry Forrest, sir."

Bob Iger, head of ABC Sports, read the piece and told producers at ABC's *Wide World of Sports* to get in touch with Collins. Shocked that *Wide World* had any interest in what he was doing, Collins told the producer that the event wouldn't work for television. "It's about as exciting as watching grass grow."

"Don't worry about that," the ABC rep said. "We make grass growing look good." With that, it was agreed. What had begun as an alcohol-fueled argument was about to become a spectator sports event. Collins wouldn't be around to see it happen, however. After the 1979 race he received orders from the navy transferring him to a new assignment, and the Ironman was suddenly without a caretaker.

Though he was dubious about its relative value, Collins knew that he had at least created something people were interested in doing. He wanted to see it survive in order for them to enjoy it. He asked a local gym owner named Hank Grundman if he was interested in taking it on. Hank and his wife, Valerie, were co-owners of the Nautilus gym franchises on Oahu. They had offered Gordon Haller free access to their place in order to train for the first race on the chance it might make for good publicity. Hank had gone further, investing his own time in helping Collins to organize the race and supporting athletes during the actual competition.

Valerie, on the other hand, had no interest in the affair and took no part in it. She thought it was crazy to race in it, crazy to work so hard to put it on, and crazy to get out of bed so early to watch it. So when Collins came into the gym with a box filled with registration forms, finishing records, and a handful of the nuts and bolts he used to make the trophies, she thought Hank was crazy to be so thrilled to have it. She viewed it as a distraction from their business that they could ill afford.

Against her protests, Hank took it on anyway, and Valerie wound up a reluctant accomplice. She remembers begrudgingly helping with registration activities for the 1980 race. Hank maintained enough enthusiasm for the both of them. "He came back to our condo the morning of the race as the athletes were finishing the swim and woke me up. He told me, 'Val! Look out the window!' I glanced up in time to see who I think was Dave Scott getting on his bike and taking off, but I remember being unimpressed," she remembers. Hank went back to the race shortly afterward and Valerie rolled over and went back to sleep. That was the extent of her involvement that year.

The argument over assuming responsibility for the race drove another small wedge into the widening space between Valerie and Hank, and soon after the 1980 race they filed for divorce. Hank got the Nautilus franchise in the settlement, leaving Valerie without a job. That was stressful enough, but what she felt even more profoundly was a sense of emptiness. "I was always an organizer of things. I didn't miss the gyms when I left. That had always been Hank's idea and his business. But it was scary to be without a direction," she says. When a storm washes you overboard from the only ship you've ever known, you reach out for anything to hold onto. She asked him if he'd let her take on the Ironman. Even today, she doesn't know why. She didn't even like endurance racing. There was no way to predict that it would ever draw a profit, nor was it even her original purpose. It was just there. All she could do was swim as hard as she could and see where it took her. "I wasn't really into the race, but I had an idea to turn it into something really wonderful. I had never done anything like that before, had no idea what I was getting into. I think if I had, I'd have never done it," she says. Hank gave it to her without argument.

Valerie's relationship with the Ironman was unique from the very start. Before she did anything else, she began talking to the athletes who had competed in the previous two races or had expressed interest in signing up. She asked them all the same question: "If you could compete in the best race ever, what would it look like?" The answers she received inspired significant changes for the 1981 race. They also shaped her vision of what Ironman would become during its first decade, and through her example would constitute the foundation of what so many dedicated fans and athletes believe is the race's spiritual meaning. Ironman was less her business than she was its caretaker.

The athletes changed her concept of the whole thing in fundamental ways. She addressed applications and acceptance letters to "contestants" rather than "racers" or "competitors," signifying their belief that it was a race more against the course than each other. Because those first Ironman races required the athletes to arrange their own support and no one had a clear idea of what they'd need, an ethos evolved among the participants that amplified the concept of sportsmanship. If an athlete or their crew needed help, anyone could give them aid. Crews gave food and water to their own athletes' archrivals, because at the end of the day the only real adversary was the competition itself; the winner was only first among equals. What mattered most was the camaraderie of having suffered the ordeal.

Participation in the race increased quickly. It was no longer just Hawaii residents, either. The 200 participants in the 1981 race came from around the world. Wherever they came from, they were the only people doing what they did, and were viewed as obsessive weirdos. Yet on that tiny island far removed from anywhere else in the world and among total strangers, they felt more at home than anywhere else. That was what made the Ironman so great to them. Valerie realized that Ironman had turned from a curiosity into a pilgrimage for a growing endurance diaspora. "I never looked at it as a race. I was throwing a party, and I wanted it to be the best party in the world," she says.

The party started getting unruly, though. Entries for the 1981 race exceeded expectations—and Honolulu's capacity. Valerie needed more room. She looked for viable alternatives and found one on the big island of Hawaii. The west side of the island was less densely populated and the Queen Ka'ahumanu highway had just been finished. It would make for ideal accommodations and racing if she could negotiate the new challenges it would present. With so many athletes on a highway course, the self-supported format would no longer be practical. There would have to be dedicated aid stations. That meant supplies, volunteers, and rule changes. It was going to be different.

Valerie began seeking volunteers in Kona. Only a couple of people on Hawaii had heard of the Ironman, but what they lacked in numbers they more than made up for in enthusiasm. There were only 92,000 people living on the entire island in 1980. Kona's small-town dynamic lent itself to success. People of widely varied interests often came together to support each other's activities. When word got around that a long-distance race coming to town needed volunteers, people offered their time for a multitude of reasons. Some people were endurance racing buffs. Others thought it would be a hoot to see what kind of person actually ran such a race. The majority were just being good neighbors happy to help someone in need. That latter reason was how Gerry and Jane Bockus got started. One of the first people Valerie contacted for help was a member of the Kona master's swim club, who was a friend of a man named Curtis Tyler, who was good friends with the Bockuses.

Like every first-time event, there were a few minor hiccups in that first year on Hawaii. Nonetheless, Valerie's perfectionism caused her to feel mortified by the mistakes she made. She remembers thinking that the event was a catastrophe. It shocked her when the athletes threw her a party to thank her for what she'd done. It renewed her courage, but throughout her tenure she never stopped fearing failure. "I had a tiger by the tail. I was terrified all the time that something would go wrong. It never went away," she says.

Yet her faith in what she was doing grew stronger after the 1981 race. She developed a strong empathy with the athletes for their motivations for coming to the race. "It was the experience of a lifetime for them," she says. "I made the Ironman motto 'more than a race.' And it was. It was a party. It was a vehicle to accomplish something. You got to know the personal lives of the competitors. It was compelling. Back in the early 1980s they were all considered kooks. I remember one athlete who came from the Midwest. He worked in an office and would train indoors for long hours during the winter. He came to Hawaii and had a blast at the race, but when he got back home everyone in his office just looked at him and asked, 'Did you get *that* out of your system?' It was so hard for many of them to be misunderstood like that. Even their families had a difficult time understanding what possessed them to do this. I developed a kind of mother instinct to take care of them."

Athletes accepted the virtual adoption by the hundreds. Scott Tinley, a top competitor who turned professional and won the race twice, says that "Ironman was a brilliant accident. Valerie got the race from her divorce. She had no kids, so we became her kids." They kept the letters she sent them on their refrigerators. She would receive phone calls at all hours of the night from people around the world, just wanting to talk. What had started as something for her to hold onto through her own typhoon had become a mission to provide a spiritual life jacket to others.

That didn't mean it was all parties and chatting with international athletes. The race barely made enough money to stay afloat in its first three years on Hawaii, let alone enough to earn Valerie a living. Yet organizing the Ironman was a full-time job for her. She couldn't do anything else. She lived hand-to-mouth, and can't remember today how she got by during those lean years. There were also a few more lessons to learn in the art of race directorship. She remembers with sheepish humor a polite yet highly emphatic suggestion she heard from multiple participants in the 1981 race: "I had measured the distance on the bike course with a car odometer, which meant I probably shorted it a little. But what the athletes were most upset about was that I had described the course as 'flat' in the race brochure. They came back and told me, 'Don't call that a flat course!' You can't really feel just how steep the road is when you're driving a car. They could certainly feel it on the bike, though!

"So the next year Gerry Bockus measured out a new course. He went out there with one of those little wheels they use to measure distance. I don't know how long it took him to do it, but he had to go back out over several days. That wound up being the bike course we used for several years."

Her ideals and commitment infected the town of Kona. Looked upon as freaks in their hometowns, Ironman athletes were received as conquering heroes in Kona. Local establishments hung posters of the most prominent athletes on their walls, and offered free ice cream or soft drinks to any that walked in if they'd just give an autograph. *Wide World of Sports* continued to broadcast the race and applications increased every year: from 108 contestants in 1980 to 381 in 1981 to more than 550 people in February 1982. (Prior to 1982, the race had been held in February. Valerie held a second race in October 1982 to change the annual schedule. Ironman has been held in October ever since.)

But this exponential growth was only a prelude to bigger changes. The 1982 race produced one of the greatest moments in sports history, and the epochal turning point that secured Ironman's future. It would become another of those "…and the rest is history" milestones, with the messy details swept underneath.

In 1982 Anheuser Busch was looking for a way to grab attention for a new product, tentatively named Budweiser Light. The company explored the possibility of sponsoring the Ironman. In exchange, they wanted to capture footage of the athletes in the race for commercials. A man named Rodney Jacobs approached Valerie with a deal for a three-year, $15,000 contract. It was good money, but *Wide World* had already negotiated exclusive film rights. Valerie explained to Jacobs that they'd have to negotiate with ABC first. "But he was a smooth talker and told me, 'Don't worry about that. I know the guys at ABC. This is how the industry works. We'll make everything okay with them. Trust me.' And I did trust him. Big mistake," she remembers. Valerie took Jacobs at his word and signed the contract with Budweiser.

What ensued was a year of cat-and-mouse between Valerie and Jacobs. She asked him frequently if he'd gotten in touch with the people at ABC. He'd always respond that he'd "just missed them." It came to the week of the race, when everyone was arriving in Hawaii, before she finally pinned him down. Frantic, she demanded that he talk to *Wide World of Sports* producer Brice Weisman and sort things out. "And he said, 'Oh, Brice? Well, then! Just tell him I'm here.'" Again, she did as he asked. Weisman exploded when he got the news. To Valerie's dismay, she found out that Jacobs had a reputation for being two-faced, and he wasn't welcome at any of the major networks. She confronted Jacobs in no uncertain terms at a dinner with the representatives from Budweiser. "I looked right at him and said, 'You lied to me.' And he just smiled and said, 'That's just business, baby.'"

Despite his frustration, Weisman sympathized with Valerie and worked out an impromptu deal with the Budweiser crew. They could film the race, but the *Wide World* film crew had first priority on coverage and the commercial team had to stay out of any shots. Everyone felt things had been settled until about midway through the race, when Weisman confronted Valerie with more bad news. The Budweiser team was not holding up their end of the bargain. They were getting in the line of the ABC cameras and ruining multiple shots. Worse, their team was helping some of the athletes by giving them water. With the aid stations now on the course, the rules stated that athletes could not receive outside assistance.

Weisman took his aggravation out on Valerie by putting her on the spot in front of the camera. They began interviewing her about the developments on the course. At one point the commentator told her that the Budweiser crew had been spotted giving wet sponges to Scott Tinley. He asked her directly how she felt about front-runners being given illegal aid and whether it influenced the fairness of the race. Terrified as she was, she maintained grace under fire. "I said, 'Well, I suppose it gives them less advantage than the ABC crew gives the lead athlete by letting him draft his bike behind their camera van.' The guy with the microphone turned to the cameraman and said, 'Cut. We're done.' And that was it. So that kept it from getting aired," she says.

It was a small victory in a battle she knew she'd ultimately lose. Out on the course, Rodney Jacobs was poisoning the financial lifeblood of Ironman. Valerie could only sit and wait at race headquarters to find out how fatal the damage would be.

That evening, after the winners had crossed the finish line, Weisman took Valerie aside to one of the ABC vehicles. He began admonishing her that the Budweiser crew had ruined all their footage and that he doubted they had anything usable for the annual telecast. Beneath her stoic appearance, Valerie felt the bottom drop out of her world. It became almost impossible to even look strong in the face of Weisman's criticism. He began showing her footage, pointing out how each shot had the Budweiser crew in it. She was fighting back tears when suddenly there was a commotion outside. Valerie remembers one of the ABC crewmembers knocking on the van and telling him he needed to get back outside. "'You need to see this,' the guy told him. Brice just said 'Yeah, sure,' and kept showing me tape," she says. Another few minutes later there was another chorus of shouts. The crewmember returned, pleading for Weisman to stop what he was doing and get outside. Weisman brushed off the crewman a second time. Then the shouting began again, this time without stopping. Valerie remembers that the crewman came in upset, pleading with Weisman to get out of the van.

He left and Valerie stayed behind, her only company the faint light of the television screen and the images of an unraveling future. Still, she held back the tears and eventually brought herself to step out of the van. Diana Nyad, a world-record-setting long-distance swimmer, spotted her and put her arm around Valerie. "She looked at me and said, 'Don't let those guys get to you, Val.' I nearly broke down, but I was able to hold it back." It didn't matter to Valerie if they got to her. What they had gotten to was what mattered most. For all she knew, they'd destroyed the Ironman. But she only knew part of the story. Back at the finish line, history was being made.

Julie Moss was a 24-year-old college student who had signed up for the Ironman as a unique way to complete her thesis work in exercise physiology. By her own account, she had not trained to be seriously competitive. Yet almost 11 hours into the race she found herself in the lead coming down the final stretch of the run. The effort had completely exhausted her and she was severely dehydrated. She was reduced to walking by the last mile, even as her closest competitor, Kathleen McCartney, closed the gap. The drama increased as Julie collapsed within 200 yards of the finish line. For a brief moment she lay back on the asphalt and appeared incapable of going on. Somehow she got up, her legs wobbling. She ambled forward, but within 50 yards of the line she stumbled backward and fell again. With her body becoming less responsive, it took the help of a few volunteers to steady her before she could walk again. With less than 20 yards to go, she fell a third time. The crowd watched breathlessly as McCartney ran past; she didn't notice the fallen Julie because of the crowd gathered around her. McCartney only found out that she'd won when race officials put the gold medal around her neck and told her. ABC cameras showed her celebrating in complete surprise for a moment, then turn back toward Julie with a look of anxiety. What she saw, what the camera crew had so urgently rushed Weisman out to see—and what Valerie didn't see—would be seen around the world and hailed as *the* defining moment of Ironman's history. Julie had fallen for the last time. Unable to get up and cross the finish line on her own two feet, she did the only thing she could: she crawled.

Valerie found Julie in the medical tent afterward, sitting up on a cot after getting medical attention. She looked up at Valerie plaintively. "Valerie, do you think second place is good enough to get a slot to come back next year?"

"I told her, 'Sure, Julie. You can come back next year.' But all I could hear was the voice in my heart saying, 'Are you kidding? This is *over*. There's not going to *be* an Ironman next year.' I was certain that this was the end of everything," Valerie remembers.

The crew from *Wide World of Sports* had a different view. Moss' finish changed everything. ABC rushed production of the Ironman segment and had it ready to go in two weeks. It turned out to be the most-watched episode of the show's history. People mistakenly believed they were seeing a live event and swamped the ABC switchboard asking if Moss was okay and demanding the network to continue coverage of her condition. In an unprecedented move, ABC aired the broadcast a second time the next week. Entry applications for the next Ironman race poured in from around the world. Ironman didn't die; instead, Iron-mania was born.

However, Moss' crawl to the line didn't fix everything. There was still the matter of Rodney Jacobs to deal with. He schlepped the Budweiser coverage—now formatted into a documentary—around to whatever local broadcast stations he could convince to play it. ABC received word of this and told Valerie to get Budweiser under control. She ultimately had to fly to Anheuser Busch headquarters in St. Louis. Though Valerie was contractually bound and had no legal say in how they used the footage, the AB executives determined that pursuing their own broadcast would create a battle with ABC that would damage Ironman. Taking a short-term loss on the one show could lead to a long-term profit with an event whose stock was rising. It was simply good business. So they told Jacobs to knock it off.

Weisman never spoke to Valerie again, nor made any gesture of apology. He later gave an interview to a newspaper about the telecast, which someone clipped and sent to her. At one point they asked him if he knew what they had when he saw it. "Absolutely," she remembers reading. "We instantly knew it was going to be a hit."

What had started as a bet, came in a cardboard box, and found its patron saint through a divorce had become an international phenomenon in the short span of four years. Unimaginable change brought unimaginable consequences. Valerie had more people applying than Kona could accommodate. She capped participation at 1,200 entrants, believing it was the greatest number of people who could be in the event without overcrowding the party. To cover the excess demand, she considered new races in other locations. She took on a paid staff to help her keep things organized as her annual party in Kona began to evolve into a full-blown global series of events. With so many people interested in coming to the Ironman, it became evident to Valerie that her old way of doing things, with discretionary slots and judging applications based on sincerity and creativity, couldn't continue. Some kind of qualification system had to be set up.

Not every homespun element was tossed out immediately. In 1984 she and business partner Bill Schwartz arranged licensing contracts for the first two Ironman qualifiers in Japan and New Zealand. She and her group worked to put together the specifics of how an Ironman should be produced, but the elements that mattered most were the least tangible and thus the most difficult to put into words. This was overcome with a personal touch. Valerie's friend and Ironman acolyte Earl Yamaguchi traveled to both countries to supervise their setup of the races. The experiences encouraged Valerie that the spirit of the thing could be replicated. "We didn't write down everything explicitly, but what we found in working with the people at those races was that they were very excited to put on an Ironman event, and they were passionate about making it everything it was supposed to be," she says.

Meanwhile, in Canada, a group of enthusiastic triathletes in the town of Penticton, British Columbia, led by a woman named Lynn Van Dove began running their own 140.6-mile triathlon in the same format as Valerie's. In 1986, Valerie granted them an official license to become Ironman Canada. That race was joined by a fourth qualifier in Los Angeles. With new events came new sponsors. Ironman New Zealand was backed by Dominion Breweries and named "the Double Brown Ironman" after one of its more popular brands. The Los Angeles event was sponsored by Ricoh electronics. In 1984 Timex negotiated a licensing deal for an Ironman-branded watch. Originally called "the Triathlon," Timex finally bought rights to the Ironman name and logo in 1986. It quickly became the company's most popular watch, and remains so today. By the time Valerie sold the Ironman franchise, the licensing deal with Timex was worth more than the actual race series many times over.

Other business interests saw Ironman's growing value as well. In 1984 a group tendered an offer to buy it from Valerie. A price was agreed upon, provided the group's review of Valerie's financial records matched up to expectations. They turned out to be predators. "This company came in with several accountants and picked apart everything in our records. They accused me of falsely characterizing the worth of the company and tried to sue for a lower price. It wasn't about the money for me, though. I wanted to sell the race because I was already feeling tired. I was always just so scared that something would go wrong, and I had wanted out from the moment I started with it. But when I saw what these people were doing I realized what they *would* do to it if they got hold of it, and I couldn't let that happen," she recalls. Though the group came at her with what she calls "a dream team" of lawyers, she fought tooth and nail to keep Ironman away from them. She finally won the case by summary judgment. It wasn't the only complication to emerge from the race's success. Valerie faced another difficult decision in 1984 that would have an everlasting impact on the character of Ironman.

Ironman had attracted the curiosity of elite athletes as early as 1980. In addition to Scott Tinley were Dave Scott and Mark Allen. (Combined, the pair would win 14 of the 16 races held between 1980 and 1995. Dave Scott would set the record for most wins by a single person with six.) Long-distance triathlon had accumulated enough participation to begin building a kind of pyramid. As the awareness base grew broader, the potential height of its talent increased. The consistently exceptional performance of these men in Hawaii and in other races demonstrated that they were of a professional caliber. The problem was that they weren't getting professional-grade compensation. Endorsement deals were difficult to come by due to the relatively small popularity of triathlon compared to the marathon, which was coming into its heyday. Unlike athletes in bigger sports, the Ironman pros didn't get paid just for showing up. Prize money helped them to cover the expenses of getting to the race, which meant it was barely enough to make it worth going to their next race. Competing was all they cared about, though. None of them thought they were going to make a fortune in such a fringe endeavor. Nor were they trying to. They just wanted to make enough to keep doing it. While there is no doubt they had unique physical talent, it was evident that even more important to their success was a psychological, perhaps even spiritual capacity to engage in such long-distance training on a daily basis. People described them as everything from "phenomenal" to "exercise addicts." Whatever the case, they were obviously different.

Valerie cared about the pros as much as any of her Ironman competitors and felt that something should be done to help them. She also recognized that other triathlons were offering prize money while Ironman did not. There was the potential concern that the other races would draw the big-name athletes away from Ironman and consequently hurt its television viewership and participation rate. The matter came to a head in 1985. Two years prior some of the top pros, including Tinley and Allen, had formed a team of athletes sponsored by a currency trading company called J David. In addition to each individual receiving $500 monthly stipends from the company, the athletes had been able to negotiate deals with organizers of another long-distance triathlon in Nice, France. But everything fell apart within a year of the team's formation when it was discovered that J David was a Ponzi scheme. They lost their power as a negotiating bloc the next year when Mark Allen broke ranks and signed an individual contract with the Nice organizers.

What had looked like the auspicious start of a players' union turned into an every-man-for-himself arena. Back in the poorhouse (many of them had also invested in J David), they became desperate. A lifeline presented itself in the form of a man known as Larry King, the husband of tennis star Billie Jean King and a sports promoter who had learned about the Ironman. He convinced the athletes that there was still a way. If they stuck together and attended or boycotted races as a unified group, they could pressure organizers to put up cash rewards. The athletes agreed. Even some who had not been part of the original J David team, including reigning Ironman champ Dave Scott, joined the cause. King also saw an opportunity for himself. He was personally acquainted with the organizers of the Nice event. If he could choke Ironman out of its pro contingent, there was an opportunity to woo ABC to broadcast the other event—and get a bonus for himself in the process.

With his "union" in hand, King paid Valerie a very intimidating visit in Hawaii. Valerie remembers King telling her about his plans in the language of threats, saying that he was "giving her fair warning that he was out to leave her in the dust" and that "You're going to have to give prize money to your top athletes or your little party is going to be over." Indeed, in 1985 the majority of the top athletes who had been competing in Hawaii also went to Nice. Scheduling their race less than a month prior to Valerie's, the Nice organizers intended to give the athletes too little time to recover from the exertion in order to run well in Hawaii. But once again, one athlete broke the picket line on the boycott. This time it was Scott Tinley. "Most guys didn't even think they could finish Hawaii that soon after running Nice," he remembers. "But I didn't care. More than anything, I just wanted to be there. So I decided 'What the hell' and went. I didn't expect to do that well, but I felt pretty good so I gave it a shot." He went on to place first in the 1985 Ironman, his second of two wins.

Though Tinley was known to march to the beat of his own drummer, the others marched together all the way to Bob Iger at ABC. Iger called Valerie after a meeting with the disgruntled athletes, telling her that there were grumblings of continuing the boycott if they didn't get offered some form of payment either in prize money or royalties from the television broadcast. He bluntly explained ABC's stance. She remembers: "He told me, 'Valerie, as far as ABC is concerned, triathlon is a wart on an elephant's rear end.' I think the athletes didn't understand the scale of things. The triathlon media had given them all this adulation, but Iger told them it was small potatoes. ABC was getting better ratings out of bowling and boxing in those days. I understood how the athletes felt, and I knew that ABC was watching for what I'd do. They never pressured, but they definitely took a wait-and-see attitude."

A way out presented itself when a man approached Valerie with an offer of $100,000 for a prize purse for the Ironman (she prefers to keep his name and intentions confidential). Though she wasn't sure exactly how, she knew the amount would change things significantly for the event. She asked for advice from two other race organizers. Fred Lebow was in charge of the New York Marathon, which offered prize money. Mike Aisner supervised the Coors Classic bicycle race, which did not have any prize money but still attracted superstars like Greg LeMond. They each expressed different misgivings. Aisner advised her to stay away from it outright. Lebow said it could help grow the sport, but there would be strings attached. "He told me that the athletes would be demanding, that if I offered money once, then there was no going back. They would come to expect it, and cutting it off would be worse than never having offered it at all," Valerie says.

Valerie ultimately decided to accept the prize money offer. She was happy to do it and believed in her decision, but what she hated was that she had been brought to decide in the first place. She had come through the Budweiser fiasco thinking she could put such disputes behind her as long as she was careful, but King and the prize money issue made her realize that the only thing behind her was the line she'd crossed. Though not in the way he intended, Larry King did put an end to Valerie's little party. It was no longer an event at which people could gather and celebrate their collective passion. It had become a professionally staffed, professionally contested sport. Lines had been drawn within the congregation. There were company employees and race volunteers. There were locals and foreigners. There were professional competitors and age-group participants. There was Ironman, and then there was everyone else. Things had changed, and they were going to keep changing.

She was inundated with new sponsorship offers almost immediately after the prize-money announcement. "As soon as people found out there was money on the table to be won, everything changed. Everyone wanted to be a part of it. Frankly, I was surprised at just how much it changed people's perceptions," she recalls. The bigger Ironman got, the more people would come trying to get a piece of it. That was the first time she genuinely began thinking of how she'd one day get out. "The thing with King, that kind of stuff always wore me out. Once it got into the business and politics, I really wanted out. There are *tremendous* cutthroat politics in big sports. I just wanted my event, and I had no stomach for the politics," she continues.

Offering prize money was probably the second biggest decision Valerie made about Ironman, next to assuming control of it in the first place. Even people who have long been associated with the event—some as far back as 1980 and who have personal relationships with Valerie—have all sorts of memories and opinions about it. Ironman participants and fans today enjoy interacting with the growing body of elite sponsored athletes. The event series gives "everyman" participants unprecedented access to the professionals. To the minds of a large, vocal population, however, the dark half of that legacy is the cozy, almost nepotistic, relationship Ironman has with its corporate partners. From hiring practices to licensing deals and promotions involving free entry to races with the purchase of select wet suits and bikes, there is a concern that Ironman has put the pursuit of revenue ahead of athletes' dreams.

What's remarkable is that none of these things are new developments. Like the Ironman wristwatch, Valerie aggressively licensed a wide spectrum of products bearing the famed "M-Dot" logo of Ironman. She was unique from the very beginning. The Boston and New York Marathons, as well as most major endurance races at the time, were run by nonprofit groups. By contrast, the first thing Valerie did with Ironman was incorporate. Ironman was *owned* by Hawaii Triathlon Corporation.

Valerie says, "I'd had no experience with endurance races, so I didn't know how the others were doing things. It never occurred to me to call any of them, and having just come out of a business it just made sense to me to set it up as a business. That's how I was comfortable managing money so I went ahead. It turned out that it was the best way to go. I don't know how the other races do it organizing things by committee. If we had done Ironman that way in the beginning it never would have happened. I always asked for help and advice, but at the end of the day you need to have one person who makes decisions, otherwise the decisions never get made. So that's what I did."

Likewise, while the money from the Timex and other licenses were a welcome source of income for her, it was of secondary importance. "The mission statement for Ironman was to have a positive influence on the lives of everyone it touched. That didn't just include the athletes or the people who came to see it, but the people they encountered when they went back to wherever they'd come from, as well. We wanted to touch the hearts, souls, and minds of people. So, for me, merchandising and licensing races was a way to spread that experience. We simply couldn't get everyone who applied into the race, and I wanted to provide them with the opportunity to somehow get close to that experience. Whether it was a race or a keychain, I wanted everything that had our logo on it to exude excellence. That was what mattered to me," she says.

She demonstrated the sincerity of her beliefs in how she conducted the daily "business" of taking care of Ironman. Her employees became concerned early on that she was too attached to her athletes. The all-hours phone calls kept coming in, as did the letters. She sent out more than 400 birthday cards every month. Even when they capped race participation and instituted a qualifying system for the Hawaii race, Valerie held 50 or so slots which she doled out at her own discretion. "People got pretty creative in how they begged to get in the race," she remembers. "One time I got a package of letters from an entire first grade class asking to let one child's father into the race. Another man promised to name his unborn daughter after me if I let him in." He got a race slot, but the girl was named Emily at birth. Not that it bothered Valerie. The man wound up making a few more trips to Kona.

She also frequently gave slots out to older applicants, who liked to call themselves her "Iron Gents." But even 50 slots were precious few to give out. She initially reserved them as a means to retain some sense of that intimate graciousness she'd been able to share with her athletes back in the days of 50-person races and shoestring budgets. It was one of her final gasps of denial that those days were gone. "It was hard to give out those slots," she says. "No. It was *brutal*." Each person that got in meant another slot that couldn't be given to someone else. Every yes carried the weight of a dozen nos.

Every invitation was an effort to go back to simpler times long past. Her nostalgia for the spirit and vibe of the early days became its own burden. Valerie grabbed onto Ironman for all it was worth during her own personal maelstrom years before. Her hope that it would somehow carry her through the storm had been redeemed. Now both she and the race had arrived on shore, but it was a shore that was unfamiliar to her, and she grew weary of feeling lashed to the race. Struggling against the bonds only made it worse.

Another epochal year for Ironman came in 1989. In what was later dubbed "the Iron War," Dave Scott and Mark Allen raced shoulder-to-shoulder for all but a mile of the race, with Allen winning by a mere 59 seconds, the closest finish in the event's history. Both athletes proudly displayed their sponsors' logos on their race jerseys. Among them were Nike, Bud Light, and Brooks running shoes. Both men wore sunglasses made by Oakley, which began making a name for itself in the endurance sports industry. *Wide World of Sports* was there to capture the breathtaking drama again. The program only had one more year left on its contract with Ironman, and it did not renew afterward, taking with it the sponsorship that had once saved Ironman from extinction. Not that anyone was worried about it by that point. Things were very different. Valerie's little party had grown up into a flourishing professional race series with events around the world and a lucrative brand name. NBC quickly scooped up the broadcast rights. The burgeoning community of athletes was able to read news of the deal in half a dozen magazines dedicated to the sport.

There were dozens of employees and scores of proposals and thousands of athletes and millions of dollars involved. It was just too much for Valerie.

When she took on the race in 1981, a friend and fellow race organizer gave her a piece of advice: "Don't stay so long that you can't look at the scrapbooks." She never forgot that.

"I stayed too long," she admits. It doesn't come out as remorseful or sad. Her voice simply drops the exuberant, melodic tone that it held while discussing everything leading up to that moment. Even when thinking back on the pressing sense of guilt while singling out those 50 discretionary slots, there was still a lilt in her voice. Though sad, it was still a song. But when she gets to the moment when she walked away, the song ends abruptly. For Valerie, the song had begun dropping its pitch from the start, every battle to maintain the integrity of her vision stripping away the high notes as she went along. In 1989 Valerie sold World Triathlon Corporation for $3 million to Doctor James Gills, a Florida ophthalmologist who had grown to love Ironman through his own participation. For many athletes who had been there for Ironman's first decade and witnessed those that followed, that was the day the music died. Yet for her, the band had stopped playing long before.

"I was tired of being terrified and just plain tired. It became political. There was so much business to take care of. It got to the point where I couldn't see the athletes anymore. The first priority was to preserve the atmosphere. Dr. Gills understood what it was about and I was confident he'd take care of it. It was the best opportunity to get away, so I did," she says.

Though she believes that Gills had nothing but the best intentions for the race, Valerie confesses that the transfer of ownership was a peculiar and not entirely comfortable affair. She never met the man, and only spoke to him briefly by phone on a few occasions. Otherwise, the deal was crafted by her lawyer and representatives from Gills' office. They were Dave Yates, president of Gills' World Triathlon Corporation, and David Voth, who would later serve as the company's president. Both had participated in the Ironman, which gave Valerie confidence in her choice.

However, as the time to sign the deal approached, the attorney negotiating on behalf of WTC began trying to renegotiate certain terms, ultimately demanding the price be reduced on the day Valerie's attorney showed up to conclude the deal. Her lawyer simply closed his briefcase and announced, "We're done." The WTC representatives quickly regrouped and signed the deal as agreed. Dr. Gills expanded Ironman to include several more races throughout the United States, South America, Asia, and Europe over the next 19 years.

In 2002, WTC bought the rights to the Nice triathlon. The event that had threatened to end Valerie's party became Ironman France. In 2008 Jim Gills sold WTC to Providence Equity Securities, a large private equity firm, for an undisclosed amount estimated between $50 million and $80 million. Past winners Mark Allen and Dave Scott both went on to write about their experiences and develop successful endurance sport coaching businesses. In 2012, they sued author Matt Fitzgerald for writing an unauthorized account of their epic 1989 race. Among their complaints filed in court was that Fitzgerald had slandered them by calling them "exercise fanatics," "mentally unbalanced," and practicing "fringe religions."

Scott Tinley became a race organizer and started a charity called the Challenged Athletes Foundation, which provides services to amputees and people with other disabilities seeking to participate in athletics. He wrote a back-page column in *Triathlete* magazine for nearly 20 years until he was let go in 2010. Apparently the editorial staff decided that his writing about the sport's heritage and history didn't align with their marketing toward the younger crowd of athletes just getting into the sport. He suffered from depression for several years, which led him to study the phenomenon both in himself and other athletes. It culminated in a PhD and a book on the subject. Today he teaches at San Diego State University.

In 2012 he wrote a pair of articles revealing a much darker perspective of his days as a pro athlete. In one titled "Haven't We Met?" he wrote, "For the recovering athlete, there are feelings of absence and vacuity" and that "We kill the things we love." In the second piece, bearing the grim title "Native Bones and Lost Cities," he wrote that "Now that I'm on the other side of the mountain...I wish I could be back."

He lamented the current state of Ironman, saying it was "the institutionalization of success." It became commercial and corporate for him. "If you can't find what you need here, someone will get It for you," he wrote. After he retired from professional racing in 1999, he couldn't bring himself to even go to Hawaii to see the race for more than a decade. There was a personal level to his angst as well. "You know that Dave Scott doesn't hold any weight in Kona anymore when even he can't get onto the pier to greet me at the finish of my farewell race," he ruefully commented in an interview with triathlon website Slowtwitch. He tried for years to fight that process of institutionalization through the printed word, but by 2011 he decided he "couldn't make a difference anymore." "Capital opens up sport for people who don't give a fuck about its past," he grouses. He maintains that money isn't the problem, though; it's the insatiable lust for more. He believes all was lost for Ironman the day Valerie sold it. He draws comparisons between Dr. Gills and *Wall Street* greedmonger Gordon Gekko. In recent years his writing style has become darker, his stories about the history of Ironman more layered with shades of grey. More and more, people wonder if his bitterness is getting the better of him.

Each year, the old pros become less recognizable at Kona as the attending athletes become further removed from that generation. Even today's top competitors are becoming marginalized. In their place, another division has cut through Valerie's communal place, in the form of a red carpet. In 2013, WTC put a big marketing effort around celebrity chef Gordon Ramsay and former pro football player Hines Ward participating in the race. They attended the prerace press conference alongside the pros. Ramsay himself was featured on the cover of *Triathlete* magazine's vaunted pre-Kona issue. After the race, retired soccer star David Beckham announced he would begin training for Ironman. For as hard as they worked for everything they have, many of the old pros seem unhappy with what they have. Or maybe it's that they, too, can't stop themselves from wanting more.

Valerie escaped the buyer's remorse. Her story ended the moment the deal with Dr. Gills was signed. There was no return, no reprise, no gradual fading into the background. She moved to San Diego in 1990 shortly after the deal was completed, then moved on to Florida to help take care of her ailing mother and father in 1995. She never returned to Hawaii. She doesn't know how many Ironman races there are in the world today. At the time she was interviewed for this book she was not aware that WTC had created an equally expansive series of 70.3-mile, or "Half-Ironman," races, or that the company has expanded to running a third series of races using the same distance as the Olympics. She doesn't know who the Ironman World Champion is. She doesn't read any triathlon-related news. The only triathlon she ever participated in as an athlete was in the early 1990s. She didn't hate it, but she didn't enjoy it either. In 2009 she was invited to attend the USA Triathlon Ceremony held to induct her into its Hall of Fame. She declined due to her obligations to care for her parents. USAT offered to pay for nurses to care for them while she made the trip. She still didn't go.

What she did carry over was the one and only thing that ever really mattered. Twenty-five years later Valerie still keeps in touch with Emily, the girl who was almost named after her, just as she does with hundreds of others. Friends from around the world continue to call her. In her own way, Valerie never left Ironman. She took with her the parts she loved the most. "I never cared about finishing times. I liked the pro athletes as much as anyone, but I always found myself cheering for the everyman athletes. I always wanted to make sure the guys in back kept coming to do the race. That seemed to be the most important thing to me. When someone started talking to me about some new bike or diet or training plan, my eyes just glazed over. It was about the people," she says.

The story of John Collins maintains its position at the forefront of Ironman's lore. The 15 men who undertook that first race are a potent symbol in the eyes of the sport's most dedicated participants. The sport's culture finds a way to tell every newcomer the legend of that first race, binding the mystique that makes Kona so appealing into its lucrative origin story. Valerie Silk has largely been written out of it, perhaps because you couldn't describe her endurance and heroism without remembering the unpleasant details of her obstacles. Those parts have been edited to "…and the rest is history" and swept under the rug. The majority of modern athletes' perceptions of "what it's all about" is informed by those iconic moments caught on the ABC cameras and broadcast around the world. Time has eroded the portrait of the woman with boundless grace behind the cameras as well as the memory of what she stood for.

Few people remember her, but Jane Bockus is one of them. When asked what she remembers of Valerie, the words immediately spring forth. "She was a lady—a *lady*." Valerie's portrait remains clear in her memory, as does her idea of what Ironman was supposed to be. Jane witnessed the next steps of Ironman's story. The rest wasn't just history to her. It was a valuable lesson in good intentions and where they can lead. As a volunteer who helped both races from their beginnings, it would eventually become her life's mission to keep Ultraman from repeating the messier parts of Ironman's history.

What would have happened if the ABC cameras hadn't filmed Julie Moss crawling across that line? What if Valerie had never offered prize money? What if she'd kept the number of race slots down instead of offering aid stations to accommodate a larger participant pool? What if qualifying for the race meant being judged of good character rather than simply how fast you were? Would Ironman still exist today? And if so, would Valerie still be running it? What kind of sport would it be, and what would it mean to those who participate in it?

Perhaps it would be Ultraman. Sometimes it's been better. Sometimes worse. It's always been different.

chapter five

So You Want to Be an Ultraman?

"At one point in your life you either have the thing you want or the reasons why you don't."

—Andy Roddick

THE FIELD OF CONTESTANTS at Ultraman Hawaii varies from year to year, but the starting line has reached or been very close to capacity in the last five years. That the established limit is only 40 athletes leads to the false impression that the ordeal's distance and cost make it exclusive to all but the most extreme challenge seekers. In reality, there are frequently dozens more applications than what the race can allow. There happen to be 46 for the 2013 race by June. You need more than the cash and cojones to get in, though. There are a couple of deadlines to meet, some roadblocks to be navigated, and a few criteria spelled out in black and white. For instance, one must either be a former Ultraman World Championships official finisher or qualify by finishing one of the other Ultraman races. If it's been longer than a year since you've logged an official finish at an Ultraman, you must have a recorded official finish at an Iron-distance race (not necessarily a WTC Ironman-branded race) or an event that the Ultraman board of directors assesses as equivalent to an Ironman. While still an indicator of exceptional athleticism, multiday running and cycling races are not always considered equivalent because they focus on only one discipline. Item 4 on the application form explicitly asks entrants to STATE YOUR SWIMMING ABILITIES RELATIVE TO THE

6.2-MILE DISTANCE. History has shown that if you're not up to the challenge of the three-day race, you'll likely find out during the first three hours.

The most important items on the form have nothing to do with physical ability. They address prerequisites of character. These are the questions for which you have to read between the lines and answer outside the box. Question 6 is sort of a big one: WHY DO YOU DO ULTRA ENDURANCE SPORTS, AND WHY DO YOU WANT TO PARTICIPATE IN THIS EVENT? Extra paper is allowed if you need the space. There is also the final note in the instructions on the form: IF YOU CANNOT MEET THESE QUALIFICATIONS, BUT STILL FEEL YOU ARE QUALIFIED FOR FURTHER CONSIDERATION, INCLUDE A LETTER OF EXPLANATION. More than one person has received such consideration and gone all the way to the finish line, but they are few, far between, and exceptional—even among this group of unique people.

The bottom line is that you can't just wave a check at Jane Bockus and expect to get a slot. It's not that she and her directors don't want your money. Indeed, there are significant expenses in putting the whole thing on and quite often they would love to have it. But there's something else they need more, and they're not willing to make compromises. The 40-contestant limit is a hard line. And having more than 40 applicants doesn't guarantee 40 people getting into the race. You can't just be a good athlete, because you don't just "do" Ultraman. You become part of it. There have been years when fewer than 20 people started the race. There were even two years that the race was canceled due to lack of applicants. That's how dedicated the organizers are, and it demonstrates the initial point of divergence between Ironman and Ultraman. This is an enterprise for preservation rather than profit. They'd rather have no race at all than one that didn't uphold their principles.

The kindred spirits Jane Bockus and Sheryl and David Cobb seek are hard to find, but they've found them a few at a time. Those additions have become a large, dependable group of passionate athletes who return year after year. Though Suzy Degazon will be missed, seven women appear on the starting roster this year. The record attendance by women in a single year is 10, set in 2009. There is even a healthy population of sponsored athletes who make money through endorsement deals. The field has it all. Ultraman has evolved survivability by culturing diversity.

Just because the athlete pool has filled enough to keep it from evaporating between years doesn't mean it's gotten any easier to filter them through the registration process, though. Ultraman is a destination found only on the road less traveled. It's the nature of the pilgrims who reach it to move in mysterious and sometimes confounding ways. Their lives are hectic and eccentric, but the results are the same. Late applications and trouble paying the registration fee keep several athletes on questionable status well into July. Miro Kregar is delayed by problems making a wire transfer from Slovenia, for instance.

There are dozens of similar outstanding issues to be addressed late into the registration period. This is only the beginning of the administrative and logistical headaches that the Cobbs will contend with right up until the race starts in November. Still, the biggest hurdle for many athletes is within themselves. Though the 2013 race is only four months away, the 2012 event is only eight months in the past. Physically and financially, there's not much time for athletes to catch their breath. Athletes who return to the island in multiple consecutive years are rare. Most can't keep up with the stress of finding ways to finance the journey while also maintaining the required level of fitness. Additionally, filling out the registration form requires a great deal of soul-searching. Some have to search more than others.

Gary Wang knew he'd come back even before he crossed the finish line in 2012. It's a non-negotiable for him. Being there among those people refreshes him. He loves what he's found in Hawaii. He can't get enough of it. Despite a finish that suggests Yasuko Miyazaki could be champion with a little more training, her focus is already on her new marriage and having children. Kathy Winkler is also done. Her medical problems during the run were too big of a warning sign that she can't recover properly anymore. Whatever it takes out of her to do something like this, she can't get back. Amy Palmeiro-Winters wants nothing more than to return. She has a score to settle with the fates that have frustrated her last two tries. But now she has a new obstacle to overcome: getting in. For the last two years, she's been able to get a slot because of her compelling story and her successes in other ultra endurance events. But now there are so many people trying to get in who have either competed in Hawaii in the past or in one of the other Ultraman races that Jane's hand is forced. Giving Amy a third shot would necessarily come at the price of excluding someone who'd earned a spot according to the black-and-white rules. Amy is told that she needs to qualify for Hawaii before returning. It only adds to her frustration.

Just as disappointment doesn't always discourage, success doesn't always motivate. Despite having won the race for her third consecutive time, Amber Monforte isn't so sure she'll be back. The 2012 race took her to a level of pain she hadn't felt before. She also has her new husband to spend time with, a new home to settle into, and a new job to get up to speed on. Ultraman is only one part of a life that has suddenly become very crowded.

Men's champion Alexandre Ribeiro is of a totally different mindset. Triathlon is the superstructure of Ribeiro's existence. He's been racing since he was 16. He'll be 48 this year. He's turned his multiple championships into a lucrative reputation for himself in his native Brazil, where he runs a coaching business. It allows him to work and play at the same time, and is one of the biggest reasons behind his success in Kona. Even his fellow athletes marvel at his ability to balance work, play, and time with his children. Though an indefatigable energy is evident in his daily routine, the secret to his success seems to be an absence of the kinds of distractions most people have. No inordinate amount of time is wasted on social media or games or collections or clubs or other hobbies. It's too easy to label him as one-dimensional. The perpetual, beaming smile on his face, somehow enhanced by his shaved head the same way as his brightly shining eyes are by the subtle crow's feet radiating from the corners, exhibits his belief that being "well-rounded" isn't the panacea of contentedness. His is the wisdom of blissful austerity. If he could be distracted from his passions, then he wasn't passionate enough about them in the first place.

Amber Monforte changes her mind and registers for the 2013 race by April. Home is where the heart is, and her heart is in Kona. "It's the people," she says. "I just love being there around them so much." So the application is filled out, the registration paid, the commitment made. But it's not the same this time around. "I signed up, but I'm hesitant. I don't know if it makes sense, but I'm excited to see the people, but not as much to race."

She's in for a fourth year in Kona, but the terms of the contract she makes with herself are different, largely as a consequence of the changes in her life. A registered nurse by trade, one of the drawbacks of her profession is that changing jobs often means starting at the bottom of the scheduling totem pole each time. She starts at the new hospital the week after the 2012 race, and it's almost completely on the night shift. The hours, not to mention the harsh winter temperatures in the Lake Tahoe area to which she and her husband, Ryan, moved, make it nearly impossible to get outside to train. Not that it's a major blow to her regimen. Several of the athletes routinely take a few months off before resuming their longer workouts.

If only that was the extent of her problems. The night-shift hours lead to other complications. She had trouble adjusting her sleep patterns, alternating between restless, sporadic periods of sleep and moving through her days like a zombie. She tried registering for a few races in the early spring to get back in a routine, but found herself dropping out of most of them. "It's hard to race well when all you want to do is lie down on the sidewalk and take a nap," she laughs. But the humor deflects the seriousness of the situation. By April, Amber knows something is wrong. She should have adjusted to the schedule by that time. Blood work reveals that the night-shift hours have caused her thyroid to stop working properly. Her doctor goes so far as to suggest she quit her job. Since that isn't really an option, she goes on some medication and things improve.

She's hardly back to training before she turns her ankle on a trail run, injuring it so severely that she winds up on crutches. It takes another four weeks before she can return to serious activity again. She finally gets in a few good runs before her first serious endurance contest of the year, and perhaps the race that is the second most dear to her heart: the Western States 100-mile trail run. The course is so hilly and rugged that anyone who can finish it in less than 24 hours receives a gold belt buckle. Some of the water crossings even require rubber rafts.

This year, the temperatures soar into the 100s. She crossed the line in less than 23 hours last year. This time it takes 26, and she's happy to have finished it at all. "It just didn't feel good, especially with the heat. I really wanted to quit early on, but I had friends come all the way from Lake Tahoe just to pace me. I sort of felt pressure to keep going for them. You don't want to let someone like that down after they come all that way for you. In the end I was glad I did it," she says.

Yet the heat may have been more helpful than she realizes. Amber feels less fatigue after this year's run when compared to 2012. She theorizes that the temperatures slowed her down and therefore kept her from doing more damage to her muscles. Given her fitness at this point, the impact the double marathon in Kona had, and the challenge looming ahead, it's possible she's better off for having not gone at it so hard. She's only been on her bike once since the second day of Ultraman 2012. Most of her racing gear is still packed in the boxes she and Ryan used to move into the new house. There is a lot of work to do, and precious little time to do it. Only time can tell if she'll be ready to race in November.

The best description of Amber's streak in the Ultraman World Championships is "dynasty the hard way." She has never caught a break during her run, and every race seems punctuated by its own special obstacle. She almost decided not to start the first race she won in 2011 after her then-boyfriend, professional triathlete Conrad Stoltz, broke up with her five weeks earlier. They'd come to Kona early so Stoltz could compete in the world championships of the XTerra triathlon—a form of racing that involves riding mountain bikes and running on rugged trails—and then stay while Amber made final preparations for Ultraman. Stoltz, perhaps the greatest athlete ever to compete in XTerra, waited until he won his race, taking the title for the fourth time in his career. Then he dropped the bomb on her. He was leaving her and going back home to South Africa.

The pair met during Amber's brief period competing as a professional athlete herself. "Professional" is a relative term. Twenty-five years after Valerie Silk's efforts to help the most serious athletes in triathlon, there are still two very different classes of professional triathlete. Very few receive endorsement deals numerous and well-paying enough to make an actual salary. The vast majority must compete for prize money only, hoping they can accumulate enough wins to garner attention from sponsors. Amber's stint lasted only two years, and though at one point she climbed up to fifth place in the overall women's standings in the XTerra race series, it wasn't sufficient to garner attention from sponsors.

XTerra is a tiny sector of the greater triathlon culture, itself a niche sport. With the race series contending with financial peril during the same years, there simply wasn't enough money to go around. Stoltz, on the other hand, had managed to make enough of a living at it. His family also maintains a large farm in his native South Africa. That was what fomented the breakup. The couple had already once planned to marry, in 2008, only to delay the ceremony over disagreement about how they would balance their time between South Africa and the US. To demonstrate her commitment to the relationship, Amber sold her home and quit her job in Reno, Nevada, shortly before going to Kona for the race. It made no difference. He gave her his final decision and flew home without her. "I was in a tailspin," she says of those days. Devastated, directionless, and suddenly without one-third of her support crew, she spent hours on the bike just crying until she stopped riding at all. Having broken the women's course record while qualifying at Ultraman Canada in 2010, starting Hawaii at that point felt out of the question. It was only with the insistent encouragement of the other competitors that she began to pull it together. "They'd come and ask me to go for a ride with them. They'd tell me they weren't taking 'no' for an answer," she remembers. She gradually began to accept their embrace, and discovered a new family that would change the course of her life—the Ultraman *Ohana*.

The hits kept coming. After getting back on track emotionally, Amber faced some of the toughest competition in Ultraman's 30 years. A professional Ironman triathlete named Hillary Biscay decided to compete. But the Goliath of that year was reigning six-time women's champion Shanna Armstrong, who had won the race for the first time in 2003 at 29, a tender age by ultra endurance standards. Shanna was 36 and by all indications in her prime. Time and experience had helped her chop another two hours off her finishing time. She completed the 2009 race in just less than 26 hours and in seventh place overall. She'd only been beaten in one race, in Canada in 2009 when she finished behind three women, including Amber. Finishing nearly three and a half hours ahead of Shanna in Canada meant Amber had a real shot. But Biscay was an X-factor and there were doubts about whether Amber's heart was fully in it.

Biscay opened the race with a record-setting swim, starting the 90-mile day one bike leg 22 minutes ahead of Amber. Amber's strongest discipline is cycling, however, and she chased Hillary to the south end of the island, cutting the gap between them to less than five minutes by the end of the day.

On the second day, following a much more difficult cycling leg winding 170 miles to the north along the eastern shore of the island, Amber erased those remaining five minutes and put herself ahead by another 31. Exhausted by the effort to keep Amber in sight during the previous two days, Hillary ultimately reconciled herself to defending her second-place spot. That fight was also tooth and nail. Shanna also slowly carved into Hillary's lead during the bike leg, and by the start of the third day the pair were separated by less than 10 minutes. The former champion managed to get ahead of the pro Ironman, but Hillary dug deep and held Shanna off, maintaining the runner-up spot by a mere four minutes. All three women set new course records that year. Shanna retired from racing after that. Hillary returned to Ironman and focused on starting a new triathlon apparel business and spending time with her new husband, Maik Twelsiek, also a professional Ironman athlete. But she didn't forget about Ultraman or Amber.

Amber returned to the mainland to pick up the pieces from her breakup with Stoltz. Essentially homeless and without a job, she spent the first part of 2011 touring the southwest United States with her dog and most of her earthly belongings in a van. She spent time visiting friends and looking for a new job, which she found easily enough. While she had won the 2011 Ultraman Hawaii by a much safer margin of more than three hours, the year leading up to it wasn't the easiest. Things really began to turn around when she met Ryan. They got engaged in May and married in September. Between a few minor injuries and the wedding planning, there was less time to train. She wasn't in peak form coming to Kona the third time, resulting in her closest call yet against Winkler and Miyazaki.

And now, despite Kathy and Yasuko both bowing out, this may be the toughest race of Amber's career. All Ultraman athletes readily, even proudly, admit that they have limits. The pride comes from their abundant faith that life is about conquering limits, and that they battle against their own as often and intrepidly as possible. What none of them want to admit is that sometimes the limits win. They are so loath to acknowledge the prospects of failure that it's left to subtle implication, but there it is nonetheless. Like completing Green Beret training or summiting Everest, finishing the Ultraman wouldn't be such a big deal if the odds against it weren't so huge. In the strange physics of human competition, failure is the antiparticle of achievement. The two interact at the quark level of an ultra endurance athlete's psyche, generating those universal forces of ambition, courage, and hope. Amber looks forward to pushing the envelope every time she goes out, but this year she may find that her greatest adversary is her own body. Her will remains an unstoppable force, but her legs always threaten to become immovable objects.

Cory Foulk is heading into a battle of different intangible forces, mainly ego and perceptions. Competing in this year's race would give Foulk the record for most Ultraman Hawaii appearances, with 15. He certainly wants to do it. At 54, he's in better physical condition than most men half his age. There's just one problem. Though Foulk has recorded Ironman race finishes in seven different age group categories during his life and is widely regarded as an institution within Ultraman, he isn't qualified to race. Because his last official Ultraman finish was in 2011, the rules state that he needs to demonstrate the ability to finish by completing an Iron-distance event. He hasn't done one yet. Nor does he have one on his calendar.

He's put all his eggs in another, bigger basket: the Race Around Ireland. Starting and finishing just northwest of Dublin, the 1,300-mile bike race is one of the crown jewels of ultra endurance cycling. Competitors ride nonstop. The winners sleep less than an hour a day on average. If he finishes, Jane will consider it an adequate equivalent to an Ironman. But he'll still have to answer the question on the application regarding his ability to finish the swim.

Then it's just a matter of paying the entry fee, which is its own peculiar difficulty. A resident of Hawaii for nearly 30 years, Foulk has gotten perhaps a little too comfortable in his relationship with the event and the people who run it. He mails in the application and casually tells Sheryl Cobb that he'll "bring the money by." When the time he mentions to her rolls around, it turns out he's gone off to another of the islands for the day. He forgets to reschedule. It gets to the point that his spot in the race is in jeopardy before he sends Sheryl a flurry of text messages and leaves her a voice mail to let her know he'll be by with "the dough," but he doesn't mention specific times again. Sheryl, and indeed everyone, is familiar with Cory's antics when it comes to stuff like this. It makes it somewhat maddening to deal with him, but it's the same element within him that endears him to the family of athletes and has made him something of a legend in Ironman.

Foulk is not alone in untangling his way through the administrative parts of the application. Duncan Cairns also needs to qualify, as his last official Ultraman finish was at the Canadian race in 2010. He's scheduled to race Ironman Canada, which takes place before the Race Around Ireland. It would qualify him ahead of Cory, which isn't a big deal but does mean that Foulk would take the last slot reserved for prior finishers. The last two spots go to any first-time finishers at the two other Ultraman races in Canada and Wales.

There are only two weeks allowed for qualifiers to make the decision, though, leaving the potential entrants precious time to consider everything that goes into actually making it happen. If no one takes them, the slots open to other applicants, and this is where Jane's discretionary power comes into play, much like the discretionary slots Valerie Silk used to hold when she ran Ironman. These are the slots for the people who don't qualify according to the letter of the law, but stand the test of its spirit. They're the crazies, the wild at heart, the ones who fall out of the blue and into Jane's lap. They hear about this race, and they don't know why, but they just have to get to it. And if they're sincere about it in a way that only Jane is somehow sure of it, then it means that Ultraman needs them just as much as they need it. There's no definitive way to know what will come of it, but it's always been something special. Jane is a divining rod for these things.

Ultraman's selection process is meant to preserve its authenticity and sense of family. It's another cobblestone in a road built of good intentions. And though the organizers have bypassed the purgatory Valerie Silk wandered into with her discretionary Ironman slots, they've begun to notice a few hot coals along the shoulder. As they work through the selection process for the 2013 race, Sheryl and Dave Cobb begin to wonder if they need to change the policies. The solutions aren't easy, because it's more an issue of things that could be a problem rather than things that are. These are often just the sort of issues that plague endurance racing events. Caught up in the daily "improvise-adapt-overcome" management of actually pulling off an event, directors have little time to think about the bigger picture needed to develop a multiyear growth strategy. As a result, yesterday's potential problem can suddenly become today's crisis.

The prime example this year is 58-year-old Kurt Madden of Big Bear, California. On the face of it, he ought to be a cinch to get in the race. It is the 30th anniversary of the inaugural Ultraman, which Madden won to become its first world champion (though the title didn't exist at that time). His return adds a sense of nostalgia to the occasion.

But while everyone is happy to have him, it demonstrates a potential flaw in the way the system is currently set up. Though Madden remains a highly active ultra endurance athlete and has a current Ironman finish qualifying him to race, he hasn't actually been involved with Ultraman in some years. His last finish was in 1985, and other than a few times spent as a support crew for other athletes, he's been pretty scarce. In a way, he demonstrates how someone can take advantage of the underlying ethos that shapes the rules—once an Ultraman finisher, always an Ultraman finisher. You're a lifelong member of the *ohana*, Hawaiian for "family."

The Ultraman family has always opened its home to any long wayward son or daughter who knocks on the door. But the expectation has always been that the dutiful sons would outnumber the prodigals. Madden is a reminder that, with only 40 slots available for the World Championships, it doesn't take many people to create issues. Madden hasn't done anything wrong. Therein lies the problem. It wouldn't even require every previous finisher to apply to create havoc. In fact, it wouldn't take more than a half dozen, and that's the potential crisis. There are more qualified finishers than ever before in the event's history. There are also more people qualified to have their first go in Hawaii. Both populations will keep growing—the latter of the two at an exponential rate. Conflicts are bound to emerge, and it's likely that no solution exists that will satisfy everyone.

As with most issues like this, Sheryl insists on engaging the problem before it comes to a head. It's one of the driving aspects of her character that have made her Jane's number two on the Ultraman board of directors. David is less involved with the management of the race series due to the more structured hours of his job. He's also the quieter of the couple. But when he does speak, the North Carolina native and former Air Force intelligence sergeant has a knack for characterizing things with salty Southern wisdom. He boils the qualification issue down to beer math: "You got two races with up to 40 people, so that means you could have as many as 80 new people trying to get 40 slots for the World Championships every year. There's just not enough room to give everyone a shot that wants it."

There's a corollary to that problem. The Canadian race was turned into an official Ultraman event back in 1996 as an initiative to spread the race's ideals, so that people who couldn't travel to Hawaii could still experience the Ultraman spirit. Wales was added as a location closer to European athletes in 2011 for the same purpose. But developments took an unexpected turn. Those competitors who have already qualified in either Canada or the United Kingdom and finished in the World Championships tend to prefer going back to Hawaii, while the major impetus among first-time athletes at the qualifiers is to punch their ticket to Kona. The result is that few veterans show up to the qualifiers, leaving them stocked entirely with rookies year after year. This not only diminishes the effort to "share the spirit" but contributes to headaches for the race directors. To begin with, they have to work that much harder at promoting their races to make potential competitors aware of their existence and get their interest to sign up. It's the opposite of what Jane intended. Instead of everything growing outward from Hawaii, it's all feeding back in the same fashion as the Ironman series.

Then come the problems of actually getting through the races. Without the seasoned athletes to help guide the rookies, snafus and blunders are more frequent at the qualifiers. The problem is compounded in the UK by weak turnout over the last three years. There were 29 athletes who participated in the inaugural race there, but foul weather made for a wet and dreary weekend of racing. That was the suspected reason that only 11 people came out the next year. But after that race ran under gorgeous conditions that year there were still only 15 registrants for the 2013 race, and all of them first-timers. The numbers themselves threaten the race's existence. Given the high costs involved just to get the permits and equipment necessary to put on any endurance event, no matter where it occurs, endurance race production is an industry with extremely narrow margins.

If participation doesn't increase, Ultraman's first effort at growth in 20 years may die off. One possible idea is to change the criteria for the World Championships, requiring applicants to have a more recent finish at another Ultraman event. It would resolve the issues of participation numbers and experience at the same time, and hopefully enhance the Ultraman spirit. Then again, it might not. The only reason past finishers may be coming back is because the door is open. Will the wayward sons be so eager to return if conditions are placed on their homecoming? No one knows.

What's at stake are the fates of people like Dene Sturm, currently one of three people on the alternates list. It will be a banner year for her if she makes it. She's already won the lottery for an entry slot to the Hawaiian Ironman. She doesn't have big ultra endurance race résumé. She hasn't been to one of the other races to qualify for Hawaii and she doesn't even entertain dreams of doing this more than once. She just wants to do it once—not because she wants to tell people she did, but because she doesn't ever want to have to remind herself that she didn't.

Dene left her parents' home in Montana right after high school, in search of freedom and adventure. She found it in Alaska, where she started working as a waitress to finance her explorations of the great white north. She found adventure when she took a job as a cook on a tourist boat, ferrying visitors around to choice fishing locations and on wilderness expeditions. She so impressed the owner that she was soon taking people out on hikes as a guide. To further entice her to stay with the operation, they offered to pay her airfare to Hawaii and let her stay in their time share for six weeks every year. She saw the Ironman for the first time on one of those vacations. "I told myself then, I was going to do that some day," she says. Years later, she finally took the leap. When she moved to Hawaii permanently, she left her car back in Alaska for fear she wouldn't stay. That was 13 years ago. Today she says she has no intention of going back to Alaska, or anywhere else for that matter.

Dene's been racing on the islands all that time. She raced her first half-Ironman in 2003, and participates in the local races around Kona nearly every weekend. Perhaps her favorite event to date was the "Monster Mango" race, an Iron-distance triathlon that requires entrants to use support crews instead of providing aid stations, in the style of the original Ironman.

When she's not racing, she volunteers in support of friends. She met Sheryl at one such race, who in turn introduced her to Jane. That was the beginning of her involvement in Ultraman. If someone is putting on a triathlon, you can count on Dene to help. She's split her time between crewing for athletes and working as a bike course official with her boyfriend, Doug. But she's always wanted to race Ultraman herself. Dene is the archetypal water girl who dreamed of suiting up and stepping onto the field with the team just once.

Everyone who knows her says that she deserves to get in. She has done as much or more than anyone else in Hawaii to keep the sport alive and well. Her enthusiasm shows through in every aspect of her involvement, right down to her fashion. All of her equipment, from her race jersey and shoes to her bike, are painted in her favorite color, bright neon green. The only thing more electric is her smile when she's out on the road. She's one of the most ebullient, tireless members of the group. She's the biggest fan of this sport you'll ever meet. It's what makes everyone root for her. She hasn't qualified for a slot, but she's *earned* one. How she's earned it represents all the intangible, indescribable things that are essential to the heart of Ultraman.

Rules and intangibles are natural enemies. The more people who qualify according to the rules, the less room the directors have to let someone like

Dene slide in the door without protest. There's a fine line between ohana and nepotism. Jane has never been much for explaining herself, and that's bred a certain degree of misunderstanding among the most dedicated athletes who worry about the possibility of not making the cut in future years. Some of them use terms like "the Hawaii connection" and "the ohana mafia." People surmise that certain people get in because of a special relationship with Jane or Sheryl. They're incorrect, but that doesn't stop the rumors from spreading.

As recently as five years ago Jane would never have thought that she'd face dilemmas stemming from growth and popularity. It's about the only type of problem she and Ultraman haven't gone through. She and Valerie Silk are remarkably similar in their trials. While they faced the most difficult and enduring problems of keeping an extremely unique race alive, neither of them went through the aggravation of actually getting it started in the first place. Though Jane showed more initial interest in Ultraman than Valerie did in Ironman, she came to be in control of the race the same way that Valerie did: the man who started it simply couldn't keep doing it forever. How Ultraman got started and found its way to Jane is the story of Curtis Tyler.

chapter six

The Race of Your Life

"Don't ever allow yourself to feel trapped by your choices. Take a look at yourself. You are a unique person created for a specific purpose. Your gifts matter. Your story matters. Your dreams matter. You matter."

—Michael Oher

JUNE 5, 1969. Despite the warnings of the naval officer who notified them of the accident, Curtis Tyler's parents went to Korea anyway. They arrived at the 121st Medical Evacuation Hospital in Inchon, South Korea, 12 days after it happened. The first question they asked doctors was why he'd been placed in a straitjacket. They were told that despite having been unconscious until that very day, coming out of a 16-hour surgery on his shattered leg and fractured skull, and being in casts and traction, Tyler had managed to attack the orderly attending to him when awoke. His bed had been near the hospital's helicopter landing pad, and in his disoriented state he woke up believing he'd been captured by the North Koreans.

Getting hit by an enemy rocket might have done less damage than the lowest bidder who assembled the LARC-V amphibious cargo vehicle he'd been on. Essentially a boat with wheels, the vehicle's hydraulic system suddenly failed while Tyler and his group were rounding a cliff. With nowhere else to go, he jumped over the side hoping to get clear of the 15-ton behemoth. He didn't. The doctors had done their best, but they couldn't save the vision in his right eye. He'd never walk the same way again, and would probably be in a wheelchair by the age of 40. They knew nothing about his fractured pelvis and wrists, or the breaks in his spine, or that his shoulder joint was shattered. Their failure to treat those issues would leave him with chronic pain for the rest of his life.

Tyler had been a top graduate from college and his Naval officer training course. His family had a long military tradition dating all the way back to his namesake, who'd fought in the American Revolution. With a degree in geology and prestigious assignments on oceanographic vessels, he'd been a rising star in the junior officer ranks. Now it was all over. Beyond his physical injuries, he was paralyzed by a single question, and it wasn't about the straitjacket. His father was the first one he asked.

"Why me? What did I do to deserve this?"

"You know," said his father, "there's a silver lining in the darkest cloud. Something good is going to come out of this."

"You've got to be kidding me. What good could come out of this?"

"I don't know, but I'm going to pray about it, because God knows more than we do."

That was easier to believe, since Curtis knew absolutely nothing. Physically and spiritually, he was in total darkness. It was very much the end of life as Curtis Tyler knew it. Therein lay the very silver lining he and his father couldn't yet perceive. With no possibility to continue what he knew, it was the opportunity to discover that which he didn't. The end of that life marked the beginning of a new one.

Curtis recounts these events fluidly, as if they happened yesterday, with a serious, measured tone and deep voice. At 65, he still cuts an impressive figure, standing over six feet tall, with broad shoulders and evident vigor. His hair cut and demeanor very much give him the look of a navy man. His face grows stern and intense when he talks about things he believes in or pauses to think. There's a dignity about his presence reminiscent of Colin Powell. You can't tell he's blind in the one eye. See him walk by, and you might notice the limp in one leg. Walk with him through the breezeways of the Keauhou Sheraton, you'll notice the confidence of his stride. His mind is incredibly sharp. The memories come easily, and he changes gears between events and their cultural context at will. He analogizes principles of his Christian faith to the beliefs of his Hawaiian heritage as smoothly as he translates between Hawaiian and English. He is simultaneously founder, historian, and theologian. He speaks of the early life of Ultraman as if it were his own. In many respects, that's exactly what it is.

Maybe his new life was his silver lining, but it wasn't an easy transition. He almost didn't make it out of Korea. Two of the four engines on the plane from Inchon to Tripler Army Hospital in Honolulu gave out, forcing it to make an emergency landing. Once back in Hawaii, he set about making life harder for himself.

"I was a terrible patient at Tripler," he says. "I screamed, yelled, threw food. One night I was at the end of my rope. I was sitting in my wheelchair in a hallway at 1:00 AM and a resident asked me what was wrong. I told him I couldn't take the pain anymore. He said to me, 'There are some things that we can do to help people, other problems we have to let nature take its course. We screwed some things up. I'm sorry.'

"Later I heard rain pounding against the window. It occurred to me that *Wow, I came close to never hearing wind or seeing rain again.* It reminded me of Hawaiian proverbs: *No rain, no life. When the heavens weep, the earth flourishes.* The Hawaiian word for law translates to 'how is the water divided.' All this came to me, and made me realize I had to develop a new perspective on wind and rain."

After that he was done being a broken, condemned man. He stopped wondering why bad things had happened to him and started healing. He was not dead, and if he could find a way to enjoy the rain, he could live and flourish again.

Though his parents had raised him in Kona, his father had since taken a job in New England. When he was done at Tripler, Curtis was flown to St. Aubin's Naval Hospital in Queens, New York. He didn't stay there long. The St. Aubin's staff "babied" him, in his words. "Everyone kept telling me that I couldn't do this or that. I wanted to get better, and they said there were rules against me doing things. The Hawaiian culture holds a strong belief in *mana*, an innate sense of the blessing of your own creation. We are given gifts and talents at birth. Often we associate restraint with treatment, be that chemical or physical restraints. But there are verbal restraints as well. We tell people 'You can't do that' or 'That's impossible,' and by doing that we don't recognize a person for who they are, which is stealing their mana. We should never let anyone steal our mana. So I finally said to them, 'Those are your rules. My rules are different. I'm tired of this. I want to get well. You don't know my limits. I do.'"

They transferred him to the VA hospital in New Haven, Connecticut. The staff there found he had developed osteomyelitis, an infection of the bones. When he finally got over that, he decided it was time to begin training for his comeback to life. Because of the limited mobility in his leg, he thought he'd try swimming. He went down to the local YMCA to look into it. "They looked at me and said they couldn't let me in with crutches because I might slip and fall. So I asked them if I could crawl in. They looked at me a little apprehensively and I asked if I could slither in. Then I asked them if someone could bring me in a wheelchair and just dump me in. I told them to give me a chance. They finally let me try."

He was swimming a mile a day within a month. Then he started riding a bike. By 1973 Curtis was a certified scuba instructor and volunteering as a swim instructor at the YMCA. Yet diving off the Eastern Seaboard was a bit too cold for his liking, especially when he remembered how warm it was around the Hawaiian islands he grew up on. So he decided to pack up and go back. He was a new man setting out to find a new life.

He got a job as a scuba instructor at one of the local hotels. While there he met the establishment's tennis pro, who happened to be a girl he'd known in his younger years. They fell in love and married. It was also at the hotel that he met a businessman who became interested in his story and capabilities. The man asked Curtis if he'd ever considered going into insurance, to which he replied no. But within another year he gave up the diving job and became one of the first life insurance agents on the island of Hawaii. "I got to do a lot of good for people," he says. "I wasn't always the best at it because of, unbeknownst to me, some brain injuries from my accident. But I was able to serve the community."

Through all of this, he was still swimming on a nearly daily basis, always at least a mile and oftentimes four or five. He taught open-water swimming and was active in the local masters swimming club, and even began organizing a few races of his own, as he felt it was time to get out of the insurance business. That's when Ironman came into the picture.

It was Curtis' friend and fellow swimmer Moe Matthews who heard about it first, from Valerie Silk in 1981. Honolulu was no longer big enough to accommodate all the people coming to her party. She wanted to know if there were people in Kona interested in helping to host it. No one in the Kona masters swim group had heard of the Ironman before, but it sounded like fun. Moe, Curtis, and their respective wives volunteered significant time to help put everything together, even helping to design the course. Like everything and everyone else associated with Ironman, things for Curtis just sort of happened. The next thing he knew, he was the swim course director. That was just the beginning.

Ironman's first year on Hawaii brought a man named Conrad Will from Del Mar, California. He and Curtis developed a friendship. They shared their strong enthusiasm for the Ironman with another of Curtis' friends, Alex Smith. As they explored ever farther from Kona by bike, Conrad and Alex began to envision a bike race around the entire island. They asked Curtis what he thought. It sounded great to him. In addition to their collective enthusiasm for endurance racing, the three men had become concerned about the direction in which Ironman was headed.

"We began to see Ironman grow. [There were 385 entrants in the 1981 race, 546 in the February 1982 event, and 919 in October 1982.] And then they started closing the roads and sponsors came in. I saw all these guys come in. And whenever anyone brings money in, they want things in return. The thought in the community was that it was getting to be too much. It was too impersonal. It was too much of a competition, too media- and money-driven," Curtis says.

"We talked with the race directors and Valerie about reining it in. I was the Ohana Liaison for the event, working the tables where the families came in. Prize money hadn't come in quite yet, but it kept getting bigger and bigger. From some peoples' perspective, who weren't involved, the wonderful journey that was Ironman became an inconvenience. A few of us never imagined that we could accommodate 2,000 bikes on the pier. But they've done it, and I commend them all. It's a wonderful race." But the thing of it for Curtis was that it turned into a race. It didn't start out that way.

Alex, Conrad, and Curtis evolved the bike race concept into a triathlon. The first thing they did was bring the idea to Valerie and ask her if she'd be okay with it. Realizing that it wasn't meant to compete with Ironman, she gave no objections. Things moved quickly after that. Curtis' main focus initially was to figure out the actual mechanics of the course. How could a group of people get all the way around Hawaii in three days by swimming, cycling, and running? Where would they stop? Where would they sleep? What was possible? What was safe? The naval officer and geographer in him came to the fore as he began resolving the logistics of such an undertaking. But as he surveyed the roads for a viable physical challenge, it became apparent to him that a spiritual journey was overlaying itself on the route as well.

"My wife and I spent a lot of time with a triathlete that came from the high mountains of Colorado," he says. "He and I measured the bike and run course so it would seem natural. The distances worked out, and stopping on top of the volcano on the first day captured the essence of things. Pele is one of the great elements of creation. The athletes stayed in the barracks at the Kona Military Camp on the first night and in the gym at Kamehameha Park on the second night. People asked, 'Why not go to a hotel?' But being together like that each night reinforced the collegiality of the event. Mana is the catalyst for the individual, but the support crews and camaraderie is what catalyzes a safe and successful completion of the event. We're all family. A human family. Part of being a family is being related by blood, but also by spirit and ethics, and the concept that we're on this earth not above or below someone else, but as servants."

With the course and rules arranged, Curtis put the word out. He was a member of the USA Triathlon board at the time, and asked friends if they knew anyone who'd be interested in participating. Applications trickled in, including from some of the highest-caliber triathletes in the world. Kurt Madden had finished seventh in the 1980 Ironman. Jim Mensching was ninth. Ardis Bow finished 11th and sixth in the women's category of the two races in 1982. Among the other 25 entrants were several with top-50 finishes.

The Ultraman might have been obscure and fringe, but it was also elite. The only thing it was not was a race. Curtis never had to emphasize that point. From the outset, the physical proportions of the course, the punishment doled out by the conditions, and the constitution of the people themselves reinforced the principle Curtis discovered. There were no time cutoffs. You could take as long as you needed or wanted to finish each day.

Still, the collision of athletes and elements resulted in tremendous upheavals within many of the participants. Curtis saw the extraordinary and the extreme. One man became so angry during the second day's bike one year that his support crew (who also happened to be his wife) abandoned him. Curtis found him climbing a tree on the side of the road, trying to pick fruit to eat. In the 1985 race, a competitor named Peter Bourne developed frostbite and hypothermia while riding his bike over the Kohala Mountains less than 10 miles from the second day's finish line. He abandoned the course and rode to the finish in his crew vehicle. It was a crushing disappointment for a man who'd finished in the top five the previous year. The next morning he came to the start of the run course in jeans and a T-shirt, figuring he'd help crew someone else, until Curtis walked up to him.

"What are you doing, Peter?"

"I didn't finish, so I'm here to cheer everyone else on."

"You can still run."

"Aren't I a DNF?" asked Peter, confused about what Curtis meant.

"Well, yeah. But there's no rule saying you can't still go on."

It was a moment of clarity for Bourne. Bad things had happened to him and he didn't have an official time for the second day. But no one could tell him he couldn't keep running. That decision was entirely up to him. The only question was what he was going to do about it.

He ran.

Peter has been coming back to Ultraman ever since. He picked up three more DNFs in that time; he also finished fourth in 1986. He stopped competing long ago but now in his sixties, he still comes to Kona every year, helping as an official or race staff. Much of that passion is owed to that pivotal moment with Curtis. "Ultraman was always difficult to train for, but I wanted to come back because I just liked being around Curtis and everyone else so much," Bourne says. "It was such a special group of people that you felt a part of, and the event itself sort of became like a mantra for life."

Bourne may be one of Curtis Tyler's greatest success stories. He's a major part of Ultraman's enduring legacy. Jane Bockus and many of the most faithful Ultraman athletes and supporters frequently talk about whether people "get it" when it comes to the ethos of the sport. Bourne most certainly gets it, echoing Curtis' own description of what it's all about.

"If you think about what the Ultraman is, it is a microcosm of life over three days," he explains. "You see the worst in people and the best in people. We all have a good side and an evil side. When we're not on top of our game, we can lose touch with our core principles. When you are in your worst despair and anguish, thinking about the rest of your life ahead of you and what you're going to do with it, if you can grasp onto this concept that you are a unique and special being, then you can find aloha and tame that evil. Those who love us and those who we've helped to nurture will be there with us. Kurt Madden wasn't a rich man. Ardis Bow was a local artist. The athletes that came to Ultraman were maybe people of small stature to the rest of the world, but of great power and love."

"Life deals you some pretty tough blows sometimes," says Curtis. "But the only way you can lose your ability to make a true difference in life is if you let someone cut your heart out and take it from you. That has to do with your ego. Your ego is what lets you feel hurt when someone points at you and puts you down. I believe that ego is the root of evil in mankind. I found in my own life and difficulties, from which I was not to recover, that once I triumphed over self-pity, once I triumphed over blaming other people, once I triumphed over feeling sorry for myself, then I could quiet the evil of my own ego and find the power of my mana. This is a wonderful thing to know, because when you're lying in your hospital bed wondering *What have I done to deserve this?* you can realize that you are unique. That's what allows you to remain connected to your mana and not let your ego pull you down with 'I can't.'"

For all the passion and spirituality bound up in the event, the outside world found a way to place exigencies on Curtis and his partners, which made organizing Ultraman an endurance sport unto itself. As busy as he was with Ultraman, Curtis stayed on board with Ironman until about 1990. He got an up-close look at all the things that happened as the race grew and changed, and says it reached new lows along with its highs. Seeing how other events tried to compete with or steal the Ironman name led Conrad Will to copyright the Ultraman name. The irony was not lost on Curtis. Inspired by what he believed the course represented and his memories of his journey out of that hospital bed in Inchon, he'd dedicated countless hours to writing a highly detailed pamphlet for the race describing the spiritual and cultural foundation of the Ultraman journey. On the front was the Ultraman logo, which had been trademarked. The cover and the contents could not have been more diametrically opposed.

"There used to be a triangle surrounding the petroglyph man in the Ultraman logo, representing the triune self and god. Heart, body, mind, occupying the three corners of a pyramid, one of the strongest geometric structures. So yes, it was weird to copyright and trademark that. It felt like the antithesis, but we saw what happened with the Ironman, with people trying to capitalize on something as an intellectual property. There was a thought from Conrad that if we were to protect the meaning of it, then we'd have to do it as intellectual property.

"When you look at copyrights you see that it's a product of Western ideas, to protect intellectual property. Look at the athlete participation waiver with Ironman, or any event for that matter. You can see it's a product of fear. It's people not wanting to be held liable for things. These things are to protect us from people who would steal our mana, and this is a very Western thing. But the Hawaiians did not believe in ideas of property or ownership. Even in Christianity, we say that it's better to give than to receive. So these products ultimately cause us to question our very principles. Is this who we are and what we want?

"And this is what the journey does. It peels us like an onion. It takes us down to our core and shows it to us. And then some people find out that they don't like who they are, to the point that they don't think they can go on. And then someone comes along and says, 'Yes, you can. If I have to stay out here all night, whatever it takes, I'm going to help you finish this. Let's hug. Let's go sit down in the grass and cry together for a minute.'"

There's a profound bit of Ultraman heritage buried in that statement. For 20 years, athletes have been crossing the Ultraman finish line with nothing more on their minds than getting that hallmark hug from Jane Bockus, the epitome of fairy godmothers. They've all thought it was just *her* thing. It's not. Before Jane, people got their hugs from a brawny, straitlaced war vet. But it's not completely a Curtis thing, either. It's a Hawaiian thing. It's a family thing. It's an *Ultraman* thing.

"Hugs were always part of the event," Curtis explains. "My father and I hugged, and people thought that was strange, but it's an important tradition among the Hawaiian people known as *honi*. It is the exchange of the *ha*, the breath of life. One person breathes out and you breathe in their ha, then you breathe out. In that way, you share their essence. We show that we're prepared to share all of each other, both the pretty and the ugly."

With very few compromises, Curtis and his friends built the purest sport possible and defied all odds and conventional wisdom to keep it going. But nothing lasts forever. The three men had incorporated as a business to run the race, just as Valerie Silk had with Ironman. Gradually, Conrad and Alex decided they couldn't continue with things and sold their shares to Curtis.

By 1991, he also began to tire out. He'd even been elected to office. He was spreading himself too thin, and decided it was time for him to step away. "It became a financial hardship, and I had other things I needed to do in my life. It wasn't burnout," he explains. "There needs to be some new blood coming into it. Just as with the Ironman, I know this needs to be taken to another level, and I don't think I was ready. You take something as far as your resources allow you, and I'd just come to the end of my time and means.

"It goes back to that idea that you don't own anything. A Hawaiian bird catcher would work his entire life on a feather cape, knowing that he'd pass it on to his son without finishing it. He knew that because his father worked on it all his life and passed it to him to continue. That's how it works. Ultraman doesn't belong to anyone. It's a never-ending story. When one door closes, another one opens. When we die, we can't take all the wealth in the world with us. We have to think about who we are and what we've done for others and how we put service above self. To me, this is a very intrinsic part of how Ultraman came to be."

Forty-four years after the accident that ended his old life and marked the beginning of his new one, Curtis still visits a pain clinic on a monthly basis to help him deal with his injuries. He likes it because it reduces the need for medication. Security officials at airports hassle him constantly about his knee brace. It frustrates him to be told he can get a pre-check clearance for $100 when he's already given so much of himself to his country. Yet he still calls being in the military one of the best experiences of his life.

"It's not about the glitz or glamour, it's the journey. Some people don't think about what they could or should have done with their lives until they're near the end. I found out what's important at the age of 21. That's what Ultraman is for. It gives people the chance to discover that at an early age. If you really want to learn something, you teach it. That's what I did. I catalyzed that experience for people so they could learn about themselves, and I learned so much about myself at the same time. That's why so many of them continue to come back. I could write those principles down in that pamphlet, but you've got to feel them to learn them."

As with many other things in his life, Curtis succeeded as a catalyst because he reacted to everything around him with faith and compassion. He didn't just catalyze people's experiences in the Ultraman year by year. He catalyzed Ultraman's evolution into a self-sustaining entity. Curtis discusses the race like it's his own life because in so many profound ways it is. Conversely, people who read about his inspirational transformation wonder just how powerful the forces of faith and love must be to have kept him going. They can experience a microcosm of that over three days during Thanksgiving— just sign up for the Ultraman.

On most Thanksgiving holidays, Curtis is too tied up with family affairs to visit the Ultraman finish line. He's there in spirit, though. It's getting along just fine in his absence, cared for by the able hands of a woman who knows the man and the journey all too well. And as she begins to contemplate when her time with Ultraman will end, Jane knows she's chosen a worthy successor. But soon enough both she and Sheryl will face a difficult test of their resources.

chapter seven

Rivalry, Rematch, Redemption

"Somewhere behind the athlete you've become and the hours of practice and the coaches who have pushed you is a little girl who fell in love with the game and never looked back.... Play for her."

—Mia Hamm

DAVID COBB PUBLISHES THE OFFICIAL start list on the Ultraman website on July 8. There are only 36 names total. Cory Foulk and Duncan Cairns are tentatively in, pending that they meet certain requirements. The other two slots hinge on the results of the Canadian and British races. Fifteen of the 36 are coming to Hawaii for the first time. The other 21 contestants make a veritable all-star lineup, and perhaps one of the most exciting in the race's history. Kurt Madden is the first to ever win the race. Cory Foulk will have the record for most finishes if he qualifies. Defending champion Alexandre Ribeiro holds the record for most wins in Ultraman history, and the third-fastest overall finishing time.

The women's race will be just as dramatic as the men's competition, if not more so. Each of Amber Monforte's championships have been marked by a defining challenge. Her third title defense now has its signature obstacle. That signature is the second name to appear on the alphabetized roster of athletes, and it is a familiar one. Hillary Biscay, the pro Ironman athlete who pushed Amber to the brink in 2010, is coming back to Ultraman.

Biscay's return to the race is both unexpected and meaningful. Signing up for an endeavor like this is difficult for anyone regardless of background. The actual race is the easy part. Putting your name on the application form and sending in the registration check is about much more than those three days of competition. It takes an inordinate amount of training just to be fit enough to make the cutoff times each day. This invokes consequences. There are only 24 hours in a day, seven days in a week, 21 weeks until the race begins. Many athletes will spend 20 to 25 hours a week training. At that rate, they will perform more rigorous physical activity in their first six days of preparation than the majority of American citizens will in the entire 21-week period. On top of that, they still have to work to pay the bills.

A person reaches an inflection point. Sport changes from pastime to lifestyle. Side effects may include, but are not limited to, abandoned hobbies, strained relationships, and the wholesale sacrifice of free time. Like Vito Rubino said, this is a deeply personal decision and it leads down a long, lonely road. What used to be an escape from life's worries becomes its own obligation, almost like a second job. Of course, it's easier if the sport actually is your job in the first place. Some people think that because Biscay is a full-time professional athlete, hers is a much smoother road to Kona. It's her job to train, after all. On the contrary, her pro athlete status is extra baggage she has to carry to Hawaii.

Ironman is a highly competitive sport among professionals. Some athletes bank an entire year of preparation to win just one race, Hawaii or otherwise. It's a precarious and often volatile psychological balancing act for these competitors. A professional race begins with a tremendous leap of faith. You can't endure all the punishment and deprivation required without an unshakable belief that you can win. But for the dozens of athletes every weekend who don't finish on the podium, an Ironman ends with a stoic acceptance of reality. Preparation is of only relative importance. A stomachache or flat tire can happen to anyone. You can have a bad day. And someone else can have a really good day. The odds are always against you. To compete at the elite level, you need to partition your mind as a timeshare between the wild dreamer and the Zen pragmatist. Then you need an emotional elevator that can bear their combined weight every time they exchange residency.

The pressure is magnified by the financial realities of professional endurance racing. For all its progress in the last 30 years, Ironman is still a sport owned and managed by a private equity company. Outside of Hawaii, the prize money for first place at the major Ironman races—about half of the events in the series—is $15,000. The other half of the events only offer $5,000. In all races, second place gets half as much as first—barely enough to cover travel fees.

Athletes depend heavily on sponsorships to make ends meet. The more successful an athlete is, the more lucrative deals they can negotiate. When times and race results aren't so good, they rely on friendships and hope they can negotiate a few pairs of shoes and a bike to race the next year. Hillary's is the life of feast and famine. It's been good, bad, and ugly, but never stable. She neither regrets her situation nor envies anyone else's. "It's a choice," she says of her lifestyle. "Some people sit in offices 75 hours a week at jobs they hate to make the big bucks. We choose to spend our hours doing what we love and make minimal profit. But in turn we don't deserve charity from those who do the hard yards in the office for the money."

The bills still have to get paid, however. Many Ironman pros have branched out by using social media to increase their value to sponsors. They blog, do interviews, write for triathlon magazines, create independent YouTube channels, and make videos. So whenever they're not aerobically beating the living daylights out of each other, they must generate content to promote themselves. When they retire from racing, most of them go into coaching or work for companies in the endurance sports industry.

Becoming a professional triathlete means giving up just about everything you have in life to pursue something that will consume whatever's left at the end of the chase. No one in triathlon likes the term "exercise fanatic." They all agree that it's an ignorant attempt at pigeonholing by people too lazy to get a real understanding of the sport. But it's difficult to ignore the professionals' monastic level of devotion. If they aren't fanatics, they're the next closest thing.

The lifestyle commitment is the foundation of Biscay's dilemma. In career management terms, she's coloring outside the lines. The physical toll will knock her out of professional competition for months—she will essentially be taking leave without pay. There's also the high-risk, low-reward proposition to her reputation. From a PR standpoint, Ultraman is a no-name race with little publicity value. But if she loses to an "amateur," it can look bad. Though few people realize it, it is no less difficult for her to make the sacrifices to attend the race than anyone else. And while those unfair professional-athlete stereotypes follow her, it's not in her best interest to dispel them. Image matters in professional sports. The more successful you look, the more successful you'll be. The nature of Biscay's trade requires her to maintain the larger-than-life image of a superhuman who makes a large salary from endorsements and appearance fees, and reinforces her credibility and value as a spokeswoman for the brands she must court. It also gives some people the notion that she's a prima donna. Yet, as with everything in Biscay's Ironman career, her ability to appear at Ultraman depends on her ability to keep up appearances.

A statuesque blonde originally from California, Biscay holds the record for the most Ironman races completed among professional women competitors. In a group of athletes who routinely rest for two months between races, she stands out for her ability to compete on back-to-back weekends. Hillary has won just one Ironman in more than 60 outings, in Wisconsin in 2008. She's finished either second or third 24 times. Hillary competed in the 2010 Ironman World Championships in Hawaii just one month before she raced Ultraman. Out of 50 professional women triathletes who ran in the race, she finished 39th.

All in all, she's had a very successful career. A second-place finish at Ultraman should be icing on the cake, but coming in second to Amber got under Hillary's skin—and for more reasons than the 35 minutes separating them. Hillary's sense of rivalry with Amber is palpable, and even if she's the only one who senses it, that doesn't make it any less real. Like all rivalries, her competition with Amber is as much about events off the course in 2010 as any on it. What happened that year and the relationship the two share underscores the rift between Ironman and Ultraman. It is a fault line that is razor thin, yet it reaches all the way down to their mutual cores.

In the three years since that Ultraman race, Hillary has competed in 11 Ironman races, placing fifth or better in more than half of them for a total prize-money haul of $11,500. To make up the difference, Ironman's most prolific athlete has possibly put herself in the running for the superlative of "most industrious." She runs a website that she updates at least twice a week. She has a small coaching business and hosts an annual triathlon camp in the off-season. When she goes to races she schedules time to meet and interact with fans or amateur enthusiasts. She's worked as an announcer at other Ironman races. In 2012 she launched her own line of triathlon race apparel. That's in addition to maintaining relationships with her eight branded sponsors. This is where appearances come in. While image isn't everything, for a pro athlete trying to stay in the black through the ninth season of her career, it is most certainly a *big* thing.

Sponsors are the major source of logistics and funding for pros. In addition to equipping the athletes with free items, they also pay bonuses that help to offset the costs associated with traveling to races. Those bonuses not only depend on the athlete's race performances, but also the relative visibility of each event. From a marketing standpoint, not all Ironman races are created equal. WTC has expanded the race series to numerous locations throughout the world, only to pull the plug on some events within a few years due to lack of athlete interest. Locations like Korea and China just weren't enticing to European and American athletes, and there was not yet a large enough population of local triathletes to sustain the moves. If a tree falls in the forest and no one is around to hear it, it flops as an advertisement for the chain saw. That's the narrow space within which Hillary has to wheel and deal. Ultraman attracts her because it is a wild frontier of endurance. Yet she has to convince her sponsors to support her cutting down trees where no one will hear them fall. Some chain saw manufacturers are less supportive than others. If Hillary doesn't want to take a financial beating on this deal, she has to finish in at least second place.

Hillary is coming because she wants to. But unless she wins she may wind up in a place she does not want to be. The consequences she faces and the influence they have on her approach to Ultraman created the wrong impression with some people in 2010. Because she had obviously demonstrated the physical aptitude for the course and the availability of slots that year, Biscay was able to get into the Hawaiian event without first racing in Canada (the only qualifying event at the time). She was one of seven first-timers, but even out of those there were a few who had volunteered for or crewed the event before. Complicating things, her finances and schedule kept her from arriving in Hawaii until the Thursday before the race, while most of the other athletes had flown in a week or more ahead of time. Being uninitiated to the race's tradition of ohana, she didn't understand the importance of the family-gathering aspect. Arriving late to the welcome banquet further aggravated some of the race staff and veteran athletes. What normally would have passed as rookie mistakes instead got filtered through stigma into a vial of suspicion. In their eyes, Hillary was some combination of self-important pro and know-it-all Ironman just here to check off a block on her race résumé. She didn't get Ultraman and she didn't belong, so there was no point in trying to explain it to her or otherwise encourage her to stick around.

Her anxieties about performing well didn't help things. Ultraman was not the first time Hillary and Amber had met in competition. They'd raced against each other once during Amber's brief time in the professional ranks. Hillary won that race, and based on the result she thought that she stood a fairly good chance of winning in Kona. What she didn't realize was that Amber had been sick with stomach flu during their first meeting, and had stopped at every port-a-potty on the course during the race. Minus the impromptu breaks, Amber probably had a faster time.

Miscommunication and speculation formed bad impressions of Hillary. Her brief remarks about having met Amber before were taken for cockiness. By the start of the race, more than a few people were itching to see Hillary get beaten. The race atmosphere was saturated with metaphor. If not an explicit belief, there was the underlying sentiment among the crowd that if Amber or Shanna crossed the finish line first it would symbolically vindicate Ultraman and humble Ironman.

For her part, Hillary felt that there was a concerted effort to give Amber the home-field advantage. Amber was "the favorite daughter," as she put it. She wasn't aware of Amber's recent breakup with Conrad Stoltz or the severe impact it had on her. From Hillary's perspective, there was a Cinderella story being written and she'd been cast as the wicked stepsister. It put a cloud over the race for her.

As fatigue and soreness set in over the next few days, the uphill mental battle grew as steep as the volcano. Underneath the blanket of subtle antagonism, Hillary felt a genuine sense of vulnerability no different than any other Ultraman first-timer. She remembers feeling it especially during one key moment in that race. It may have been the best chance of the entire weekend to put things right. Before the run began on the morning of the third day, the athletes, crews, and race staff all gathered into a circle and joined hands. The group spent a few moments in the predawn darkness to reflect on the race's principles. Not understanding what was going on and feeling unwelcome, Hillary hung back from the group. "It was just sort of weird," she remembers. "I didn't get it." No one made an effort to explain.

Unaccustomed to competing in multiday events, Hillary wasn't prepared for the stress Ultraman puts on an athlete's metabolic system. She finished each day so wrecked that she couldn't get down enough food before hitting the sack. She woke up each morning severely behind on caloric intake, but the impending physical activity prevented her from eating a large meal. Then she'd get going and her system would be unable to take on anything large. Late into the second day's bike ride, she realized she wasn't in control of herself or her bike. She wrote on her blog of the experience: "To be totally honest, from here on out all competitive fire was gone and I was driven entirely by the desire to Get. Off. My. Bike. And not die."

By the third day, the vicious cycle had made a complete wreck of her digestive system. The tables turned with her stomach, preventing her from chasing Amber at best speed. "I became mostly nonverbal right about the time I did start seeing signs of the Kawaihae stores. Dave asked me to weigh in on a personal situation he was describing and I replied with, 'My stomach hurts. I can't talk right now.' Soon thereafter began the search for the missing package of Immodium that we had so diligently procured during our extensive prerace shop-a-thon.

"Again, I got to the point where I didn't want to have to speak or even motion for what I wanted in terms of fuel or drink. Sometimes I wouldn't even take what I did want from my crew because I couldn't be bothered to stick my arm out or break my rhythm to put ice in my hat. But, at some point around mile 35 or so, I realized that pounding gels plus Coke plus Red Bull couldn't hurt. So that's what I did, and carried on doing all the way to the finish…. I had not hurt this bad since I had to make a pass at mile 25 to win Ironman Wisconsin two years ago," Hillary remembers. She crossed the finish line completely obliterated, made it to the picnic area where the massage tables were, and collapsed. She lay there for nearly an hour while medics administered an IV.

There was one final twist. Because Amber broke the course record, Jane extended to her the extra reward of waiving her race entry fee for 2011. Hillary misunderstood the gesture and thought that the fee was waived simply because Amber had won. What she therefore didn't understand was why Jonas Colting, the 2007 men's champion and a close friend, didn't receive the same treatment when he won it. She took it as a hurtful parting shot.

No one would blame Hillary if she never came back. But not everyone in the ohana let her down. Among those who helped her rethink the experience was none other than Amber, who came to visit during her time roaming the southwest when she was looking for work. Ironically, Amber had been totally unaware of the antagonism others had stirred up between her and Hillary. The pair had dinner at the home of a mutual friend and longtime Ultraman athlete, and kept in touch by email for some time afterward. It didn't clear up all the confusion. Three years later, Hillary still thought Amber had gotten the registration fee waived for beating her. But it did sharpen her perspective of what happened. As the 2011 Ultraman began a year later, Hillary wrote:

"Last year at this time I had the pleasure of partaking in this three-day suffer-fest. Truly, I suffered in ways that I had never suffered before. And I loved it."

So once more unto the breach. Though diminished, she'll face the same skepticism and stigma. She'll face Amber and the elements, the uncertainty and unknowns, the limits of her own mind and body, the tremendous pressure to win and the stark consequences of failure. For her, that's what it's all about. If you're certain, safe, and secure in your life, then you're just not living enough.

At one time she had the secure life. The daughter of a doctor and a schoolteacher, Hillary had been a collegiate swimmer good enough to qualify for the US Olympic trials in 2000. She started competing in triathlons about the same time she began working on her graduate degree in English at the University of Southern California. Though her parents worried that teaching college English might be a difficult and relatively low-paying career, they were at least encouraged that it was a profession. Their anxieties increased when Hillary entered a doctoral program to specialize in African American women's literature—not exactly an area of widespread interest. But they were hardly prepared for her next decision.

In 2004, two and a half years into the program, she decided to take a sabbatical. Her results in amateur triathlons the previous year had been good enough, and she wanted to explore her potential as a pro athlete. "Dad thought my academic track was niche, but at least it was a career path," she says. "Becoming a pro Ironman athlete was a step into crazy town." It didn't help that she was hit by a car and broke her hip in two separate training accidents in the same year. It took another year before she finished third at Ironman Arizona—collecting $5,500 in prize money in the process—that her parents took a brighter view of things. "When I finally got a paycheck, my dad was like 'Okay, you can maybe make a living doing this.'" Her sister, a Harvard Law grad, thinks Hillary's choice of career is "nuts," but she's still fascinated by it. With that tacit support, Hillary decided that the sabbatical would morph into a permanent vacation. She committed to a triathlon career and never looked back.

It hasn't been easy. Economically speaking, competition among professional endurance athletes is a race to the bottom. "Getting sponsorship keeps getting harder. It's not an easy environment to work in because a lot of athletes take shit contracts. But they have to, because they're desperate for money. Even people with good contracts can feel tons of pressure over one bad race performance. It's a tricky balance for any sport. That pressure to perform sucks the fun out of it. So you're always on this roller coaster. I have friends that will have a bad race, and they have to pretend they're okay on social media. But I see them on a personal level and people will go into a hole for months over a bad race or injury. But that's what we choose to do."

The mental fatigue accrues the same way as the physical does. Some people think it gets harder to feel excited to jump in a cold pool at 5:00 AM or imagine your butt on a bike saddle for six hours as the knees stiffen and the back aches more persistently. But in truth the mind is its own organ. Its patience can wear thin and nerves can snap just as easily as an ACL. A big concern among pro athletes is what's referred to as "overuse injuries," muscular damage that results from pedaling too many miles. The mental analog is cynicism. Hillary has gotten a taste of that as well.

"As Ironman gets more crowded, it gets less fair. I remember racing Ironman Hawaii the first time as a pro, and after we hit the Hawi turnaround on the bike course, we rode back the way we came and saw this seven-mile pack of age-groupers. And some are obviously trying to draft [following one cyclist too closely in order to gain an aerodynamic advantage], and others are trying to follow the rules. But there's just too many people, and you can't police them all. But the biggest thing for me is that I've done this so many times. When I retire, there's no appeal to me to competing as an age-grouper. It would just feel anticlimactic."

Hillary has an exceptionally clear understanding that this won't last forever. And she may be one of only a handful of pros who are actively preparing for the future. She's made friends with other athletes and watched how they have dealt with the inevitable end of their athletic careers. One, a former top-three finisher at the Hawaiian Ironman, is now in medical school. Another does marketing for different endurance sport companies. But perhaps her greatest influence is Paula Newby-Fraser, who won the Ironman a record eight times. "I trained with Paula right after I turned pro. I noticed that she always had lots of projects on the go. She made jobs for herself."

Observing how others' stories were ending made her acutely aware of the need to shape her own destiny. "Once you're out of competition, the shelf life of a pro athlete is *very* short. You can only rely on your racing success for two years after you're out. After that, you need to have accomplished something as a coach or whatever other career you get into. I remember working with a friend and former Ironman Hawaii champion, and a friend posted a photo of us together on Facebook with the caption 'Hillary hanging with a world champion.' All the comments came in guessing it was [current champion] Mirinda Carfrae. When you say 'world champion,' that's about how long people's memory lasts."

And that's why she has the blog, the clothing line, and the occasional gig as a race announcer. She's making jobs for herself and starting projects to lay the foundation for version 2.0 of her life in sports. Ultra-distance races are the recreational analog of that effort. She can't stay in the pro pack forever and she won't do age-group Ironman. That leaves only the places she's never been before. "I've always been a little fish in a big pond type of girl," she says. "When I first turned pro, some people told me that I should spend an extra year as an amateur and enjoy winning races. But winning isn't enjoyable if it's easy. I wanted to run headlong right into it. I have a need to work and take risks, to feel like I'm fighting for my pay."

That's what's at the heart of her return to Ultraman this year. She's looking for a fight and some payback. But not with Amber. Hillary's dissatisfaction with her performance in 2010 had nothing to do where she finished in the standings. It was how she got there. The score she's coming to settle is with herself. "Winning alone isn't enough. I could have won that race and still felt bad about it. That race was so hard, and I was so messed up at the end. I felt like I messed some things up so bad that I never really got to see what I could do at the end. I just want to come back and do it right. If I can have the race I want, regardless of how I finish, I think I'd be done with Ultraman." Win, lose, or draw, she'll be off to explore different races and distances—if she can just find a little redemption. She readily admits that this course is brutal no matter how prepared one is for it. This can't be a regular thing for her. She's not like the others.

Meanwhile, Amber is getting back to her old self. Her ankle mends and her energy levels bounce back within a few weeks of starting the thyroid medication. In July she runs another 100-mile trail race in temperatures soaring over 100 degrees. Just three weeks after finishing the Western States in 26 hours, she crosses the line only four minutes over the vaunted 24-hour mark. In August she and her husband, Ryan, fly to California for a short vacation. They spend five days visiting friends along a 540-mile route from San Francisco to Los Angeles. They ride their bikes the whole way.

Dene Sturm is still on the bubble. There are also the two other Ultraman races in Canada and the United Kingdom, which offer World Championship slots. How those races go and whether all four slots are claimed will have a significant impact on her chances. All she can do is sit and hope that the patron saint who presides over this event will answer her prayers. She's waiting on good news from the woman they call "Ultra Mom."

chapter eight

Ultra Mom

"I think it's important that all of our family remembers that we really haven't done anything to earn this. We're just the recipients of a tremendous legacy. I use the word 'custodian,' and we want to pass it on the best way we can."

—Virginia McCaskey, owner of the Chicago Bears

JANE AND GERRY BOCKUS MET on an evening flight from San Francisco to Hawaii in 1966. She'd been with Pan Am as a stewardess for two years; he worked as the airline's director of communications in Honolulu. Though he was no stranger to the talented and beautiful women who staffed the planes, there was something about Jane that piqued his interest. After dinner was served he walked back to the galley, where she was cleaning up. It was a meeting of the era's icons—the jet-set media executive and the diva of the skyways. Only an opening line worthy of a Cary Grant movie would do. "You're the only stewardess on this plane with a decent pair of legs, so I thought I'd come talk to you," he said.

She'll never forget her first impression of the man she'd eventually marry: *Who's* this *guy?* But Gerry's combination of abruptness and easy confidence lent itself to a disarming charisma. They spent the next hour getting to know each other. Among other things they learned was that both their grandfathers had been born in Gananoque, a small town in Ontario along the St. Lawrence River on the border with the United States. After a while he returned to his seat to sleep and she got back to work. Jane didn't think about the surprising gentleman with the coincidental background again until she went to the terminal to collect her luggage. As she reached down to pick up her bag from the carousel, a hand shot out from behind and grabbed it for her. There was Gerry, as abrupt and charming as before.

"I checked your schedule. You don't fly out until tomorrow night at 11. Have dinner with me. I want to take you to meet my parents so my dad knows that there are other people from Gananoque." She agreed, and met his parents on their first date. They decided to get married in 1970. The honeymoon didn't last long. Jane and Gerry moved to Kona the next year. Though Hawaii was more serene than the hustle of Oahu, it added two days to Jane's commute to her base of operations in San Francisco. The long periods of separation put an unbearable strain on their relationship. Gerry ultimately decided that perhaps it had all been a mistake. They separated in 1972.

What the hassles of modern life tore asunder, fate put back together. On July 21, 1973, Jane was working on a flight from Tahiti to New Zealand. Per the route schedule, her crew got off the plane that night and handed it over to another crew that would take it on to Los Angeles the next evening. At that point, it became Pan Am Flight 816. It departed Faa'a International Airport at 10:06 PM local time. Thirty seconds after takeoff, the Boeing 707 banked sharply to the left and fell. It crashed into the ocean in a matter of minutes. Only one person survived.

Gerry was in Kona when he heard about the crash. Knowing that Jane routinely worked that flight, he frantically began making calls. He finally reached someone who confirmed Jane had not been on the aircraft. What he felt went far beyond relief. He called her at her home in Woodside, California, after she got back. "I miss you. I need to see you," he said.

Naturally, she was reluctant. Their reunion took place the next time Jane passed through Honolulu outbound from San Francisco. She didn't rush back into his arms, but they both realized that the love was still there between them. It would take time to find it. They remained in contact over the next year, getting together whenever their schedules allowed it. The winter of their separation passed with the seasons. They remarried in 1974. Jane gave birth to their daughter Elizabeth in 1975. She quit Pan Am the next year.

Hawaii is an unmistakable paradise. It is peaceful, beautiful, and unspoiled. But keeping it that way means rejecting anything that can besmirch its shores. No weed can take root in paradise, and certain attitudes and lifestyles from the mainland are as forbidden as its flora and fauna. The decontamination process occurs through the sacrifices made to be worthy of paradise. Gerry paid his toll to the big island by quitting his Honolulu-based job as communications director with Pan Am in 1971. Though the biggest island, Hawaii in those days had a tiny population and even smaller job prospects. There was definitely nothing at the executive level he was used to. He landed a government job working as a metrologist for the Hawaii State Department of Weights and Measures.

Jane's forfeiture had no attached real dollar value, but she felt its loss regardless. Growing up in Canada and taking frequent family vacations to their cottage in Vermont, she had a lifelong passion for skiing. She gave up winters on the slopes and took up the island's native recreational passion of canoe racing. What they gave up to become part of the island, the island returned to them in kind. Their sacrifices led them to an intersection of fates with Valerie and the Ironman.

Jane and Gerry got involved by way of Curtis Tyler. He and his wife had their first child at the same time as Jane and Gerry. The couples met in childbirth classes. The Bockuses and Tylers became very close. Gerry had served in the Marines before working for Pan Am, and he and Curtis hit it off well. (They still get together regularly with a group of other veterans who like to call themselves "the Sandwich Island Club.") When Jane and Gerry's daughter was born, Curtis became her godfather. Likewise, Jane is godmother to Curtis' son. "We're attached at the hip, the head, and the heart," he says of the enduring friendship.

So when Curtis was made the Ironman swim course director and tasked with finding boats to help mark it, he remembered that Jane was a member of the Keauhou Canoe Club. Jane agreed to help and ask if anyone else at the club would. Naturally, everyone was willing to join in on the fun. They lined up their canoes along the length of the 2.4-mile course in order to provide swimmers with a straight line to follow. The swimmers went out along the right side of the canoes and came back on the left. Jane remembers that it turned out to be a nearly impossible feat for the paddlers to keep the canoes aligned with all the thrashing from the athletes. The next year they found proper buoys to mark the course, but the canoe club still played a significant role as dock support.

Wide World of Sports first came to cover the event in 1982, and production managers immediately realized the challenge they faced in tracking the athletes along the bike and run courses. Because there were no cellular networks, the race relied primarily on radios. But even radio signals had difficulty reaching over the hilly 56 miles between Kona and Hawi. ABC crews responded by installing temporary lines for their own personal phone network. Crewmembers all reported to a call center they set up at the Kona Surf hotel, now the Kona Sheraton. Jane remembers it looking and sounding like a Jerry Lewis telethon. The ABC folks began referring to it as "the war room."

The only thing left to do was find the people to man the phones. ABC offered $100 per volunteer to any local civic group or club members who would answer the calls. "We realized with enough volunteers, we could buy a new race canoe," remembers Jane. "So the club jumped on it." It became a yearly tradition. Because of her experience and organizational skills, Jane was nominated to direct the whole operation. Though she never saw much of it, she experienced more of those early Ironman races on Kona than even some people on the course.

Jane continued to work under the ABC umbrella until 1994. When ABC gave up broadcast rights, WTC negotiated a new deal that gave them more control, including the war room. Jane kept doing the same thing, just for WTC. She got an official event staff shirt and the new title of tracking director. That lasted until 2002. At that point, technology rendered the war room obsolete. Special ankle bracelets with radio frequency identification (RFID) chips allowed remote tracking of athletes, and laptop computers and cell phones reduced the need for additional communication infrastructure.

Diana Bertsch, the Ironman Hawaii Race Director, hardly wanted to let Jane go. As it happened, the aid station coordinator quit the same year. Diana asked Jane if she would be willing to assume the responsibility for organizing the numerous aid stations throughout the course. Jane replied that she would, under one condition. "I remembered that Sharron Ackles, the race director before Diana, had always given $100 to the local clubs and groups that ran the aid stations as thanks for their volunteers. I asked Diana if she'd continue to do that."

Diana called back to WTC headquarters and confirmed the deal. Jane took the job. She stayed until 2008, when Ultraman grew into such an enormous task that she simply couldn't dedicate enough time to both. Today, Ironman gives about $500 to each Kona organization that works an aid station. Though Jane is no longer aid station director, she still works as an aid station volunteer for the event.

The Bockus family moved to California in 1990—the same year Valerie left Hawaii and the Ironman behind—to help their daughter's chances at college during her last years of high school. Jane continued her work with Ironman and Ultraman, flying back to Kona every year. Her 33-year streak in Kona is unbroken and, as far as anyone knows, unrivaled. From the quiet background of the aid station tents she has seen as much of the event's history as anyone. But for all the anticipation of the drama that will unfold before her from year to year, it's the memory of the war room and Valerie Silk that got her hooked for life.

Ironman in the 1980s was radically—almost unrecognizably—different from what it is today. There were some minor adjustments made to the course over time. Instead of two transition areas, everything is now consolidated at the pier. The bike course loops a bit longer through town as well. But when you hear people like Curtis Tyler actually talk about it, you begin to think they're describing a totally different animal. From the itinerary of festivities programmed months in advance to the digitized athlete check-in to the projected finishing times of the winners, the actual mechanics of the modern Ironman come off with all the polished optimization of a well-designed airport. It also has the same crowded, hassled feeling. Since the Boston Marathon bombing in 2012, it has incorporated a security zone with guarded checkpoints. It even has its own version of the VIP lounge—a streamlined, to-the-front-of-all-lines program known as Executive Challenge. In the words of program manager Troy Ford, it offers a "high touch" experience, complete with special spectator seating for family members and private dinners with the top professional athletes.

All of this would have been considered taboo back in 1982. In its early years, Ironman was—by equal parts circumstance and design—an unprecedented endeavor. The athletes weren't the only ones engaging in high adventure. Just putting it together was an enormous undertaking. Many of the logistics had to be figured out on the fly. Everywhere you looked, you could see life going off script. Improvisation didn't just abound in Ironman; in many ways, it was the *very foundation* of the race. Whereas outsiders saw incomprehensible bedlam, many others, like Jane, found indescribable beauty in the chaos. What she cherished most about those experiences—and what fueled the passion that brought her into Ultraman—was the spectacle of people rising to the occasion time after time. Paramount among them was the woman who always seemed to rise above it all, Valerie Silk.

Valerie's influence and inspiration are still evident in Jane's voice when she speaks of her. In principle and practice, Jane is a mix of Curtis Tyler's and Valerie Silk's legacies. It's Curtis' torch she's running, but it's Valerie's cadence and gait she imitates. She humbly shakes her head and smiles at the suggestion that she equals her idol by virtue of her tenure going three times as long. "I could only hope to be the kind of woman she is," she says.

It is remarkable that, for as much admiration as Jane has for Valerie, they have never been closer than mere acquaintances. In fact, they never held any discourse at length. Though learning about it did nothing to change Jane's perception of her hero, she never knew the extent of Valerie's inner turmoil and personal battles. Just as she hid her tears and despair from Julie Moss after exiting the ABC van that fateful night, Valerie never gave any hint of her insecurities and heartaches. To some extent, it was a matter of protecting Ironman. But for the most part, as a woman of grace she thought that private matters should be kept private. What she gave to everyone else and the act of giving itself were public domain. But her relationship with Ironman itself was between the two of them.

People don't know it, but Jane emulates Valerie in this aspect as well. There are topics she won't discuss with anyone. There are things she's done to preserve Ultraman that seem to contradict her principles. Some of them defy reason. She refuses to explain decisions and actions that are uncovered despite her efforts to conceal them. It could mislead one to conclude that her motives are driven by a belief that this is her race and sometimes she has to do things her own way. But in this, she's of the exact same mind as Curtis Tyler. To her, it's she who belongs to Ultraman. It is a spiritual institution. As soon as you begin obsessing over every letter in the law, you start boxing the spirit in. Every "t" you insist be crossed or "i" that must be dotted is another nail in that coffin. No one's ever questioned her. They trust Jane to do the right thing, and she trusts Ultraman to lead her to what the right thing is. That instinct hasn't failed in 30 years.

Such incidents have been few and far between, and are as exceptional as the owner of an international race series who helps put together crew gear and info packets for athletes at every event. She has a unique leadership style for a unique organization. Her brand of principled improvisation wouldn't fly in anything so self-important to call itself a league. The label itself demonstrates an inherent level of ego—the root of all evil, according to Curtis—within such an outfit, and therefore necessitates a commensurate amount of bureaucracy. It binds itself in red tape to keep the pretentiousness from ripping itself apart. There are too many people for the directors to communicate their rationale clearly to everyone, let alone have a close personal relationship with the majority. Misunderstandings and hurt feelings are inevitable. "And this is why we can't have nice things," goes the saying.

Jane saw that happened with Valerie in the years before she left Ironman. The main reason she's kept Ultraman small all these years is because of the sheer logistical constraints of the island, yet knowing what Valerie had to contend with as Ironman grew has been the bedrock of her faith in what she's doing. Like Curtis, she believes that there's nothing wrong with Ironman. She still volunteers at the race. It provides people with something as good and valuable as Ultraman does, only different. That's the key. The world already has an Ironman. It needs something different. Ultraman is that something, and Jane is committed to keeping it that way. It has not been easy.

Jane began working with Ultraman in 1984. Curtis Tyler initially approached her during Ironman preparations in the war room in 1983. After hearing him describe the event she agreed to help however she could. Between 1984 and 1987, she was limited to only helping with the swim on day one and at the finish line for the run on day three. Her job coordinating delivery services for the local newspaper kept her tied to Kona during the weekend.

By 1988 she had a few more people working for her on the distribution and could organize a short absence, so that year she was able to go all the way around the island for the first time. It was a fortuitous trip. During that race she became acquainted with Klaus Haetzel, a German athlete with an intense passion for endurance racing. He was a regular at Ironman, traveling to Hawaii to cover it as a journalist whenever he wasn't actually competing. He made sure to say hello to Jane the following years. Though the Bockuses had moved to California by then, Jane still flew back to Kona to help with both Ironman and Ultraman. She even took Elizabeth with her for Ultraman that year. Haetzel planned to race Ultraman again in 1990, but canceled his plans when the Berlin Wall fell in 1989.

The wall wasn't the only thing to crumble under pressure. Curtis Tyler determined that 1990 was his last year as race director of Ultraman. He'd been making a big push to grow the event into something resembling Ironman. He allowed 58 participants in 1989. There were only 49 registered in 1990, but his real goal had been to get as many as 80. Curtis believed the race could be expanded, but the efforts he made to promote it and get sponsorship, combined with the comparatively meager results, exhausted him. "Curtis was going to make it too big. He wanted 80 athletes," Jane remembers. "It's reached capacity at 40. He had to do wave starts, and it was just too big. I think he got burned out trying to do it."

Curtis took it as an indication that it had been a pipe dream all along. Maybe building some things didn't mean that people would actually come— at least in enough quantity to redeem one's faith. There was no Ultraman in 1991.

Klaus contacted Jane later in 1992, asking if there was going to be a race that year and explaining that he had organized a large troupe of German athletes who were ready to participate. Jane contacted Curtis, who wasn't excited about the idea of putting the event on for a dozen people. A man named Don Ryder called her and pledged his help. Jane called Curtis to ask his blessing. "Keep me out of it," he told her. "It's not a USAT-sanctioned race and it's not insured."

It was agreed they had his permission to call it an Ultraman—just not to anyone who might get Curtis in legal trouble. Jane borrowed a truck from her father-in-law and she and Don pulled the whole thing off themselves. It was manageable since, without any advertising or announcing, there were nowhere near as many participants as there had been in 1990. Only 11 athletes showed up—all Germans, with the exception of one local. Seven of them finished. Good times were had by all.

If anything, it served as an ironic vindication of what Curtis had perhaps sought the previous years. He had left the event to die, and its heart refused to stop beating. His faith rejuvenated, he came down to the finish line after the run. "Curtis was so pleased with the whole thing that he brought trophies after the whole thing was over and no one had gotten killed. He had a few left over from the previous year and got the names etched on them in time for everyone. It was a really sweet gesture," Jane says.

Jane and Don decided to make it official the next year by getting USA Triathlon to sanction the event. They were successful in getting the event certified and insured, but unforeseen events made it costly. Hurricane Iniki hit Honolulu hard that year. Jane and Don decided to put the race on out of their own pockets, and gave all the registration fee money to relief efforts. It was the first major moment Jane demonstrated her beliefs in aloha and *kokua*. There would be many others.

Also in 1993, Don introduced Jane to a friend of his from Canada, Steve Brown. Don had approached Brown about assuming control of the effort to put on a second Ultraman. Jane came out to meet Brown and take a look at the course. She gave her blessing, though final approval rested with Curtis since he was still officially the owner of Ultraman. After Steve Brown got the Canadian race going, he determined that he was also in it for the long haul.

In 1994, Jane, Don, and Steve decided they wanted to adopt the race. Curtis was happy to pass it on. The three caretakers incorporated in preparation for the buyout, naming their company Ohana Loa, LLC. Jane bought a 50 percent stake in the venture. Steve and Don split the other half evenly. Because Curtis still owed royalties on the Ultraman trademark to Conrad Will, Jane assumed the last few years of payments. Other than that, she, Don, and Steve owned the race free and clear. The future was wide open.

It seems funny looking back on it now. Never more than 40 customers, and oftentimes there weren't enough to keep the lights on. Only three owners. Only two races. Zero interest in profit. As far as business models goes, it's impossible to make it any simpler. Yet in less than 30 years, it got so very complicated. What happened?

Love happened. People love sports. Love is an emotional thing. And when things get emotional, they get complicated really fast. One thing that got complicated was the love triangle around Jane, Gerry, and Ultraman. He didn't bat an eye when she ponied up the cash for the majority ownership in the race. "The money came from funds I had and he knew I was passionate about it," she says. "This is what I love to do, and he knows that."

For the first several years he was supportive both morally and physically, helping to haul bikes from the day two finish line in Hawi back to Kona so that the support crews wouldn't have to deal with them during the run on the last day. He also helped by setting up and tearing down the stage equipment at the start and finish lines each day. But then something catalyzed a precipitous decline in his enthusiasm. He stopped going out, and gradually became more withdrawn from Jane and everyone else in the ohana during Thanksgiving week. These days, he stays home with the football games and has dinner with friends.

Sheryl jokes that she has to walk on eggshells near the Bockus residence in the days leading up to the race. "Gerry and I get along great every other week of the year," she says. "He likes everyone just fine. He doesn't hate the race. He just doesn't want to have anything to do with it." She gives him his space. As for the couple, they don't discuss the matter. Gerry understands and respects that Jane has to do this, and Jane understands and respects that Gerry has to *not* do it.

He busies himself by working on a couple of old Haflingers, a type of jeep used by the Austrian army during the 1960s. He even travels to Haflinger enthusiast conventions in Europe. Jane goes with him. When he's not doing that, he'll turn on the football games and read the newspaper. He holds the paper up, which keeps him from seeing the screen.

But his disinterest can't bring Jane down. She's positively ecstatic each and every year. "I get energy from the athletes. I have more energy during Ultraman than at any other time during the year. It's what they put themselves through. A lot of it has to do with that it's something that's within themselves. They don't have to finish first, that's why we don't bill it as a race. Sure, it has a start line and a finish line and there's a clock running, so it *is* a race, but it's more than that. It's a family reunion," she opines. The thrill and the energy she gets from Ironman and Ultraman for two weeks in October and November have been enough to keep her working for them tirelessly for three decades. The fruits of that labor have been a prosperous family and the addition of two more weeks of Ultraman goodness in Canada and Wales.

And yet it's been labor nonetheless. Jane and Don put on an Ultraman race in Hawaii every year between 1992 and 2000. They never turned a profit, and on multiple occasions they lost significant amounts of money. Still, the registrations would come in every year. People loved doing the race, and Jane loved to put it on. So she kept investing her own personal finances to keep it going. Still, by 2000, it was becoming untenable. But in that year a man named Vito Bialla offered what they thought was a godsend. In a way, it was. His involvement in Ultraman marked a pivotal moment in the race's history—one that galvanized Jane's conviction in how it should be managed for the rest of her life.

Bialla had as unique a background as anyone else in the Ultraman family. His mother emigrated from Austria to the United States after World War II. Vito had a difficult childhood, and after his mother married a man from Louisiana he ran away from home at the age of 13 and again at 16. He made good on his final escape effort by joining the army when he turned 17. Though they told him his mother's background made him perfect for service in Germany, he wound up going to Vietnam. An extraordinary athlete, he kept up with his training during his time in the service and even had a shot at qualifying for the Olympic swim team. Those dreams were dashed by the American boycott of the 1980 Summer Games in Moscow.

Figuring that his opportunities for athletic glory had passed, he turned his energy toward business, ultimately becoming a successful headhunter in the corporate world. He enjoyed his accumulated wealth by getting into sailing, drinking Bordeaux wine, and smoking fine cigars. That changed in the 1990s, when he met his second wife, Linda. She was a hard-core marathoner, so to impress her he invited her to go for a run from his house to the local yacht club. It was maybe a mile. Vito was embarrassed and frightened when Linda, unimpressed, dragged him out for the uphill run back home. Somehow, though, the humiliation and physical torture encouraged him. Linda had given him two things: a challenge and the encouragement to meet it. So he turned into a dedicated runner himself. Vito finished the Hawaii Ironman in 1995. He married Linda shortly afterward. During their honeymoon, they ran the Venice marathon.

Just like that first run that got Vito hooked on running and Linda, the Biallas' dual love of endurance racing and enjoying life together became mutually encouraging pursuits. They got into ultra endurance events in short order. Linda finished the Western States 100-miler. Though Vito twice failed in his effort to finish that race, he notched his first of eight Ultraman finishes in 1996. In the meantime, Linda also inspired him to purchase the triathlon apparel company Zoot. He left most of daily operations to Linda, and they took it from a small outfit based in Hawaii to one of the sport's preeminent shoe and apparel makers.

Meanwhile, he kept coming back to race Ultraman every year after 1996. His passion for business led him to begin wondering about the event's potential for growth, and he started talking to Jane, Steve, and Don about a financial involvement. They realized from the beginning that Bialla had a greater vision for Ultraman, and thought perhaps he would add a degree of business expertise that the race lacked. "Vito had a different perspective," remembers Steve Brown. "He thought there was potential for spectators and mass marketing. It represented a philosophical change, and gave us cause for thought. Maybe he was onto something. The board wasn't enthusiastic. Some of his ideas weren't logistically feasible for Canada. He thought we could expand the field of athletes to between 125 and 200 people."

By 2000, the fiscal strains finally outweighed the board's anxieties. Ultraman was in desperate need of cash, and Vito had it in abundance. Steve Brown and Don Ryder sold all their shares in Ohana Loa to Vito. Jane also let go of a small portion of hers so that Bialla would have a controlling interest. Determined to get things turned around, Bialla set about talking to his business connections about sponsoring the race. With short-term survival guaranteed, he began strategizing a plan for growth.

As part of that, he completed an unprecedented personal feat in 2000—two Ultraman races in as many weeks. He called it "the Ultraman double." Going to Hawaii early for that year's race, his first race was on an experimental course he'd created to make the race more accessible for media and spectators. Instead of going around the island, he began and ended each day's leg in Kona. This alleviated logistical problems and had the added benefit of actually reducing the overall finish time by avoiding the huge climbs during the cycling phases of the race. Bialla went on to finish the "traditional" race the next week, and decided that they'd go with his new format in 2001. The idea was to hammer out the logistical details during the next couple of years, grow participation to nearly 100 athletes, and then pitch the idea to bigger sponsors and media outlets.

Things didn't go according to plan. Not going around the island's perimeter killed a lot of the race's magic for the athletes and volunteers. Instead of tripping through the most scenic portions of the island during the bike leg, the race course took the athletes on redundant out-and-back trips through the moonscape of the lava fields on the west side of the island. The area is notorious for its punishing winds and rolling hills. Its most scenic points are the rare glimpses of greenery from the resorts down by the water. Within two years, athletes were bailing and the local volunteers were grumbling. The race had more money than ever, but it was still dying. Something had to be done. It was up to Jane. At the end of the 2002 race, she told Vito that she was out. "It was boring," she says. "Not going around the island killed the fun for everyone. I told him he could do whatever he wanted, but I wasn't going to be part of it anymore."

Jane's ultimatum suddenly left Vito in an extremely vulnerable position. He might have had 51 percent of the stock in Ohana Loa, but Jane had the overwhelming majority of love and support of the Ultraman family. He was only the CEO of the company; Jane was Ultra Mom.

In the end, it was Linda Bialla who might have had the biggest influence in convincing Vito to change his mind. A relentless competitor in every aspect of his life, the increasing challenges to his idea might have only served to encourage him to stay the course. However, this was one of the few occasions on which he backed down. "Ultraman is like a church," he says. "You can't own that. It's not about money or growth. It's about the athletes. It's not that it needs to stay that way. It's just that's the only way it can be."

Vito relinquished his shares of Ohana Loa shortly after the 2002 race. He gave the whole thing to Jane—lock, stock, and barrel. She paid him back for the few shares she sold him, and he gave her the rest at no cost. Don Ryder had gone home to take care of his parents and would not come back to Ultraman for some years, but Steve Brown was still very much interested in being involved. He asked Jane if he could buy back into the company.

She refused him. Her reasons signify things about her relationship to both Steve and the race, things that still play a critical role in how Ultraman is managed.

"Steve's a Virgo, like me. Very meticulous. Only he's better on details. He's an accountant. He looks at the bottom line. And that's where we've had...I wouldn't say conflict. But he sold his shares to Vito, as did Don. And then later I wound up with 100 percent of the company. Steve wanted to buy back in, but I won't do it, because I want to have control over where this thing goes. He would love to have races everywhere and make lots of money. I wouldn't say that's his ambition, but that's the direction he wants to go with it. And that's not what it's all about. This is why I've tried to control as much as I can by holding on. And eventually it will be passed on. I know I can't physically carry on. I've never been a triathlete. But you don't have to be one to understand this," she explains.

Only 15 athletes signed up for the 2003 Ultraman, fewer than half the number who came before Bialla's experiment. Participation recovered over subsequent years, but for Jane that troubled time would always evoke within her a "never again" sentiment. Not selling shares back to Steve is more about her fear of letting go than of giving to him. Yet holding control alone has not guaranteed smooth or even safe sailing for Ultraman. Thanks to Vito Bialla's penitence, she owned everything about the race—including its baggage. Carrying that burden is a task that has gone on far longer than restoring the attendance in Hawaii. Added to that weight are all the standards she's sworn to uphold.

She's carried it well for the last 10 years. That the race has lost virtually none of its character is a testament to her resolve. That doesn't mean that things haven't changed, though. The race has survived, grown, and even prospered. It has expanded. In that regard, it ultimately did realize certain elements of Vito Bialla's vision. That necessarily meant business deals. In her mind and heart, Jane maintains stark lines between what Ultraman is and what it never shall be. Some of those lines have narrowed over time, but they've never been compromised.

For Jane and her small group of administrators, taking care of Ultraman has become a delicate balancing act between preserving the race's life and its spirit. The history of Ultraman is a monument to the success of Jane's character and leadership. Jane is working on major plans for the race's future. New blood and old ways will challenge each other, and once again she'll have to negotiate a balance between them. The test begins far from Hawaii, where the first pages of Ultraman's annual story have been written for several years.

chapter nine

Hometown Antiheroes

"I always turn to the sports pages first, which records people's accomplishments. The front page has nothing but man's failures."

—Earl Warren

JULY 31, 2013. Less than 41 miles from the US border and 160 miles almost due east of Vancouver, the town of Penticton, Canada rests between two north-south-running lakes: Okanagan Lake to the north and Skaha Lake to the south. Known as British Columbia's wine country, the hills of the Okanagan Valley are resplendent with vineyards and fruit orchards. Penticton itself is nicknamed "the Peach City." With a population of fewer than 37,000, its tallest building is a 15-story condominium complex on the north end. Main Street runs between the two lakefront beaches. It serves not only as the central vein of business and governance, but also a living timeline of the town's evolution. The sign on the front of the Erickson Building tells you that it was raised in 1922, in case its distinctive brickwork and inlaid concrete columns don't make it clear enough. With its three-floor glass-and-metal-frame office spaces flanking the modest concrete central foyer, City Hall is the most progressive design. Fittingly, it's at the extreme end of the street. It's a juxtaposition that hints at the character of a town that wants to evolve yet is afraid of and perhaps resistant to change. It's not the only such indication.

There are lots of serious triathletes in Penticton. Many of them were born and raised here. Like the miners and viticulturists of the outlying hillsides, they do it because that's what they grow up knowing. Others have transplanted themselves here to be closer to kindred spirits. A great deal of the town's pride and identity are wrapped up in its involvement with Ironman. Theirs was the country's only Ironman-branded event for several years, and even when other, bigger cities obtained race licenses it retained the "Ironman Canada" title as a sign of the sport's gratitude and the town's heritage in it.

But the title belies the true story of that heritage. It's a story fraught with ego, politics, and dispute, with half occurring on the sports page and half on the front page of the local *Penticton Herald*. The identities of its villains depend on whom you ask. Most of its actors characterize themselves as victims of one kind or another. Heroes are hard to come by. What is certain is that when Valerie Silk's race migrated to Canada, it brought with it all the little diseases it contracted in Hawaii. The town caught the fever. Even after it subsided, the infection remained. Thus far, Ultraman has been immune to the plague.

Things change, though. Take Peach City Runners and Adventure Sports, for instance. It shares ground-level space with a collectible coins shop in the Board of Trade Building on 212 Main Street, halfway between the Erickson Building and City Hall. Today it is Penticton's only triathlon retailer, as well as the headquarters for Ultraman Canada. It used to be the office of Ironman Canada.

On July 31 the store has a steady trickle of customers. Twenty-nine of them are the participants in the 13th edition of Ultraman Canada, the second-oldest Ultraman event outside of Hawaii and a qualifier for this year's World Championships. Jane is already here. She's in the upstairs conference room, setting up tables and paperwork for registration. She comes out almost every year—partly in the role of CEO, to ensure the race is produced according to Ohana Loa standards, and partly in the role of Ultra Mom, to welcome all the new members into the ohana. She has many friends here and everyone looks forward to seeing her working registration, but the director of Ultraman Canada is Peach City's proprietor, Steve Brown. He's also one of Ohana Loa's four board members.

Steve is a complicated figure in the history of Penticton triathlon. The best way to describe his relationship with the citizens these days is "the loyal opposition." His critics hear the opposition and forget about the loyalty. Neither Ironman nor Ultraman would exist here without him. Yet he still fits the characteristic profile of those who involved themselves in the early development of Ironman: a person of noble deeds surrounded by ignominious rumors. Perhaps he's a failed hero. The story of how triathlon came to Penticton is one of bitter fights over ego, politics, and money. Steve did at least as many good deeds for the town and the sport as he did ill. Following the ironic lot of failed heroes, he was punished for his good ones.

The story goes back all the way to the beginning of Ironman Canada. The first time Penticton hosted an Ironman race is a matter of semantics. If you believe that anyone who swims, bikes, and runs 140.6 miles in less than 17 hours (the standard was still 24 hours in the early days) has completed an Ironman, then the year was 1983. But if you maintain that a person only truly finishes an Ironman if the event is officially licensed and sanctioned by World Triathlon Corporation and bears the obligatory M-Dot logo over the finish line archway, then it didn't occur until 1986. If it doesn't sound like a big deal, try telling people of either persuasion that they're wrong.

The event started as the brainchild of Ron Zalko, a Vancouver fitness club owner who had participated in the Hawaiian Ironman in 1981 and 1982. He returned from Kona seeking to replicate the experience in Canada. To do it, he had to go somewhere far enough removed from a big city to avoid traffic but big enough to provide the necessary logistical support. Penticton welcomed the idea. He and his business partner started putting the word out by leaving information brochures in the chamber of commerce building. One of them got picked up by Lynn Van Dove, a woman who had recently organized Penticton's very first triathlon during the Penticton Peach Festival. Van Dove contacted Zalko and expressed interest in helping put on the race. To her surprise, he asked her to be the race director. So began a short and tumultuous partnership. Passion is the force that drives these races. But to succeed, pragmatism must guide passion. The Zalko–Van Dove team had plenty of enthusiasm, but they were short on diligence.

The first issue arose before word had barely got around. Zalko, in his exuberance, had assumed that, like a marathon, any race that conformed to the distances and rules of the Kona event was an Ironman. It did not occur to him that Ironman was a trademark and copyright owned by Valerie Silk, so he didn't ask for permission to use it. Valerie's lawyers called and expressed her displeasure. So the name was changed from "Ironman Canada" to "Canadian Ultra Distance Triathlon." The field for the inaugural event in 1983 had only 23 athletes—22 men and one woman. Nothing spectacular, but enough to say that long-distance triathlon had officially arrived on the continent.

For whatever reasons, Zalko became disaffected with the whole enterprise and gave up his involvement. That left Van Dove with sole ownership of the race. All it needed was to find enough people to help grow it. More importantly, it needed to find the *right* people. There was plenty of interest from the community. Unfortunately, most of it was the wrong kind, and even in retrospect it's hard to distinguish the altruists from the opportunists in the fog of overlapping perspectives. Even though Lynn owned the race, it was impossible to organize its production without substantial support from the city. Volunteers, road closures, swim course safety and marking, and setup of the large areas for athlete transition between the three disciplines all required planning and coordination with Penticton's local government, businesses, and civic groups. In a short time, a group of locals formed what would come to be known as the Ironman Canada Society. It was designed to keep the kitchen in orderly fashion. But it also provided entry for too many cooks. Whether he was in the right or wrong place at the right or wrong time, that's when Steve Brown got into the mix.

Brown was a self-described "half-decent" soccer player in his youth, earning himself a spot on a few successful club teams. Even in his thirties, he was able to make rosters primarily made up of players 10 years his junior. A severe ankle injury changed all of that in 1982. Restricted to crutches for a while and facing a long recovery afterward, he grew restless to have an outlet for his athletic energy again. His doctor recommended swimming. He didn't know how, but went to the pool anyway and began teaching himself. In time he worked up to covering a mile in 58 minutes, which he thought was "pretty good." When the ankle healed further, his doctor advised that he start with a bike and work up to running again. Brown remembers a friend observed his new health habits and suggested he try "this new sport called triathlon." He signed up for that first Penticton Peach Festival race organized by Lynn Van Dove. "I entered that first race on a total lark," he says. It wound up changing his life.

After crossing his first finish line, he had no desire to play soccer again. He joined the Penticton Pounders running club and took part in several other races during the next two years. Penticton in the 1980s was an even smaller world than it is today. In a town of fewer than 25,000 people, the grapevine worked faster than Google. Between his involvement in the Kiwanis Club and the endurance sports community, Brown's name quickly got around some small yet active circles as a professional accountant in the British Columbia health care system. Less than a year after his first triathlon, the newly formed Penticton Triathlon Society approached Steve to ask if he'd become its first treasurer. Over the next two years, Van Dove, Steve, and the other Society members worked to bring the Penticton race up to the same standard as the one in Kona.

In 1985, Van Dove convinced Valerie Silk to visit Canada to discuss obtaining a license to make Penticton an official Ironman event. After seeing what they'd accomplished, Valerie agreed. The next step was for Lynn to come see the 1985 Hawaiian Ironman to observe Valerie's philosophy in action and finalize the paperwork. A few other members of the Ironman Canada Society joined her of their own accord. Unfortunately, the trip incited personality conflicts that would later jeopardize the whole endeavor.

According to Van Dove, Society members wanted to get the license in the Society's name instead of hers. She contends that people on the Society's board of directors envied her for the way Valerie favored her. On a website called Shy Giants that she started in 2012, Van Dove claimed that Valerie and her executive staff were not pleased with the Society members' antics during this time. Even so, Valerie granted the license to the Society rather than Van Dove for the 1986 race. The corporate logo was stamped across the finish line in Penticton the same year, and with that Ironman was officially on the continent. Steve Brown continued his athletic endeavors both on the road and behind the scenes. In addition to building the race over the next few years, he finished Ironman Canada himself in 1987 and Hawaii in 1989 after winning a lottery slot. Yet he decided to leave his position as the society's treasurer in 1989 when conflicts between Van Dove and the Ironman Canada Society boiled over.

The race racked up a $78,000 deficit in its first year as an official Ironman event. According to Steve, it was the result of investing too much too early. Caught up in their own enthusiasm and ambition, Van Dove and the Society collectively invested in various initiatives to promote the race. They hired a new marketing agency, spent money on a television deal, hired an artist to design the advertising poster, and offered a generous prize purse for the top finishers. Unaware of how long Valerie had toiled through debt to make

Kona the event it was, everyone assumed Penticton would mirror what they believed was Hawaii's overnight success. When that didn't happen, everyone adjusted their expectations and budgeting—except for Van Dove. A major cut in the race's budget came out of her salary and travel expense account. She viewed it as an effort to bring her under control. Lynn accused the board of deliberately undermining her and asked Valerie Silk to reassign the license exclusively to her.

Having reduced the deficit to around $55,000 by 1987, Steve felt that the situation had reached a crossroads and spoke to Valerie about the issue when he went to Hawaii for the race. "I told Val that giving the license to Lynn would eventually lead to a financial disaster and that the board was trying to work toward bringing the deficit back to a break-even point but that it would mean some harsh measures—all of which Lynn resisted," he remembers.

Van Dove has a different perspective on Brown's overtures to Valerie. Her tone becomes venomous when she says that Steve was one of the conspirators in the background trying to orchestrate her downfall. "Steve Brown stalked me for eight years. He was one of those that couldn't stand me, because I had created something big and they all thought they should be running it. I was a girl with a toy they didn't think I had any business with," she says.

Despite Brown's warnings, Valerie decided to give Lynn sole ownership of the race license in 1989. Van Dove would later remark that Valerie "was never convinced that a society served much purpose." Valerie always maintained sole ownership of World Triathlon Corporation, and though she consulted with her volunteers and athletes about improving the race in Hawaii, she insists that it was essential to Ironman's success for the final decision-making authority to lay with one person. "If we had organized the race by committee, we'd have never gotten anything done," Valerie says. "There were just too many ideas and opinions, and at a certain point you had to have one person who could say 'this is the way it's going to be.'"

It's difficult to argue with success, especially as successful as Valerie was in Hawaii. But it's equally impossible to ignore failure, and there's no one-size-fits-all method in sports management. "Lynn was a great person, but she was a terrible money manager," Steve remembers. "You could just see the writing on the wall when that decision was made. No one argued with her particularly. It wasn't about the power to make decisions so much as it was having the necessary involvement to make good decisions. Giving her the license meant she could do things without consulting other people, and she often did. Not deliberately, but by accident. And that's what caused a lot of problems. The left hand didn't know what the right one was doing."

Lynn described the state of affairs at the time of the transfer. "After a few more years of small-town politics and obvious dirty tricks, Valerie pulled the society's license and reassigned it to me privately," Lynn says. Despite claiming that she and her small cadre of race captains had been able to hold the Society at bay and maintain primary authority over race issues, she denies the blame for any failures.

"When the license was reassigned, I inherited their $100,000 deficit," she says. No one remembers the deficit ever being that large, nor do they challenge Steve Brown's memory when it comes to numbers. Lynn's memory is one of many such instances of the fish getting bigger with each retelling. There are nuggets of truth in the account, but they're buried in a narrative that paints her as the hero suffering injustice. Even Valerie says that aspects of Lynn's stories aren't true.

After usurping full control of the event, Van Dove's relationship with the Society became even more secretive and antagonistic. "Lynn always had this paranoid streak around this race," Steve recalls. "She was always thinking other people were trying to take it away from her. She especially felt this about politicians. She would go into city council meetings with hidden tape recorders and such. Very strange." Van Dove has even put some of the recordings she took from those city council meetings on her website. "She was convinced that the ruling political party in the province somehow wanted to control the race. She was never accepting of the fact that the Board and others of us, myself included, were trying to save her from herself and her financial disaster."

All of Steve's predictions came true. Valerie Silk sold Ironman shortly after transferring the Canadian license to Lynn. Under the management appointed by Dr. James Gills, World Triathlon Corporation increased the yearly licensing fee. They were not sympathetic to Van Dove's feuds and melodrama. Ironman was no longer Valerie Silk's party for wayward endurance fanatics; it was a business, and businesses make profits and cut losses. Van Dove suddenly found herself on the wrong side of that equation.

Harboring paranoid suspicions about the local society members trying to take her race away, confronted with the very real possibility of losing it to WTC, and without Valerie to help, Van Dove had nowhere to turn. By 1990, the Ironman Canada Society had to seek outside investors just to put on the race. She sold 51 percent of her license ownership to a Canadian investor named Michael Bregman, but the situation continued to worsen. Despite Penticton's moral support for its thriving endurance sports community and the amount of out-of-town money the Ironman event brought to its economy, local businesses still hesitated to offer support. Not only had the race participation dropped so low that there was no guarantee sponsors would break even, it was also not entirely certain that the group could get the race set up in the first place.

The debt increased, and with it the calls for Lynn to resign. After the 1991 race, just two years after being granted sole ownership of the license, Lynn Van Dove stepped down as director. Ironman Canada was in financial ruin. Bregman bought the rest of Van Dove's license. Organization of the race fell to the board of the Ironman Canada Society in April 1992. With less than five months before Ironman Canada was supposed to begin, they asked Steve Brown to come back and help them save the race. He refused.

It wasn't out of spite. Steve loved the race and had good relationships with almost everyone in the society, including Van Dove. But the same objectivity that had earlier brought him to conclude the race would falter also led him to calculate the insurmountable odds against its survival. The same week the board approached Steve, they received new demands from David Gates, the new president of World Triathlon Corporation. To hold the race, the Penticton group would have to front $125,000 for the licensing fee and the prize purse for the professional athletes. More than 10 years of experience in business finance told Steve that it was a losing battle. "The money they needed, the amount of time they had to put it together. I looked at them and said 'No way.' It was an impossible mess and I didn't want anything to do with it," he says.

This is why Steve doesn't always fit in with the endurance racing crowd. To those who take part in it, Ironman is a physical testimony to an almost religious belief that anyone can accomplish anything, no matter what the odds. Theirs is a church of audacity. The core of its faith is belief in the power of belief. Pessimism is the original sin. Pragmatists are heretics—skeptics who dabble in percentages. Their numerical agnosticism holds them back from leaps of faith.

Steve is the consummate pragmatist. From the way he adjusts the Ultraman Canada registration fee each year based on the previous year's expenses and earnings to the measured tone and pace of his speech, Steve's every action is an expression of his methodical nature. Even his appearance seems a reflection of the way he views the world, with white hair trimmed neatly in a military-style cut, serious eyes staring out from underneath dark eyebrows, framed by the black, squared rims of his glasses. Whether working as support crew for athletes in Hawaii or behind the director's desk during the Canada event, he wears a look of stern thoughtfulness as easily as his lightweight synthetic polo shirt emblazoned with the Ultraman Canada logo. In a world of gregarious people wearing wildly colored spandex and living on the spur of the moment, Steve holds onto business casual and his ledger. He went to Hawaii in 2012 as the support crew chief for Tracey McQuair, a Penticton native and multiple Ultraman winner. From the time she began the swim to the moment she crossed the finish line, he never smiled. He was always in a hurry, giving short, direct orders to the crew and moving things along. To those who don't know him, he comes across as brusque. His friends know that there's a method to his madness and an underlying compassion to his leathery temperament.

"I crewed for Sheena Miller in 2009, and it was a disaster," he remembers. "We dilly-dallied around after the finish on day one and the damn restaurant on top of the volcano closed on us. Sheena couldn't get a decent meal in her and wound up sick the next morning. I wasn't going to let Tracy down the same way. I was there to do a job and it was all business until she crossed that line."

People don't know how to take Steve sometimes because the best way he knows how to show them he cares is tough love. He doesn't do hugs and flowers like Jane. He feels like he has to be that way, because his biggest concern for his friends and the athletes he loves so much is that they might get hurt. He'll never be able to allay that fear. It's been branded into him by all the times he's been hurt. His love of the sport has brought him a lot of pain over the years. He's had to be tough in order to keep loving it.

Shortly after turning down the offer to rejoin the board, Steve received a phone call from a Penticton hotelier asking him to attend a meeting with several other hospitality operators in town. At that meeting they made an offer of good faith. If Steve would agree to rejoin the Ironman organizing committee, the town's hotel owners would give $75,000 directly to him in a trust fund for the race. Their gesture honored him, but more importantly it changed the math. The balance sheets and the odds were now more in favor of the race's survival, pending his return. He couldn't refuse in good conscience. He rejoined the group and quickly afterward was elected as its president and the Ironman Canada race director.

That was the last time anything came easily to Steve as far as the Ironman was concerned. The group still had to scrape another $70,000 together to make the race happen. Then there were the skeletons in Lynn Van Dove's closet, or rather her laundry room. According to Steve, the group found things in total chaos when they went to her home to recover past records and athlete applications. Lynn "filed" the 1,200 applications for the 1992 race in haphazard locations all over her house. Steve found some of them in a plastic bag in her washing machine. They were mortified to discover that she had 300 previously unmentioned "rollover" applications for the 1992 race. Rollovers were essentially rain checks issued to athletes that had paid to register for previous editions of the race and then had not been able attend, thus allowing them to sign up later for waived registration fees. In principle, it's an effective way to avoid the administrative hassles and expenses associated with giving refunds. However, in this case, it amounted to a race desperate for money that suddenly had to let hundreds of athletes in for free. Lynn Van Dove denies that such rollovers existed, and counter-claims that there was a break-in of the Ironman Canada offices shortly before her departure. "I wonder if it wasn't Steve and his cronies trying to pull more antics," she says.

Steve addressed each problem with his customary diligence. He traded the blood, sweat, and tears of an athlete for the organizers' bad coffee, long hours, and eyestrain. Slowly but surely, the Ironman Canada Society turned the corner. Thanks to local support and a few donations from the federal government, the event broke even in 1992. Scott Tinley won the race. Steve greeted him at the finish.

Steve was formally reelected as president of the society in its fall elections after the 1992 race. Immediately afterward, the board of directors called an impromptu meeting for reasons unexplained to him. A motion was made to call for his resignation. Officially, the given reason was that Steve had violated the society's rules by purchasing a new computer. Just weeks before the start of the race, the local hospital that had loaned a couple of computers to the society years earlier demanded that they be returned. Under time pressure, Steve decided to exercise executive privilege and good judgment. For those jealous of the way he'd been treated by the hoteliers, it was the opportunity they'd been looking for. Bylaws stated that he was supposed to get approval for any expense over $2,500. The computer had cost twice that. It didn't matter that no one protested during the preparations for the race—not to mention their lackluster bookkeeping to begin with. Steve knew money wasn't the real issue. Several of the board members never forgot that so many businessmen in town had thrown their support behind Steve, not the Society.

It never even made it to a vote. The race was secure and would remain so. No matter how things turned out, arguing over whether he should remain president would create more bad blood than it could wipe away. He thinks back on that moment. "Besides, I never wanted the job in the first place. Why would I fight for it? If someone else wanted to do it, let 'em," he says. It wasn't an emotional decision. It was just the sensible thing to do. Being a sensible man, he walked out. Whatever differences Lynn Van Dove and Steve Brown might have had, they shared almost exactly the same fate. Their respective ousters occurred in a murky cloud of conspiracy and their own personal abuses of authority.

For Brown, the pain began where sensibility ended. The story made the front page of the next day's *Penticton Herald*. Though he kept it to himself, the scandalous nature of the story wounded him deeply. His wife, Maria, a first-generation Canadian whose parents immigrated from Italy, made her opinion known in characteristic Mediterranean style. "One of the board members came to our house later to give Steve a watch," she remembers. "I said to him 'you know what you can do with that watch.'" He left without asking her to specify.

Another scandal occurred during the 1993 event, when two athletes went into a coma while on the course. Suspicions fell on a nutritional product called Endura. The news reported that the Ironman Canada Society investigated the product and cleared it, but the management of the fiasco after the fact revealed more about the nature of the Ironman Canada Society than anything. The new race society president said that he "just wanted the whole thing to blow over." Another board member responded to enquiries by asking reporters, "Don't you realize how much money the race brings to Penticton?" The race director was fired shortly afterward.

By 1995, license holder Michael Bregman had become fed up with Penticton's penny-ante politics and botched results. He contacted an organizer named Graham Fraser, who ran several other races that Bregman sponsored, about taking the Ironman to Ontario. Sensing Bregman's frustration, Fraser asked if he could just buy the entire license outright. Bregman agreed. Fraser recalls that Steve Brown had also expressed interest in buying the license and taking the race over. "There was interest, but [WTC President] David Yates wanted me to have it." Fraser bought the license for $250,000, then discovered he would have to assume the race's existing debt, adding another $90,000 to the pile. But his no-nonsense business approach to managing costs and expectations, combined with his diplomacy with the local community, once again turned things around.

Meanwhile, as happy as Steve was to leave the politics behind, he missed the experience. He'd offered to let a few athletes crash at his house prior to the Ironman, and their time together left an indelible impression on him. "There were athletes from all over the world, but we all still found this closeness in the sport just sitting around and talking. It was really great to share that. I made friends for life during that time," he remembers.

That's why a few associates approached Steve in April 1993 about organizing a new race. Lynn Van Dove had run another event in the early 1980s that she called Earth Journey. It was an extreme distance triathlon modeled after Ultraman. She was able to put it on twice, but afterward couldn't find any athletes interested enough. One of Steve's friends, Don Ryder, had been involved with Ultraman since 1988 and worked with Ironman Canada since 1986. Just as Penticton had been ideal for Ironman's mainland landing, Ryder and his partners believed it was the most natural place to receive Ultraman. And who better to organize it than Steve? Brown had a different opinion. After his Ironman experience, he was even more emphatic with his refusal to get back in the organizing business. "The whole Ironman thing had just worn me out. I told them I was done being involved in triathlon, period.

"But God damn it if two weeks later I was putting the thing together," he chuckles.

He says it as if he had been swept up by the course of events, but Steve may be the only person in Ultraman history—athlete or organizer—who jumped into it knowing exactly what he was getting into. Having those Ironman athletes in his home made him realize that, for him, triathlon had changed from physical to spiritual exercise. Whatever this Ultraman endeavor might cost him in time and effort, it was worth it to keep it going.

That did not mean it went smoothly, however. The first edition of Steve's race took place in 1993, with 10 of the 11 participants finishing the course. It did not bear the official name or logo of Ultraman. Steve had not obtained the license from Jane. Nor did he adhere to the same distances, opting instead for a 10k swim, a 200km bike, and a double marathon—slightly shorter than the Ultraman course in Hawaii.

The field grew to 14 in 1994. By that point, the race had drawn Jane's attention and an agreement was reached to make it the second official Ultraman race. The 1995 race changed the course to meet the distance requirements. Unfortunately, there were only eight participants. In 1996 Steve completely abandoned holding the race when it became apparent there wouldn't be enough participants to cover the expenses. He wouldn't host the event again until 1999, when seven people registered. Interest died off again in 2000 and the event lay dormant for several years.

These were harsh times for Steve personally as well. As a regional budget director for Canadian hospitals, he had spoken out against the proposed restructuring of Canada's health care system in the 1990s. So it was not a surprise when he learned in 1998 that he had not been hired for a position within the new system. He took it in the same stride as he had his ouster from the Ironman Canada Society.

"Accounting was a tool for me," he says. "I never set out to be the world's best accountant. I liked business and solving problems. So I started looking around for what I wanted to do next. It came to mind that there were a lot of people in Penticton who were runners, but the shoe stores only carried good running shoes during the summer, as if we all stopped just because it snowed outside. It was a source of frustration for many of us that we couldn't get good quality shoes." Eight weeks after Steve lost his job, Peach City Runners and Adventure Sports opened for business in Lynn Van Dove's old

Ironman Canada office space. He continued to be active in Ultraman Hawaii as well, crewing for his good friend Gerry Van DeWitt in 2001 and 2002.

Ultraman Canada returned in 2005 with 16 participants. It shrank to 12 the next year, but rose to 15 individual competitors and three relay teams in 2007. After taking on 39 individual competitors for the 2010 race, Steve discovered that Penticton had a problem Kona had never experienced—crowding. He decided that the local road conditions couldn't sustain so many people and scaled the race roster down to 29 slots.

The Ironman also flourished during those years, so much so that its added girth became cumbersome to the small town that nourished it. The race did well in Penticton, and the Ironman brand did even better internationally. By 2000, there were 15 Ironman races worldwide, including Hawaii and four in North America. Fraser held the licenses to those four through his company, North American Sports. Even more prolific was the growth of the M-Dot's recognition. World Triathlon Corporation collected substantial revenue by lending its "official product of Ironman" stamp of approval to equipment items ranging from shoes and headbands to bikes and wet suits.

But there's a difference between legitimacy and authenticity. The space between them is defined by heritage. People discounted the three years the race occurred under a homegrown banner without considering that the coveted M-Dot might never have become so coveted without those first unbranded races or the work of the people who organized them. That attitude clashed with some people in Penticton.

As its brand became a household name, Ironman's logo took on a unique gravitas among overachievers. The M-Dot became the sigil of "been there, done that." Not content to simply buy the T-shirt, people began tattooing it on their bodies. The lines between what belonged to the culture and what belonged to the corporation began to blur. Other race organizers around the world started their own 140.6-mile triathlons, calling them things like Silverman or Titanium Man. But as the number of M-Dot branded races increased, the off brand competitors found it more difficult to draw participants. Even though WTC events cost hundreds of dollars more, people were willing to pay for the chance to cross the finish line at a "legitimate" race. A large portion of the faithful were of the opinion that if you didn't do an *Ironman* Ironman, then it didn't count. WTC had succeeded beyond its wildest dreams.

That hubris gradually seeped into Penticton. Year by year, WTC increased the fees it charged Graham Fraser. "It jumped 400 percent in one year," he remembers. The governments of Penticton and British Columbia were also trying to squeeze every drop they could from the race. Fraser recounts a $60,000 bill to have ambulances and medical personnel on hand for the event. Meanwhile, locals such as Steve Brown complained about how Fraser and WTC profited from the race and left the town with nothing. The race increased its fees for local vendors to occupy space in the race expo area. "You couldn't possibly break even with expo sales," Steve says. "You could only hope that people would see your name and come by the shop after the race."

Under continuous pressure from WTC, Fraser eventually sold back all the licenses, except the one for Ironman Canada, in 2009. His company, North American Sports, continued running the races, but now WTC had more power to dictate terms. As Ironman continued expanding across the continent, athletes didn't have to travel as far to compete. The race didn't sell out as fast as before. The competition in the pro field was not as heated, and WTC reduced the prize purse.

Never as large a town as the other franchise cities, Penticton couldn't hope to keep up with the rising costs. Yet it was in the intangibles where Penticton really shined. The entire population contributed to the event. A weeklong party grew up around the Ironman that rivaled the Peach Festival. Despite the feuds and politics within the society, the town held true to the original Kona spirit they meant to transplant. They made Ironman races the way Val used to make them. The problem was that it wasn't Val's Ironman anymore. Graham Fraser remembers that the town couldn't see the change happening around it, nor had any desire to keep up with the times. "Penticton was in a little valley, and they couldn't see outside of that," Fraser says. "They all wanted to act like it was still 1995, and those days were gone."

His attempts to communicate the greater forces at play fell on deaf ears. In a way, Steve Brown characterizes the local viewpoint. "Ironman might still be here today if the people in charge had just dealt with us differently. The people here really came out in support of this thing. Ironman wasn't just a race to this town. We made a huge deal out of it. We had concerts and group meals for the athletes. There was a bike race and a kids' triathlon the day before the main event. People would come a week early and stay a week after the Ironman. The athletes loved what we did here, and we loved putting it on for them. The WTC folks just didn't get it," he says.

But Fraser remembers that Penticton charged astronomical rates for the local convention center for the athlete banquets, and that by the mid-2000s the Kona spirit that packed the halls looked more like the ghost of Christmas future showing empty chairs. By 2011, estimates were that Ironman Canada brought $10 million into the Penticton economy. Yet its value dwindled. The license fee alone approached $200,000. The town was also compelled to pay between $60,000 and $70,000 to WTC for "marketing fees," an expense Steve challenges as borderline fraudulent. "What marketing? They never advertised the race. They sure as hell didn't advertise the town," he says.

Even bigger charges slipped by unnoticed in the form of in-kind contributions. WTC was not charged for traffic permits or overtime pay for police to conduct traffic safety. Setup, teardown, and cleanup operations were all paid for by the city. Local hotel rooms also had to be set aside for WTC executives and VIPs, all compensated by the town. Fraser and the town clashed over all of these. WTC leadership additionally decided to reduce the prize money for the athletes—from $12,000 going to the winner to just $5,000. WTC was simply doing what it had done since its first clash with Lynn Van Dove—reducing its costs and increasing profits. "People were too excited with it being a race at first," says Maria Brown, who works in the accounting and finance department of Penticton's city government. "The community didn't initially think of Ironman as a business, but it is and they gradually came to realize that's how the owners approached it."

Negotiations between Penticton and Ironman deteriorated throughout 2010 and 2011. Fraser eventually decided he'd had enough and sold the Ironman Canada license back to WTC in 2012, two years ahead of its expiration. The city government became irate, claiming that they had an agreement with Fraser to approve any transfer of the race license. Because Fraser had broken his deal, the mayor declared Penticton had the right to look for a new race producer. The little city that brought Ironman to Canada prepared to kick it out of town.

Now more than ever, World Triathlon Corporation is the 500-pound gorilla of the sport. As more people aspired to qualify for Kona, Ironman races everywhere literally sold out in minutes, allowing the company to raise licensing charges and negotiate further compromises on municipal fees. It courted executive sponsorships and celebrity endorsements by giving race slots and other fringe benefits to VIPs, much to the chagrin and sometimes the expense of the most dedicated athletes. It raised entry fees to their races each year, reaching a zenith $1,000 per person for Ironman New York City in 2012.

That opened it up to competition from a gang of smaller gorillas. Another race series began when WTC abandoned its race in the German city of Roth in 2001. The people and local government of Roth pulled together to help the former Ironman organizers hold the race under a new banner, calling the race Challenge Roth. It became one of the largest Iron-distance races in the world in less than 10 years, hosting some 4,500 participants. By 2011, the Challenge group that had kept the race alive with the help of Roth's citizens had grown their enterprise into a 21-race series across Europe, becoming WTC's most serious competitor in the process. A growing stable of former professional Ironman athletes and WTC executives defected to Challenge, observing that it had not forgotten the people who had made it successful.

At a press conference at Challenge Roth in 2013, former three-time Ironman World Champion Chris McCormack brazenly accused Ironman of becoming "the McDonald's of triathlon." Penticton decided to follow suit and terminate its relationship with Ironman. WTC offered to reissue the license to Fraser if the town would keep the race. Fraser himself went to meet with the mayor and city attorney. "I advised them to do a deal with me while I still had the license so that there would be a long-term solution after I left. The offer was that the city would get $100,000 from the race every year, guaranteed. But they had already made their decision. They told me they didn't need Ironman anymore," he recalls. Within the month, Penticton threw its lot in with Challenge. The endurance sports media reacted by saying the town had pulled off a coup.

Pulling off the actual race was another matter. WTC's response was to undercut the new Challenge race by establishing a new event in the city of Whistler, BC, and gave it the title of Ironman Canada. Penticton formed a committee to begin organizing its new event. Appointments to the board were highly political. There were a few local business owners and a first nations tribal chief, but no one with actual race organizing experience. Columnist Don Kendal wrote of the situation in the *Penticton Western News*:

> No government, at any level, is suited to running business; they cannot deliver effectively the basic services for which they exist. This has little to do with the competence and commitment of the people in government. It has everything to do with the disparate interests, externally and internally, those in government feel they must serve, and the lack of any real consequence as a result of failure. Worse, there is rarely an acknowledgement of failure on the part of government.

It soon became evident to the board that they needed serious help. Enter, once again, Steve Brown. He had remained on the periphery of the debate. Some, like Tracey McQuair, might say he was a passionate fan of the sport who couldn't help but care about the outcomes. Others, like Lynn Van Dove, would label him an opportunist circling over the beleaguered race, awaiting the right moment. Whatever the case, the city did ask him for help, and that's what he's doing on July 31. The Ultraman participants can't find him in Peach City Runners this morning, because he's at a Challenge Penticton planning meeting, working as a contracted event organizer for the city. He's in charge of the race and being paid to direct it. It's an odd place to be, considering he's gotten exactly the things he's spent years denying he wanted.

Whatever his motives, there's no denying their intensity. Steve Brown's identity is bound to Penticton and long distance triathlon. The real question is the true nature of that identity. His life in the sport is defined by a sort of restlessness. He's married to the sport, but he talks about the business and management of it as if it had grown dull shortly after the honeymoon. He speaks vaguely about growth and improvement, but more frequently and specifically about the failings and scandals that have occurred over time. If there's something he wants, he either hasn't figured out what it is or he's keeping it to himself, like the majority of his feelings.

Jane couldn't have found a more dissimilar counterpart for Ultraman's first expansion race. They are as different from each other as the paths that brought them to Ultraman, and that leads to very different philosophies about the race's past, present, and future. He is everything she is not, and maybe for good reason. The world has always rewarded her for giving it her trust and charity, but that doesn't mean it always will. She thinks that sometimes Steve is a bit too severe, but he's seen the short end of the stick too many times to be careless with his heart, and as contentious as he may sound, it's really just his way of showing he cares.

It's not all doom and gloom, though. The two months of Ultraman and Challenge make the aggravation of the other 10 worth it. This is when Steve gets to be closest to the things he loves the most about triathlon: the athletes, the families, the *action*. In the mornings he'll give rules briefings and safety warnings to the athletes and their crews. In the evenings he'll clean gear, get things ready for the next day, and secure hotel rooms for the endurance caravan. With 29 athletes, their attendant crews, and his own staff, Steve will supervise a small flotilla of kayaks, a convoy of large vans and SUVs, and a platoon of hungry, exhausted athletes across 320 miles over three days. Then he'll help set up the postrace banquet hall, call the local trophy shop and confirm the number of finisher plaques he needs and the names on them, pick them up, and host the awards party. He'll be lucky if he gets more than five hours of sleep on any given night. And if it all goes according to plan, he'll exclaim that nothing "crazy" happened over the course of the weekend.

In an odd, masochistic way, being a race director is an endurance contest in and of itself. Steve absolutely lives for this. In fact, as evidence that he can't get enough of this stuff, he's working on a third race project this weekend, and it's a doozy. Flying in from halfway around the world is the potential for another expansion in the Ultraman race series, and maybe a major upheaval in its makeup. Steve is passionate about producing races, and he's one of the most diligent men in the business. But this time he may have taken on more than even Jane and the rest of the Ohana Loa board can handle.

chapter ten

Something Aussie This Way Comes

"I think so. I think multiple NBA international teams. Twenty years from now? For sure. In Europe. No place else. In other places I think you'll see the NBA name on leagues and other places with marketing and basketball support, but not part of the NBA as we now know it."

—NBA commissioner David Stern, January 2013

"Probably most important for the long-term growth for the NBA, participation levels continue to increase among the Chinese youth, both boys and girls. Right now it's our second-largest market. But who knows in a country of 1.3 billion what the opportunities will ultimately be?"

—NBA deputy commissioner Adam Silver, March 2013

TONY HORTON LOOKS LIKE he's in the final stages of the zombie virus when he gets off the plane in Penticton on August 1. His skin looks slightly gray and there are dark, puffy circles under his eyes. Spending 20 hours in terminals and airplanes between Sierra Leone and Canada while fighting a possible case of malaria will do that to you.

Not that the 50-year-old former Australian special forces soldier is going to let on to anyone that he's under the weather. He puts on swagger as easily as a T-shirt. Jetlag hasn't taken the knavish glint out of his eyes. Though it might be the death of him, he'd hit the bars for an all-nighter on an invitation. His head is clean-shaven as a matter of practicality given the conditions of his work environment and his face is wrinkle-free except for a few shallow lines just above his eyebrows, but it's evident from the early stages of his beard that the salt is overtaking the pepper. But he has a hair trigger for double entendre and he's never backed down from a physical challenge. Tell him he can't do something and the voltage in his smile spikes just a little, silently daring you to dare him. The Ultraman logo tattooed on his calf warns he's not bluffing.

He's really not. Tony is Mr. Been-There-Done-That. He began working as a miner in his hometown of Dinmill, Australia, at the age of 19. He worked through the ranks and signed up for classes in mine rescue. That qualified him for underwater rescue training, which somehow led to a qualification for parachute rescue training. After learning nearly everything imaginable about mine rescue, he decided to embark on new adventures with the Australian army.

"I realized I didn't know anything about weapons and I wanted to learn," he says. "It just felt like something I should know about, and I figured the best place to learn about it was the military, so I signed up. I got there and was in basic training for a few weeks, then realized it was just silly. All these kids—it was a little immature for me. Then one day we're walking along and I see this poster for the Special Air Service, with these guys jumping off a bridge with parachutes. I signed up right away."

Horton was a natural fit in special ops. The secret to being one of the cool guys who walk on the wild side is remembering not to lose your cool and start running. Tony can whistle through a cemetery even when the dead are rising from their graves. That's why he's not freaked out about contracting the zombie plague. The malaria has fatigued him a bit, but you can't tell because he's always this subdued. He yearns to be around excitement, but he doesn't actually *get* excited. Maybe it's genetic. Maybe he picked up on Zen in the course of his wandering education. It's probably a little bit of both.

As good a fit as he was for the special forces, he didn't make a career of it. Once he'd learned all he could from the SAS, he went back to mining work as a safety chief. His diverse skill set made his salary lucrative enough, but people began to understand that Tony had something much more valuable than his accumulated knowledge: a God-given talent for getting things done. That's how he got his current job. A mining company hired him as director of risk management in their Sierra Leone operation. Managing risks in a west African country runs the entire gamut of health hazards, from mosquitoes spreading zombie malaria to thugs armed with AK-47s stealing copper wire to sell on the black market. "There are 12,000 workers, a 30 percent AIDS rate, and 20 deaths a month," he says.

It's not your regular 9-to-5. The only course he attended before taking this job, and maybe the only remaining subject he wasn't already an expert on in the realm of catastrophe management, was a kidnapping and ransom negotiations seminar. That happens in Sierra Leone, too. Basically, his job is to be the sheriff in a place where the only law anyone knows is Murphy's. The catastrophe of the day is a recent spate of "accidents" involving people who push their own family members in front of oncoming trains owned by the mining company in order to collect compensation. The two BlackBerrys he carries around are exploding with emails relaying grim updates. He splits his time between his office in Africa—a 20-foot-long shipping container converted to a military-style bivouac—business meetings in Johannesburg, London, Peru, Oregon, and visits to the home he shares with his wife in Australia. He once flew around the world twice in a week, and spends so much time at altitude that doctors routinely find he has a higher-than-average red-blood-cell count, often considered a boon to endurance athletes. As if his plate wasn't already full enough, he became an Ultraman finisher in Canada last year and owns a juice stand business in an Australian mall. In between checking his BlackBerrys, he's trying to get his iPhone to synchronize with the Canadian data network so he can find out if his offer to buy a second juice franchise has been accepted.

And yet somehow, the endless disasters and speculation on piña coladas just isn't enough for him. For all the pleasure he takes in being here, the purpose of his visit is the business stored on his laptop. Tony Horton has done Ironman. He's done Ultraman. He's done all kinds of races and competitions. But he's never *directed* one. That's what he's here to discuss with Steve, Jane, and the rest of the Ohana Loa board of directors: a proposal to create a new Ultraman race in Australia.

Steve notices Tony's haggard appearance as soon as he walks into Peach City Runners. "You look like a strong breeze would blow you over," he jokes. Tony brushes off his concerns, even when Steve makes the genuine offer to take him to the hospital. "No, mate. I might need some anti-malaria medication, but what I really need first is to get a SIM card that'll get my iPhone working." The juice stand is on his mind. One of the BlackBerrys that he laid on the extra table in Steve's office buzzes like a mechanical hornet. He reflexively picks it up and for a moment he's back in the Third World. The information processed, he puts the device down and switches to Ultraman. "So, when are we talking to the board?" he asks.

Not soon enough, as far as Steve is concerned. He would love to have the board's approval in hand before the prerace breakfast tomorrow morning so he can make a grand announcement. He's put a lot of time and effort into helping Tony structure his proposal to maximize its chances of success. Ironically, that's the biggest strike against Ultraman Australia going into the discussion. Tony initially approached the entire Ohana Loa board with his idea, but since their early discussions he's interacted almost exclusively with Steve. This has drawn aggravation and suspicion from Sheryl and Dave, who've been forced to get updates through indirect sources. What they've heard has made them anxious. The stickiest points have nothing to do with Tony. More than anything, Sheryl and Dave are wary of Steve's role in the affair. They've told him countless times to keep them in the loop by conducting all communication with Tony using the collective Ohana Loa email account that everyone on the board has access to. They've also repeatedly asked him for updates on what's going on. He hasn't exactly been accommodating. They're probably reading too much into the email account issue. Steve is notoriously bad at using technology. He doesn't have a smart phone and he has trouble with text messaging. It's reasonable to believe that he'd have trouble juggling two email addresses. But his evasiveness in answering Sheryl's questions is a departure from character. The accountant in him is too meticulous to forget that many times. For Sheryl, that's only the beginning in how the accounting aspect of Steve's personality causes problems.

Steve's grown used to people misinterpreting him whenever he gets involved in these affairs. Wherever he's gone throughout his long experience in the triathlon business, he's always been one of the few people with an actual business education. There are plenty of people with a story about how they ran a major race into the red. He's one of a handful in the world who have put one back in black. The difference is that you can run an event reasonably well and make ends meet so long as you know what to do with a dollar and don't hit any complications, but to make an event truly successful and turn it into something that can stand up to minor catastrophes you have to know business. Sheryl knows dollars and sense, and she's had a significant role in bringing Ultraman back to its feet after the Vito Bialla years, but she doesn't have the same understanding of business that Steve does. As a consequence, she has trouble understanding Steve.

Not that she hasn't taught him some things. One of Sheryl's early observations in their relationship was that Steve didn't provide the race volunteers food at the finish lines. Steve initially responded that the volunteers knew they'd have to eat throughout the weekend of the race and would buy food anyway, but Sheryl pointed out that the volunteers couldn't simply abandon the finish line to take a lunch break. He'd never thought of that, so he made arrangements with local grocery stores to provide a la carte meals. He still doesn't provide shirts or postrace banquet tickets to the volunteer escort kayakers; he pays them for their time instead. Sheryl takes a dim view of this approach. She makes a huge effort to make the kayakers feel like part of the event in Hawaii, but the Keauhou Canoe Club has stronger ties to the Kona race. Sheryl and Jane are still active members. Steve has had trouble in past years rounding up enough paddlers for Canada, so paying people works better in Penticton. Different strokes for different folks.

It's mostly minor stuff like that, but the two have some strong philosophical differences, too. He's mindful of the money, and she thinks he has nothing but the money on his mind. And because Australia is such a big deal that affects the community, she's more than a little nervous about the full extent of Steve's involvement in this venture. She wonders if he plans to sink some of his own cash into it and what return he expects from his investment.

Added to the Cobbs' frustration over the lack of information from Steve is just how much everyone else in the Ultraman community seems to know about it. These discussions are supposed to be kept in utmost secret, at least for the time being. Steve seems to forget this and casually introduces Tony as "Race Director for Ultraman Australia (new event coming up in 2015)" via emails weeks in advance of the Canada race. Sheryl goes ballistic when she finds out about the slip-up. There's a basis for her anxiety. Ultraman United Kingdom—the newest addition to the series—is only in its third year and already it is facing difficulties drawing participants. Popping off about an Australian event before it's up and running may cause potential registrants to hold off in the UK, possibly denying that event whatever chances of survival it has left. Steve isn't as concerned. He's already asked the graphic designer who helped put together the logos for Ultraman Florida and Ultraman United Kingdom to make a similar banner for the Australian event. It looks magnificent. The Australian flag flies within an outline of the country, accompanied by a kangaroo on the side. There's also a framework already built for the event website.

In fairness, the precedent exists for Steve to do this. He was the one who got those items worked up for the UK organizers when they began, and Consuela and Trung Lively approached him for the same assistance when they started planning for Florida. He's used the same graphic and web designers each time, and it's produced a uniform look that gives a professional appearance to all the events. In this case, however, Tony has yet to gain the board's endorsement. Steve is putting the cart before the horse.

Tony shares some blame in this as well. He's recruited three of the Australian athletes racing in Canada this weekend to help him with the event. They've been over the entire planned route in Noosa, including running through most of the double marathon course. Now they're here. They're excited to discuss all things Ultraman with their fellow participants—even the things they're not supposed to. Tony himself whips out the laptop the moment fellow Australian and past Ultraman Canada winner Nick Mallett comes in to say hi. They open up a slideshow in Microsoft PowerPoint and begin discussing it animatedly. Everyone who comes by to talk to Steve and happens to ask Tony what he's looking at gets the same response: "This is the race we're planning in Australia for next year."

It's a busy day upstairs. The registration area is so inundated with participants and crews that Jane doesn't get a break until it's time for the bike course presentation at the hotel banquet hall. It's a mandatory meeting specifically to discuss the rules and requirements—for both athletes and crews—during the two cycling segments of the course. The seminar is scheduled to last two hours. It might seem a little excessive for a bike race, but if anything is going to go wrong this weekend, odds are it will happen on two wheels.

Jane comes down before heading to the hotel and chats with Tony and Steve. They discuss finding a good time to discuss Tony's presentation before convening the official meeting with Dave and Sheryl. With Dave in Kona and Sheryl in California, they plan on using an online conferencing program to talk via computer. Jane says that she has time now, so why not show her what Tony has? They don't have to be told twice. They pull chairs up to the extra table and Tony rewinds to the beginning of the slideshow.

Tony's extraordinary talents and experience immediately show in the composition of the slide presentation. The agenda is as streamlined as it is thorough. The maps have been created and edited in Google Earth, with inset photos to show the actual terrain. Weather data for the proposed month, tide charts for the swim, moon phases. It's all there. It could be the plan for a military operation.

Each day of the event is proposed to start and end in Noosa. It's reminiscent of Vito Bialla's failed Hawaii experiment, but in this case it makes sense. Noosa is a sort of triathlon Mecca. It's famous for hosting several world-class events every year, including a national triathlon festival. Tony calls it "a fitness town." There are plenty of facilities for the athletes and crews and a large, supportive population from which to draw the necessary volunteers and sponsors. It's a gem of a location.

Tony's gone even further by surveying the site and planning a racecourse fit for the best possible viewing as well as competition. He's checked to make sure shark nets are in place to protect swimmers. He's also researched sponsors, promotion, media coverage, and increased visibility through social media. There are even a few items to dazzle the group. He's found a way to put GPS units on the athletes during the race for live-feed updates. Jane *oohs* at that. He's also timed the event to coincide with a local food and wine festival, which would help to bring greater attention to both events if they work things right with the organizers. Jane scribbles a note on her pad. By the time he finishes, it looks as if he's covered all the bases and then some.

Now comes the pitch. Tony says he can't make any more progress toward securing agreements or licenses without official endorsement by Ohana Loa. "I need your permission to put the Ultraman logo on a business card, or a letterhead with your certification that I'm an agent of the brand down there. Otherwise, everyone just looks at me like some guy off the street. They're not going to negotiate with me until I can show I'm a legitimate operation."

Jane's response stops just short of explicitly saying yes. She's enthusiastic. She's also been here before, and this is the one place where her trust was betrayed. She won't let her excitement overcome discretion. It's a difficult position to be in. As Ultra Mom, she's always been the fairy godmother of the race, granting every wish and making every dream come true. It's not her style to turn people down. So while she is the sole authority on these issues, she maintains that the board must discuss the matter and vote. It's not a complete illusion. She does rely heavily on the counsel of Steve, Sheryl, and Dave. But everyone likes it better in a world where it's Jane that says yes and the board that says no. It falls upon Sheryl to act as chief executive of rejection, and she's already skeptical of the deal. Though not able to physically attend the event due to a family emergency, she's been able to glean some information about Tony and Steve's dealings through the grapevine. The less Tony and Steve have kept her in the loop, the greater the opposition they've created for themselves.

Jane is able to deflect any pressure by saying she can't wait for Dave and Sheryl to hear the presentation tomorrow. There isn't time to go further because the first official athlete briefing is scheduled to start in a half hour at the local hotel banquet hall. Everyone leaves for the dreaded bike course safety brief.

Athletes are milling about the parking lot and inside the hall by the time the group arrives. Some make banter as they take turns emptying the coffeepots in the back of the hall. The majority are shuffling around the tables, apprehensively grabbing seats closer to the back of the room. Most everyone here is a rookie, and it shows. The group looks like a bunch of kids on the first day of school.

Steve begins the meeting with some opening remarks. He talks about the big news with Challenge and makes special mention of Tony Horton and the possibility of "a big announcement at the breakfast tomorrow." If Jane is surprised, she doesn't show it. The briefing is excruciatingly long, even if necessary. The two bike phases of the race are considered "open course," which means that there will be no special assistance with traffic from local law enforcement. Roads in major cities get shut down for marathons and even Ironman races, but ultra events are too long in distance and small in numbers to justify it. It's always been one of those things organizers and participants have had to deal with. It's emphasized time and again that the participants have to obey all traffic signs, including stoplights. It doesn't matter if you get caught at a light in a close race. Those are the breaks.

That's not the only consideration. Because the crew vehicles stop frequently to provide food and water to athletes, Steve has to address the correct way to go about things without making the race a nuisance to the community. There are also specific areas deemed too risky in which to stop and make handoffs to athletes. Support vehicles are also strictly forbidden from giving aid to athletes while moving. That's a good way to get someone killed by an oncoming car.

Athletes can't draft behind vehicles on the road, whether they belong to support crews or not. It provides an unfair advantage and it's dangerous. Likewise, crews can't drive directly behind their athlete—for too long. That's considered blocking, and is a common offense. Crews often get anxious about aggressive traffic encroaching on their athletes and think it's a good idea to shield their athlete on especially narrow roads. What sometimes winds up happening is that an angry driver attempts to pass the crew vehicle and sideswipes the athlete when they mistakenly come back into the lane too soon.

Navigational errors are especially costly to competitors. If an athlete goes off course they are forbidden from getting in their crew vehicle to get back on track. Similarly, there can be no changing bikes unless the athlete's primary bike has a mechanical breakdown. These are just the basics. Steve pores over endless "what-ifs" throughout the next 90 minutes. The athletes get restless, but they have only their predecessors to blame. The race started with very few regulations. For every rule Steve addresses that sounds stupid, there's been someone who has done something stupid enough to make the rule necessary.

He finally finishes the briefing and hands things over to his daughter, Alexis. She's working as assistant race director, effectively running the entire show while her father has been wrapped up in meetings with the Challenge board. She's split her time today between working registration and preparing the banquet hall for the safety brief. Her remarks now focus on an evolving dimension of Ultraman both as a business and community: social media. The Ohana Loa board is slowly coming to grips with how to use social media and how it will affect the events going forward. Steve is absolutely clueless about how it all works. Alexis created a Facebook page for Ultraman Canada, and there are pages for the other races as well as a designated group for the Ultraman community in general, but no one within the race leadership professes to be a social media expert. Alexis provides everyone with the locations of different Twitter and Facebook pages, and asks everyone to "tag" some key personnel if any photos or updates are posted for the widest possible dissemination across the worldwide Ultraman community. The primary focus is making sure everyone in the family sees the photos and gets the updates; there's nothing resembling a marketing strategy. Alexis concludes her remarks by scolding a final few athletes about getting their paperwork in. She gently but firmly mentions that people won't be allowed to take the starting line until the forms are completed.

There's not much socializing afterward. Everyone is exhausted from traveling in from wherever they've come and are ready to hit the sack. Tomorrow will start early, with the prerace breakfast and more safety and rules briefings. The rest of the day will be consumed with last-minute grocery shopping and preparations. A few people rush the stage to give Alexis their apologies and paperwork. The hall clears out in less than 15 minutes. Tony and Steve return to Peach City Runners to shuttle some gear and administrative items around for the next day. They find an email from Dave saying that they can make the conference call late the next night.

The prerace breakfast is an endless buffet of Canada's best. Cheese. Ham. Potatoes. Everything the athletes could possibly want is here, and they want it all. Kathleen Wood, a nurse from just up the road in Kelowna and first-time participant in the race, heaps her plate with an astonishing amount of food given her slender, 5'4" frame. A multiple Ironman finisher, she has the body fat of a Spartan hoplite. The swell of her calf muscles and definition in her quads are startling. Her metabolism must be the equivalent of a nuclear reactor. She's not the only one. Despite what they're about to go through, most of the competitors here have been going for runs and bike rides all week; some of them even got in a workout in before breakfast. They settle around the heavenly aroma of the eggs Benedict with Canadian bacon like a committee of vultures on an abandoned carcass. When the serving pan is emptied, they circle patiently for the next one to come out, lest it be cleared before they can get at it.

Steve finally calls things to order and everyone takes their seats. He welcomes Jane and introduces the primary officials, then a few key personalities here to help with the race. He counts Tony among them, and mentions that he's here for "special reasons that we'll hopefully be able to announce at the end of the weekend." Jane maintains her poker face again. Steve finally gives a nod to Barb Haines, the Challenge Penticton general manager. He then brings Jane to the stage. Her message is simple: "This weekend, you will hear three words over and over. Aloha, ohana, kokua. If you let them, they will touch your heart forever. You'll do more than finish a race here. You'll join the Ultraman family."

With the sentimental stuff out of the way, Steve yields the podium to the representative from Challenge. She gives a 10-to-15-minute presentation on the upcoming race and all the great things Penticton is doing. The audience gets restless after the first two minutes. More than one grumbles later that they feel like they got roped into a pitch for a time-share. Yet Steve's proud of what's happening in his town. He's happy that Penticton has a second chance at putting on the race it always wanted. This was his way of showing off his new baby to the world. It didn't come across the way he wanted.

There's a five-minute intermission before they get to the real business. Everyone empties their bladders and refills their coffee cups, bracing for the worst. First up is the swim brief. It's pretty simple. The course is a straight shot down Skaha Lake. The only big concern is the diapers. Six miles is a long way to go, so each athlete is guided by a support crewmember in a kayak to give them food and water along the way. While the athletes work so hard that their digestive systems close for business during the swim, the kayakers may spend up to four hours sitting in a rather uncomfortable position, with nothing to do but paddle every few seconds. They're up the creek if nature calls in the lake. The swim course directors recommend adult diapers for anyone who worries they might need them.

The bike course is covered in painstaking detail. Steve goes over every turn, four-way intersection, highway junction, and town along each day's route. Lodging between nights, start and finish area procedures, penalties, food and gas for crews. Slowly but surely, it's all explained. It finally comes to an end with just enough time for everyone to go take care of a couple of errands before lunch. The room clears out quickly. A few athletes stick around and ask each other what the whole Challenge thing was about. Steve and Tony take off quickly to try to find a SIM card for Tony's iPhone and something to fight the zombie virus. He's feeling better, so maybe he can get by without quinine. More than anything, he wants to get plugged in and check on the juice stand.

The group reassembles on the beach later that afternoon for some swim practice and to go over the kayaks with the swim course staff. It takes about an hour. Afterward, many of the support crewmembers put on their own wet suits and go for a dip. Many of them are extraordinary athletes in their own right. For many, that's how they know the participants they're supporting. Some are Ultraman veterans. Others have it in mind to try the race for themselves within a few years and are here to get an up-close-and-personal look at what it takes to finish.

Everyone disappears after that. As social a group as the Ultraman family is, at a certain point you have to attend to your own needs. There's also a certain psychological element at play. It hasn't been discussed too much, but everyone feels a certain breathless anticipation. Some big guns have shown up for this race. John Bergen won here in 2011. Inaki De La Parra is the 2012 Ultraman UK winner. There's talk that Craig Percival of Australia is also a serious contender. Michael Owen is a phenomenal runner, but the question is whether he can keep the gap close enough to use that to his advantage on the last day. Christian Isakson is the dark horse. He's never competed in an Ultraman event, but he's finished the Epic 5 Challenge, an event in which participants race five Ironman courses in five days on each of the five islands of Hawaii.

Nick Mallett says Dave Matheson is the one to beat. If anyone is the oddsmaker, it's Nick. He's something of an institution in the ultra-triathlon world, especially here in Penticton. He won the second Ultraman Canada in 1994, his first time entering the race. He won again in the 1999 resurrection, and has been coming back about every other year since. He's placed well a couple of other times and picked up his share of DNFs. At 49, age is catching up with him a bit. More than anything, he struggles to maintain a consistent training regimen due to bouts of severe depression. Then again, part of his status as an institution is based on how he's embraced the race's principles. Winning and finishing aren't as important or even necessary for him. It's all about the journey. In 2011 a breakup with a girlfriend precipitated an especially deep slump and he realized that it might be the end of him if he didn't take drastic measures. He decided to take an extraordinarily roundabout way to Ultraman by flying to Alaska and riding his bike all the way to Penticton. He went even further by chronicling the journey on a blog he titled Riding Through the Haze. Equal parts travelogue, cry of the heart, and epistle of hope, his first post concluded:

I believe that very few people have bothered to truly understand where I have come from, why I have lived the way I have and just who I am. It is easier to form false truths to explain away a life than it is to actually ask about that life. The why's and wherefore's of ones exsitance are often more complicated AND more simple than can be imagined and a troubled mind can usually be traced quite simply to a broken spirit or a tortured heart.

By the end of his 3,500-mile trek, his broken heart had partially mended and his physical fitness had sufficiently returned for him to finish the Ultraman. He almost didn't start after a harrowing accident outside of Alberta. In some ways, it didn't matter. He presaged that sense of triumph in another blog post explaining the course of his downward spiral and how the Alaskan trip began:

Now after reading my previous posts you may have some idea of what has happened to contribute to my athletic demise but that is the reason and not an excuse. There really should be no excuse because life is what it is and we all do things for our own reasons. People who believe that I failed in those last events are looking at the shallower side of what is important, the real story is that I was alive and well enough to start. I know that sounds lame to some but sometimes just to feel part of something is victory enough to someone who sometimes had trouble just getting out of bed to face each day.

Everyone in Ultraman lives to race. Perhaps more than any other, Nick races to live. Triathlon permeates every aspect of his life. When he's not racing or training, he's watching events or reading about the pro athlete standings or business dealings of the major race series. Like so many others with such strong attachments to the sport, his opinions match his passion. He has very specific ideas about what's wrong with the sport and how to fix it, and he's quite vocal about them both in person and online. Some people write him off as a fanatic, and maybe he is. But maybe that's a reason to take him seriously. Outside of Steve King, few people are as knowledgeable of the sport as Nick. So when he says that Dave Matheson is the odds-on favorite, you bet against him at your peril.

Born and raised in Penticton, Dave has competed in the Ironman race here for 11 years. The Ultraman course is his training ground. On top of that, he's been coached in the past by Kevin Cutjar, the current Ultraman Canada course record holder. Nowadays the former student has become an equal. They train together as friends. Whatever Cutjar knows about winning on this course, Dave also knows. Based on their respective times in other races, Dave seems the most well rounded out of the top men. Each of the others claims one discipline as their strength, but that leaves them vulnerable to attacks in the other two. Matheson doesn't have any weaknesses. You can't beat him on the swim, the bike, or the run and expect to put him away. You've got to beat him from the moment the gun goes off and keep beating him all the way to the finish line. People who've seen him in action are dubious as to whether anyone else in the field has enough firepower to pull off that kind of race.

The only sure bet is that there will be fireworks. There have been some tight races in Ultraman Canada's history. There have been some incredible finishes. But there's never been a deck this stacked with all-star talent. They're very close to being the best you can possibly get. It's possibly a sign that, after 30 years of building a race for the world's greatest endurance athletes, they're finally starting to come. From the sophisticated equipment they've mounted on their bikes to their race résumés and the evidence of countless training hours in their physiques, everything about these athletes radiates an aura of killer instinct. These aren't weekend warriors. They are competitors to the core, just a half step behind full-blown professionals. The fire of naked aggression flickers behind their eyes.

After dinner, Jane, Steve, and Alexis regroup at Peach City Runners for the conference call with Sheryl and Dave. Tony hasn't made it back yet. Technically, this should be for Tony and the board only, but Alexis has special reasons for being there. Beyond her position as assistant director this year, she's had a special relationship with the race as long as it's existed. She's been involved with Ultraman Canada since her father held the first race. There are photos of her working as Jane's "administrative assistant" at age eight, marking down athletes' times as they came out of the swim. Other photos show her blowing out the candles on her birthday cake at different locations around the course. It just turned out that the race typically falls on the week of her birthday. "It's pretty hard to explain to an 11-year-old that her father forgot her birthday because of a race," she says. That's the wool they pulled over her eyes one year for a surprise party. No one would have faulted her for being jealous, but instead she embraced the event. It's become a special part of her relationship with her father. It always will be, she says. "I can't imagine ever not coming to this race. It has too many memories for me." They've had some serious heart-to-heart talks about that sentiment. Beyond her capabilities to keep the paperwork straight and project the necessary authority to drive the athlete herd along the route, she has the kind of love it takes to make this work. That's a big part of why she's in this room, and why she's assistant director this year. It may be that she inherits this race from her father.

Steve cranks up the chat program and finds Dave Cobb already online. He rings in and everyone exchanges pleasantries. Sheryl joins moments later by phone. Tony's still out, so Jane and Steve have to make do for a few minutes. After making some small talk, they start giving Dave and Sheryl a preview of things by describing what they've seen and their impressions, which are highly positive. Steve explains that Jane has already seen and heard the presentation, so the Cobbs are the only ones left out of the loop. He misses how poorly that goes over with Sheryl.

Tony finally arrives and apologizes for his tardiness. Introductions are made around the room and Tony takes it from the top. Dave is able to see the slides somewhat from the live video feed, but Sheryl is dialing in from another location using her phone and can only hear what's being said. Tony reaches the same conclusion as he did with Jane. This time, a pregnant silence follows his pitch.

Dave takes it upon himself to break the awkwardness: "It sounds really good. You've done a solid job answering all the questions, I think. There may be a few more things we have questions about, though. But if the slides are as good as what you've told us, we can take this and get some thoughts together and get back to you pretty easily with what you've told us tonight, Sheryl?"

"Yeah. I mean, it sounds great from what I've heard, Tony," she says. "I obviously can't see the slides, though. So what I want to do is take a look at those and have some time to go over them in detail and see if there are any questions we can think of. At that point, we'll get together with the board and discuss it, and based on what everyone says I think we've got a good start."

Tony begins glancing from Steve to the computer and back again. He keeps a straight face, but this is obviously not what he anticipated. There's an edge to his voice when he speaks again. "I'm not sure I understand. There's not much more I can do from this point, and what I was looking for tonight was the authority to go and get the answers to whatever further questions you might have. But if there's something you want to ask now..." He trails off, opening the door. Sheryl tries to make it clear that this isn't going to be a 15-minute Q&A.

"Tony, the problem isn't that I have any specific questions for you now. It's that I'm not sure what questions I might have. I mean, you guys are all there and have apparently seen this presentation, and Dave and I haven't seen anything. So I don't know what questions I will have until I've seen the presentation and had some time to think about it."

"And another thing that we have to consider here is Florida," adds Dave. "I mean, we haven't even had that race yet, so I don't want to move too fast on this. I would personally like to see how that race goes and what the response and participation numbers are before we start cranking up a new event and steal their thunder."

"I thought Florida was already full, right?" The look on Tony's face when he looks around at everyone else is asking a different question: *What's with this stuff about Florida? I thought we were here to talk about Australia.* As far as he's concerned, Florida has nothing to do with him. That's what has worried Sheryl the most about Tony—he's only concerned as far as he's concerned.

"Ultraman UK was full the first year, too," says Dave. "And then it had a huge decline in registration and it hasn't picked back up. So I'm not ready to shift support off of one event based solely on its first year." You can't get a more pragmatic statement, or a more bitter underlying sentiment. The UK event started auspiciously enough, but it has faltered drastically ever since. The event has had all kinds of problems, from foul weather to incompetent planning. What was supposed to herald a new age of growth of the Ultraman principles and family has turned into a millstone around the neck of the Ohana Loa board members. Dave's words are meant to explain the rationale to Tony, but the tone of his voice tells everyone else what's really on his mind: *Let's not do that again.*

That relates to another problem with this meeting. Steve Brown was the one who took the lead helping the Ultraman United Kingdom director make their sales pitch to Jane. Everyone on the board voted to accept that race, so they all share responsibility in falling for some of the lies they were told. Steve sort of fell the hardest. And that's Sheryl's biggest problem with this situation. This feels like a repeat of very bad history.

Tony asks if the board is simply reluctant to make any moves toward expansion at this time, implying that he's been misled into wasting his time and money by making the trip out. Steve defuses that line of discussion and gives his endorsement to everyone that Tony isn't the type of person who'd allow a repeat of "the types of things that have happened in Wales." Dave and Sheryl assure Tony that he's not being accused of anything, nor are they close-minded.

Steve tries a different approach. "Sheryl, I understand your concerns, but what we're trying to achieve tonight isn't as much an official go-ahead as an informal one. We'd like to at least reach a consensus within the board so we can make an announcement to the people here tomorrow." Of all the wrong things he could have said, that was probably the worst. He's telegraphed how hard he's trying to push, and now Sheryl digs in to a proportionate depth.

"I'm not ready to do that tonight, Steve. Whether it's formal or informal, we need to discuss this together as a board."

Tony interjects. "I thought the board was all together now." Like Steve, Tony is a business-minded alpha male. He's used to winning, even in no-win situations. What he doesn't understand is the time frame. He's throwing for a touchdown when the only thing he should be aiming for is a first down. The harder he pushes, the more he risks Sheryl's ire. Things are about to stop being nice and start getting real.

"The board is all together," Sheryl responds. "But, no offense Tony, you're there too, and I feel like there's some kind of pressure to make a decision tonight, and I don't feel comfortable rushing to judgment."

Dave intervenes again. "What I don't understand is why we're in a rush to reach some kind of decision tonight. Even if we said yes, what difference is that going to make? I mean, Tony, you're in Canada for the rest of the week, and then you're going to Wales with Steve after this. It's not like you can do anything with the approval if we give it to you."

Tony sits back and puts his hands up in surrender. He's got no answer to that one. He sees what's happening here. Less is more—for now. Steve doesn't give up the charge. "Well, I think what we achieve is a sign of good faith," he says. "Tony has come all the way out here to give us this presentation and I think he's done a great job. We ought to give him something to take home with him."

Sheryl probably wouldn't have said anything, but Steve has ignored every signal they've given him. The only thing he'll apparently listen to is the chief executive of rejection. "Steve, I'm not saying Tony hasn't done a good job. But we have not *all* seen the briefing. I know that I've been asking to see some copy of what you guys were working on for weeks, and I still haven't seen the slides. And I want to take a look at what Tony's put together and physically see it before I make any judgments. So I don't want to feel forced into making any decisions tonight, because if that was the case and I was forced to give an answer now, my answer would be no."

And that's the ballgame. The only thing left to do is salve the hurt feelings as best as possible. That means it's Jane's turn to talk: "We're not saying no. What we're saying is that we want to take a look at it and make sure that the location and the timing are right. We have the other races to think about and when we launch this we want to make sure it has the best possible chance of filling up the first year without interfering with the other races."

Everyone nods in agreement as she looks in Tony's direction. "You have to realize we've had this experience before," she continues. "Ultraman UK is only three years old, and it's had problems getting people to sign up. We don't want to have that happen. So let us make sure that we're ready to give you all the help we can to make this a success."

Tony looks at the ground and nods. "All right. That's fair." He almost sounds satisfied. The fairy Ultra Mom has worked her magic again.

Dave gives him an extra verbal pat on the back. "Just send us the presentation and give us some time to look at it, and when we've had a chance to discuss it as a board we'll get back to you."

"About how long do you think that will take?" Tony asks. They assure Tony that they should be able to get back to him by the end of the month. They cut the conference feed and the group is once again left amongst themselves in the room. Tony gives Jane a disappointed smile. "Well, not exactly how I expected that to go."

"You just have to get used to Sheryl," she tells him. "And Dave's right. A couple of weeks isn't going to hurt anything. We'll get it sorted out. You'll see."

The day started at 6:00 AM and it's nearly 10:30 at night. Tomorrow will start even earlier and be even longer. In 90 minutes, it will officially be day one of Ultraman Canada 2013. No more arguments over what someone said or debating interpretations of rules. Just clean, honest racing and the ultimate truth of who crosses the line first. How complicated could it be?

As it turns out, really complicated.

chapter eleven

White Line Fever

"In athletics there's always been a willingness to cheat if it looks like you're not cheating. I think that's just a quirk of human nature."

—Kareem Abdul-Jabbar

AUGUST 3, 4:35 AM. Tony Horton walks into the living room of the house he's staying in and settles into an armchair with his BlackBerry. His hosts for the weekend are the nurse volunteering as the race medic and her husband, who's decided to get involved by helping set up and tear down at the start and finish lines each day. It's only their third year being involved with the race, but they're so into it that they're giving the extra bed space in their house to complete strangers.

Tony tries to get through his morning deluge of updates from Sierra Leone, but he keeps looking up frequently to ruminate on the board meeting. It's the first time he shows any sign of fatigue or distractedness since arriving in Penticton. The gears aren't turning as smoothly as they did in Steve Brown's office. He dissects every word of the conference call as obsessively as a Super Bowl postgame report. "I mean, what else do they want me to do? I did everything they asked. Made the phone calls, went down to the area, met the people, ran the course. Honestly! Was it not all there? What else could I have given them?" He crashed hard and fast when he got in. Though it all happened yesterday, in terms of consciousness he's only been out of the meeting for an hour. The angst from losing what to him was the big game doesn't subside that quickly.

Darkness is barely receding when Jane's car pulls in front of the house. Tony pockets the BlackBerry and moves to the door. Jane is her usual cheerful self, even at this hour. More than that, she's excited. It's day one. Time to race.

The drive down to the north shore of Skaha Lake only takes about 15 minutes. Tony mainly just asks Jane about how things will go. Jane explains as she drives, interrupting herself occasionally to remark on some landmark they pass on the road, usually in the form of a house someone she knew used to live in. They're the first to arrive at the park, about 15 minutes ahead of Steve Brown and the volunteers coming to help set up the start-line banner and support canoes. Tony decides to walk up the street to a gas station to grab something that can pass for breakfast. The postgame show resumes once he's out of earshot of Jane.

"I mean, if they don't want to go along with it, it's not like I'm going to just throw in the towel, you know? I'll just set it up and do it my own way. It just won't be an Ultraman-branded event. So what? I don't think Sheryl and Dave get it about Australia. They can mandate all that ohana stuff all day long, but Australians aren't into that hold-hands-in-a-circle, 'Kumbaya' crap. It's not our thing. We like to party, mate. I mean, *parrrrrty*. We'll race for three days and then drink beer for three days. You know what I mean?"

His meaning is unmistakable, but it's also apparent that the longer he dwells on it, the more straw men he builds to blame for his perceived defeat. He's somehow developed the idea that Sheryl and Dave have a hippie-like infatuation with the core values of Ultraman, and that it's directly to blame for their resistance. For most of his life, Tony's found himself in situations that demanded him to say "to hell with the obstacles" in order to succeed. Consequently, if it's Dave and Sheryl and their ideals that stand in his way, to hell with Dave and Sheryl and their ideals.

His assessment isn't entirely wrong, though. Several people who race Ultraman on a consistent basis don't subscribe to the Hawaiian ideals that Jane, Sheryl, and Dave do. And there are plenty of ultra events around the world in which regular participants develop a sense of community with each other. Nick Mallett finds just as much camaraderie at Double-Ironman events around the world, which are put on by the International Ultra Triathlon Association. Ohana, aloha, and kokua are definitely a part of what makes Ultraman special, but only one part. It's not essential to making a race special, or even successful. But it is a quality essential to Jane and Sheryl, which creates a dilemma for them. Other events aren't as restricted in their expansion plans by holding so true to similar values.

The lakeside park explodes with activity in the time it takes Tony to pick up some food and walk back from the gas station. Steve and the volunteers roll in shortly after Jane, with the athletes hot on their heels. Crew vehicles burst forth with gear and people begin loading the canoes for the swim leg. The public restroom and shower area become hot spots. It's a common scene in just about any endurance race, regardless of the distance. Because races start so early, participants often down gratuitous amounts of coffee to kick-start their engines. The result is another time-honored tradition: the prerace poo. At major events like Ironman Hawaii or the Berlin marathon, the line for the porta-potties can take as much as half an hour. Despite a planning factor of one unit per every 50-75 people at an event, they'll have better luck finding one with toilet paper in it than buying a winning lottery ticket. Even with only 29 athletes and their crews here, the latrines turn into premium real estate.

Steve King begins getting his gear wired for showtime. He arrives in a minivan specially outfitted as a mobile announcing platform. Its rear storage space is retrofitted with extra power outlets and an array of amplifiers and speakers. The atmosphere suddenly charges with a sense of urgency once the music starts and his voice comes over the speaker, welcoming everyone to the 2013 Ultraman Canada. The adrenaline starts flowing and you can see something switch on in the athletes' eyes. Doubt. Determination. Fear. Hope. Everything inside begins to well up and everything outside gets up close and personal. Then comes the announcement for the athletes to assemble on the beach.

A bagpiper begins playing. It's Steve Brown's own personal touch to the opening ceremonies, and not a bad one at that. As much as he uses and believes in the words aloha, ohana, and kokua, this is still his race and his family has Scottish roots. He then has the athletes join hands as he encourages them to race with sincerity and sportsmanship, to accept whatever happens over the next three days with open minds and hearts, and to have fun. Finally, he asks everyone to turn and join him in singing the Canadian national anthem. Everyone turns on cue and faces the Canadian flag in the park. There's no music, but the sound of their voices without an accompanying band is pitch perfect.

A few minutes later, 24 men and five women wade out hip-deep into the water. Their support paddlers wait anxiously 50 yards away. The crowd joins Steve Brown in a final 10-second countdown, and with the sound of an air horn they're off. There's maybe a minute's worth of cheering mixed with a frenetic splashing in the water, and then as suddenly as it started the beach is quiet again. Once the athletes move out of camera-phone range, the volunteers begin packing things up to head to the swim finish. Nor does Steve King linger. The music cuts out immediately. It's astounding how quickly the swimmers move out of sight. In short order they look as small and slow as a band of otters drifting along the current.

Up close, they're working like sled dogs. Craig Percival has a strong swimming background and throws down the gauntlet early. His pace takes him a minute and 26 seconds to cover 100 meters. That's only five seconds slower than the pace for the Hawaiian Ironman course record, and that's over a distance six kilometers shorter than what Percival will do today. Dave Matheson falls on Percival's heels. Four other men join the chase: the dark horse Christian Isakson, the two former champs John Bergen and Inaki De La Parra, and the X-factor Michael Owen.

There's an odd development in the rest of the pack. Twenty minutes after they start, three or four athletes have managed to drift all the way over to one side of the lake or the other, with clusters of three or four at random intervals between. Some of these folks are literally going the long way around, adding hundreds of meters to the task ahead of them. They're trying to catch a favorable current from the river that flows between the lakes along the Okanagan. All of them are competent swimmers. The different tactics highlight the difference between good athletes and the highly competitive ones leading the race. These presumed stragglers are not just good swimmers, they know how to negotiate the swells and tides of open water, how to stay on course by sighting landmarks on shore, and how to judge which way and how hard the current is pushing them. The difference is akin to the adventure seekers who climb Everest and their Sherpa guides. What the former call a challenge, the latter call home. There's no greater testimony to that than Nick Mallet, who's up in the top 10. Just a couple months shy of his 50th birthday, he's hanging right alongside guys young enough to be his sons.

Craig Percival is the first out of the water. With an official time of 2:24:28, he smashes the swim course record. Everyone cheers as he gets a helping hand out of the water from one of one of his support crewmembers. He runs up the carpet laid out from the beach to where the bikes are parked with short, choppy steps, as if he's walking on hot coals. The sensation of standing up and walking after spending hours bobbing and struggling through the water is jarring. It takes a few minutes to get the amphibian out of his system. While he reacquaints himself with terra firma, his crew frantically yanks his wet suit free. He stands and carefully pulls socks and cycling shoes onto his wobbly legs. A final application of sunscreen and a quick check to make sure he has a few essentials in his pockets, and he's on the bike in less than five minutes.

Percival is long gone by the time Dave Matheson arrives 12 minutes later. But what Matheson does next is utterly superhuman. He yanks his wet suit down to his feet and has his cycling jersey on before his crew can help him step out of the ankle cuffs. He takes a quick handful of items from his wife, Tina, and jumps atop the bike on the run. His shoes are already clipped to the pedals and he slips his feet into them as he goes. He is literally gone in 60 seconds, and in doing so he cuts Percival's 12-minute lead to just eight.

It's another 23 minutes before John Bergen and Christian Isakson make landfall. Conventional wisdom would tell them not to sweat it and to hold to their plan. But Percival and Matheson have confirmed everyone's suspicions that this race will be anything but conventional. Ultra athletes are usually very orderly at support stations or transition zones like this. They don't lounge about, but they do things methodically to ensure they don't forget something important that will cause them to stop again later. There's unprecedented urgency in Bergen's and Isakson's transitions. Crewmembers fumble with their wet suits and drop shoes. Both men ask for things with the staccato exclamations of trauma surgeons. They scramble to their feet and start jogging out with the bikes. Then they jump onto their saddles and take off like fighter jets.

Inaki De La Parra comes in at just a minute over three hours. Michael Owen arrives six minutes behind that. Another five men mount their bikes before the three and-a-half-hour mark. Then the intervals between athlete arrivals grow noticeably longer. Crews must contend with a mix of growing nervousness and boredom as the minutes drag into hours. There's even some unexpected drama when one of the support crewmembers suffers an allergic reaction to a bee sting. The medic attends to her while Steve Brown calls for an ambulance. Its arrival winds up delaying Peter Vaughan by several minutes. He gets blocked behind it as it tries to maneuver through the narrow parking area by the lakeside, and he dare not try going around for fear of getting hit or holding up the woman's trip to the hospital. It took him just over four hours to finish the swim. He has no intentions of catching the top men. At this point in the day the anxiety among athletes is governed by the time remaining before the 12-hour cutoff. Vaughan should be safe. But you never know when something like an ambulance carrying a bee sting victim will pop up. Or, less creative but equally frustrating, finding out you forgot your spare tire after you pop a flat just a few miles from transition. That's the call from Iona MacKenzie just a few minutes after Peter gets under way. Her crew has already supplied her with a refill of water and gone too far down the road for her to see, and unfortunately they've forgotten to leave their cell phones on in the support vehicle. She calls back to the swim finish for help. Steve Brown again organizes an impromptu rescue.

There's another crisis Steve can't help with. Peter Lopinski, from Poland, takes 5 hours, 2 minutes, and 42 seconds to finish the swim. Between the time left on the clock and the utter exhaustion of the effort, he is terrifyingly close to missing the cutoff. He developed motion sickness from the lake's waves pitching him around. Added to the water he inadvertently gulped during his time out there, he hasn't ingested any calories since breakfast. He's utterly depleted and can't stomach anything. All he can do is lie down and wait for his body to recover, if it can.

Things solidify at the front of the pack. Dave Matheson can't get any closer to Craig Percival in the lead, but Percival can't pull away either. They've got first and second place locked up—for the time being. Things behind them are a bit more jumbled. Christian Isakson slowly pulls ahead of John Bergen, but never out of sight. Inaki De La Parra is also able to nudge ahead of Bergen. For the most part, they're so close together that no one can tell. They have it easy for the first 50 km, a flat southward journey through the valley between Skaha and Osoyoos Lakes. They go into the small town of Osoyoos then turn westward, where they find the first of two major challenges on the bike: a climb over the Richter Pass that takes them up 400 meters in less than 8 kilometers. The type of bike these guys are racing on is built to cut through the wind, not push over mountains like this. They grit their teeth and go right over; slowing down could cost them the whole race. Percival keeps daring everyone, and they all keep chasing.

The sheer pain they endure is best demonstrated by one of the athletes farther back. Alan MacPherson has finished Ultraman UK and twice completed the World Championships in Hawaii. The Scottish-born corrections officer is as tough as they come. He jokes that his last night at work before departing for Canada was "slow." There was only one fight in the cell block. He does all this on top of living with Crohn's disease. His distinctive brogue, natural gregariousness, and penchant for heavily coating his face and arms with big white streaks of sunscreen like some kind of war paint make him recognizable, but his reputation is built on a superlative toughness—even among this crowd.

That's what makes his breakdown on the Richter so scary. He's okay on making the cutoff, but he can't get settled on the bike. His legs just aren't firing the way they should, and between the time and money he's invested in this, anxiety has worked its way into his head before he starts the climb. By the time he gets two-thirds of the way up, it's gnawed down to his last nerve. The incessant battling against the wind and the slope become too much. When he gets close enough to his crew vehicle, he gets off his bike and throws it off to the side of the road, cursing a blue streak at nothing and everything all at once. The athletes who compete in these sorts of races routinely finish them with all sorts of injuries, from blood blisters to broken bones and even kidney failure. They can push through blizzards and tropical storms because, as they say, it's all mental. That's what makes this such a critical moment for Alan. The injury is nowhere but in his mental toughness.

His crew puts him into the backseat and gives him some food. All they can do is let him stew in the air conditioning and his own obscenities and hope it doesn't take more than an hour to cool him off. Thankfully, he regains his senses after about 10 minutes. He's not happy, but at least he's moving again. When Peter Vaughan hits the climb 30 minutes later, he also dismounts. At 60 years of age, he's not too proud to walk the bike up such a steep climb. But for a man who's finished 72 Ironman races, it's humbling nonetheless.

Things are more definitive on the women's side. Iona MacKenzie came out of the water 10 minutes ahead of her closest pursuer, Kathleen Wood. Despite the time lost due to a flat tire, she's still on a steady pace to increase the gap.

Lucy Ryan and Stacey Shand hit the beach at 4:13 and 4:28, respectively. They'll finish nearly an hour behind Iona, but that's still an accomplishment. Just 20 days earlier Stacey finished the Badwater Ultramarathon—a 135-mile footrace through Death Valley and then up Mount Whitney. Temperatures soared above 130 degrees Fahrenheit during the event. Some people would consider that the capstone event of the year, if not their entire career. But Stacey is back at it less than a month later. Nor is this Lucy's only event this year; she's already signed up for Ultraman Hawaii in November. Ariane Allen will finish in 4:52, giving her precious little time to finish the bike leg.

Dave keeps putting the pressure on Craig. Though Dave's too far back to see, Craig knows he's in hot pursuit thanks to Dave's crew vehicle. Every time Dave's crew finishes delivering new food and water bottles to him, it takes off and races ahead to the next spot. Craig passes the stopped vehicle, and presently it races past him on the road. The intervals between sightings means Dave is breathing down his neck. At least he can't sneak up on him. With 10 km left they hit the final climb of the day. It's not as steep as the Richter Pass, but it's tough enough. Craig digs deep cresting the hill and keeps pedaling even as the front wheel dumps down a final, hair-raising descent. Leaving nothing to chance, he hammers all the way to the finish line. His effort gives him more than just the lead at the end of the day. His combined swim and bike times yield a course record for day one: 154.8 km of swimming and cycling in 6 hours and 43 minutes flat. Dave Matheson crosses the line seven minutes and seven seconds later. They're half an hour ahead of their closest pursuers.

Craig's crew takes his bike as he lifts himself off it gingerly. He's in significant pain. Relief awaits him in the park next to the finish line. The volunteers have taken several inflatable rafts and filled them with ice water. It makes the perfect resting spot for an aching athlete. Craig eases himself down slowly, as much out of fear of cramping as the icy water. He's stripped off his jersey because the dried salt from his sweat has turned it uncomfortably crusty, but once he hits the water he begins shivering uncontrollably. Someone brings him a blanket and he's able to tolerate it, but this is still almost as painful as the ride here. He's a little pale and his eyes are a bit sunken. He looks less like a victor than a refugee, as if he can't enjoy the moment because he's still in shock from his flight here. It doesn't seem possible that he can get back on the bike and ride tomorrow's 275.4 km course. He's cooked.

Dave looks positively chipper by comparison when he sails down the hill and into the park a few minutes later. He's beat, but he moves much more fluidly than Craig did. After he gets a few hugs from his wife and crew and chats briefly with Steve Brown and Jane, he walks over into the grass and settles into an ice-water raft beside Craig. Craig immediately perks up as the two shake hands and pat each other on the back, congratulating each other on a great day of racing. They recap the last few hours as if they were talking about last night's big game over the water cooler. They talk about various landmarks, difficult moments, and meander into a discussion about what the roads will be like tomorrow. Though they've barely seen each other all day, it's already evident that a bond is forming between them. Theirs is the fraternity of solitary suffering.

Christian Isakson is the next to roll in, at 7:20:55. Inaki De La Parra is only 18 seconds behind him. John Bergen arrives four minutes later. They're all less than 40 minutes behind Craig—still close enough to take first place. The next group of men comes in between eight and a half and nine hours. Iona MacKenzie is the first woman to the finish, at 9:28:49. Kathleen Wood is 25 minutes behind her. Lucy Ryan and Stacey Shand finish with marks of 10:17 and 10:30, respectively. Ariane Allen comes in with two other men at just past the 11-hour mark. Then the nail-biting begins. Peter Lopinski finally recovered from his stomach sickness and got on the bike after spending half an hour in the transition area. Less than 40 kilometers out, he's close enough to make it in time, but he's still got that last hill to get over. He has less than an hour before he's marked down as a DNF. His has become a race for survival.

Craig, Dave, and the other leaders left a while ago, and things have wound down considerably. They'd have stayed to cheer Peter in, but their bodies were in no state to sit around under the sun and wait. They needed food and sleep immediately. The other athletes are still in various stages of cooling off in the rafts or being attended to by the massage therapists, who have set up under canopy tents in the park. It's a full setup, complete with tables for the athletes to lie down upon. They strip down as far as they can and let the massage therapists do what they can to soothe and release muscles that have locked up from holding that extreme position on the bike for so long.

To the casual observer it all looks a bit over the top, but this is essential work. Without this treatment, many of the athletes here wouldn't even be able to get out of bed in the morning, let alone ride a bike 275 kilometers. Most professional triathletes see a massage therapist once a month, and would do it more if they could afford it. While the majority of orthopedic complications in the workplace—bad knees, hips, and backs—are the result of overuse injuries, endurance sports are all about using the muscles as long and hard as possible. It's the deliberate exploration of the body's breaking point. Tennis damages elbows. Baseball destroys pitchers' shoulders. Triathlon hurts damn near *everything*.

As the 12-hour mark nears, even the massage therapists begin to tear down their stations. The tables go empty and they know there's only one person left out on the course. Steve King keeps up the music and the commentary in the announcer's tent, but even he gets anxious. Alexis Brown tries to call Lopinski's crew on the phone. Steve looks at her as she dials. "If you get hold of them, tell them to tell him not to coast when he hits the downhill. He needs to ride as hard as he can. It's going to be close."

She doesn't reach them. Maybe that's good news. The cell reception up on the hill is pretty bad. If they're not answering, it's either because they can't get a signal or they're too busy following Lopinski on the descent. Twenty-five minutes left on the clock. And then Alexis' phone rings. "He's on his way in!" she yells.

Volunteers step out to the road leading into the park to get a better glimpse of him coming down the final mountain and across the bridge leading in. Lopinski's crew vehicle comes in with just 20 minutes left on the clock. And then Peter appears, coming around a distant bend. Everyone cheers him on. He crosses the finish line in 11:47:13— less than 13 minutes to spare. There are tearful embraces with his crew at the line, and an immense sense of relief among everyone assembled.

Peter himself looks great, considering what he's been through. He feels a little weak, but being able to stand is a marked improvement from how he felt seven hours ago. Steve King tells him not to be fooled and to down as many calories as he can before hitting the sack. It's sage advice. There's no possible way he could have replaced everything he lost from the swim. At the rate his metabolism is pumping, he'll spend the rest of the event behind on nutrition. The medic makes a special point to weigh him so she can keep track. But for now, they'll celebrate. It's not typical for an athlete to DNF on the first day, but it's not unheard of either. For the volunteers, finishing the day with everyone still in the race is even better news than hearing someone broke the course record.

The volunteers waste no time breaking down the tents and gear after Lopinski is taken care of. It's been a long day, but it's hardly over for anyone. Alexis Brown works feverishly on her laptop to get the finishing times recorded on the official spreadsheet they use for records. She's been bombarded all day by Ultraman enthusiasts around the world, asking for updates. For the massage therapists, volunteers, and support crews, tonight's preparation will be even longer than the last. The second bike leg starts in approximately the same location as day one's and finishes in Princeton, a small town about an hour and a half away by car. Everyone will spend the night there before starting the run back to Penticton on day three, so everyone has to pack to take the entire show on the road for the next 48 hours. Hotel rooms that were thrown asunder during last-minute preparations this morning have to be reorganized to make sure nothing is left behind when the vehicles get packed.

Because they're totally wiped out, the best thing the athletes can do to prepare is go to sleep. This is where the Ultraman spirit changes from principle to practice. Anyone still trying to run their own race effort is costing themselves valuable rest and recovery. The support crews take care of everything, from applying ice and cleaning the bikes to packing the running shoes and sending updates to friends and family via email and social media. It's common to see athletes' Facebook pages with photos and messages posted for friends, family, and fans throughout the race weekend—and it's obvious that the crew is making all those updates. It demonstrates how closely ultra races bond athletes and crews. After all, social media accounts are a sensitive part of people's lives. But, just like their phones, car keys, and credit cards, athletes hand them over to their crews without hesitation. During the race, the crew takes over every facet of the athlete's life outside of eating, sleeping, and racing. As tough as the athletes look during the day, they wouldn't make it through the night without their crews.

By 8:00 PM Steve Brown is back at his house, trying to get everything together for day two. Thankfully, Tony Horton is there to help. Tony's been shadowing Steve all day, learning the ropes of actually executing an Ultraman race. They're both exhausted, but the work can't wait. Inside, Alexis and Jane work to push out information across the Internet to those looking for updates. Once it all gets finished, out comes the beer, and the group takes a well-deserved break. The first day has been a success.

It's nothing compared to what lies ahead. Day two begins similarly to the first, close to the swim exit from the prior day. Everyone is up dark and early, and the sun has yet to appear over the mountains before the racers assemble at the start line. Dave Matheson is the first to arrive. He and his crew get there as Steve Brown and the volunteers are putting the aluminum frame for the start together. He's excited to get going. He's ridden half of these roads during his training, and that familiarity provides him with a strong sense of confidence. He's not sure what Craig Percival will be able to do today, or any of the men close behind them, for that matter. But he knows what he will do, and knowing that is all it takes to energize him with cheerful resolve.

Craig arrives with his crew shortly afterward. He appears significantly more apprehensive. He's all business as he checks his gear. But the grim look on his face softens as other athletes and volunteers come by to congratulate him again on yesterday's accomplishments or wish him luck today. It's almost as if he has two personalities. The real Craig is affable, humble, pleasantly dignified; Race Craig is a high-pressure combustion chamber filling with adrenaline and connected to nerves preparing to unleash a 10,000-volt spark.

Bergen, Isakson, and De La Parra have no idea what condition Dave or Craig might be in. If the leaders went out too hard yesterday, it's possible they could make up significant time today. They're also in a dead heat with each other. Anything could happen. Eager for release but penned in behind the start line, there's nothing to do in the final minutes except dwell on the possibilities. When the body can't race, the mind does.

Steve King hasn't bothered to turn the music on this morning. His setup remains packed in his van. Things will move along so quickly that he needs to be ready to go. He gives a brief overview of yesterday's racing and the standings as they prepare to get under way, then hands the microphone to Steve Brown so he can give instructions to the competitors. Then things get complicated.

The athletes will start en masse this morning. Putting 29 cyclists on the road all at once is a tricky proposition. They'll space themselves out during the first two hours, but at the beginning it's going to be a large group on two-lane roads. Furthermore, the no-drafting rules require the athletes to maintain a distance between themselves of seven meters. If they want to pass, they have to do it quickly or risk getting a penalty. Because things will certainly be fast and furious for the first hour, Steve Brown tells everyone that the first 20 kilometers are a "no feed zone," prohibiting support crew vehicles from pulling over to give anything to the athletes. It's just too dangerous to have that many bikes and cars trying to use the shoulder as daily traffic slides by. He reminds athletes to ensure they have everything they need to change a flat tire.

From the north end of Skaha Lake, they'll travel south down its east side, through the same valley they rode yesterday down to Osoyoos. Then they'll turn around and ride back to the south end of Skaha and straight through the location of the day-one finish line. From there, they'll turn south of the day-one course, up into a brutal, five-kilometer stretch of road that climbs more than 160 meters uphill. With sustained grades in excess of 15 percent, it's earned its nickname from the local athletes. They call it "the wall." Once they hit the top, there's an equally precipitous descent down the other side. That will mark the halfway point of today's course—the *easy* half.

All of these factors—the mass start, the fast and flat road heading to the climb, and the treacherous incline of the wall—come together to form a highly challenging strategic element to today's race. There will be plenty of running but no hiding for the leaders today. No one will be able to pull a quick move without his pursuers quickly matching the effort to keep him in range. But given their experience, these men know that it will be nearly impossible to break away early anyway, due to the flats. Even with their aerodynamically engineered bikes and helmets, wind resistance will equalize their efforts. The real racing won't start until they get to the wall. So it comes down to a very delicate balance. Everyone will try to keep the pace slow so as not to burn out before the climb, but they can't let anyone else slip away. It's a poker game that you pedal.

Steve Brown tells everyone to line up in the order in which they finished yesterday. Craig and Dave take their places at the front, followed by Christian Isakson, Inaki De La Parra, John Bergen, and Michael Owen. After they're ready, Steve orders all the crew vehicles to leave and get to their first positions to replenish the athletes, outside the no feed zone. Then the contestants take off.

The drama ensues quickly. As patient as the leaders try to be, anxiety gets the better of them. One guy just trying to coast gets a little close to the man in front of him, which causes his leader to panic and think he's about to be overtaken. That guy accelerates, which spooks the man in front of him. Everyone wants to relax, but no one can find their brakes.

Further complicating matters is Alexey Panferov, the first-timer from Russia. An exceptionally fit man, he's here to prove to his son that you can do anything you put your mind to, regardless of the obstacles. His personal obstacle was the loss of a kidney to cancer a couple of years ago. He's almost qualified for the Hawaiian Ironman on more than one occasion, but each time there was someone who was literally just a few seconds faster. He still wants to qualify, but he loves going long distances. He expected to be in a better position at the end of day one, but some stomach issues held him up in the water and he finished in 8:35, effectively putting him out of the running. It's disappointing, but at least this morning he's back to running with the big dogs. He doesn't intend to let the pack escape him a second time. The problem is that he's a little too intense. He rides up into the group in short order, but can't find a spot between the men who've already spaced themselves out according to the rules. He's forced to either ride closer to the middle of the road—a sure way to tempt fate and irate drivers—or slip in between the other athletes and break the draft barrier. It's impossible to pedal hard enough and long enough to pass the entire line. Without asking, he cuts in, inadvertently getting so close to Craig's rear wheel the Australian doesn't have to turn around to know the guy is riding his tail. Regular Craig would probably shrug it off, but Race Craig becomes furious.

Things get dicey as they approach the second small town on the route. The guys get too close for the race official's comfort. He comes by on his motorcycle and begins giving stern warnings to respect the draft distance. What he doesn't realize from his gasoline-powered ride is that the athletes are *trying* to keep their distance. But with a slight downhill grade and a tailwind blowing through the valley, they are flying at breakneck speed. They heed the warnings to give a little space. Things remain close even after they exit the no feed zone and slow down at intervals to grab fresh water bottles and food. Steve King is also concerned by the extreme proximity of the drafting among the athletes at times. He yells at a few of them from his own vehicle as he drives past. Isakson overdoes it a bit as he tries to comply with the warning. He allows a gap to open and has to work to catch up before they get to the wall. Technically, Steve King isn't a course official. A strict constructionist would argue that Isakson should never have listened to him in the first place. On the other hand, there's only one course official and he has to spend at least some time watching the other athletes. The unspoken rule that's evolved over the years is that good sportsmanship prevails in this event. You police yourself, and if a volunteer points out something to you, you regard it as a friendly yet sincere warning. That being the case, Isakson *is* policing himself, just perhaps not all that well the moment King drove by. You have inadvertent cheating and inadvertent interference with clean racing. Two wrongs don't make a right, but they certainly add color to the race.

Yet it's better to err on the side of safety and lose a couple of minutes than to be slapped with a time penalty. The first penalty assessed to an athlete costs him six minutes. The second one will get him 12. A third will result in a disqualification from the race. He won't even be allowed to continue participating, as athletes who fail to make a time cutoff still are. Some people need a stiffer reminder than others.

There's a difference between tenaciously hanging on to the competition and getting lost in the grip of your own competitiveness. Inaki De La Parra and John Bergen cross that line when they hit a four-way intersection in one of the small towns halfway between the start and Osoyoos. Having fallen behind the group, eager to make up time in whatever way they can, and with race volunteers in plain view waiting for them to go by, both men blow right through the stop sign. It's not just cheating, it's dangerous. Phone calls are made and the course official hunts them down, but not before De La Parra hits the turnaround to go back north and runs the exact same stop sign a second time. A violation that dangerously flagrant may well be grounds for immediate disqualification. That will be up to Steve Brown's discretion, but he doesn't even know it's happened yet.

Most of the start-line volunteers, including Steve, Jane, and Alexis, are getting breakfast in an Osoyoos diner. They're slowly filtering toward the crest of the wall. The road on the mountain is so steep and winding that it's also been designated as a no feed zone. Steve leaves early to help ensure the crews obey the rule. By the time he gets there he finds Steve King chastising one crew vehicle on that very issue.

At the top of the climb is one of Penticton's characteristic wineries and vineyards, complete with a sweeping view of the valley and roads below.

From their vantage point, the group watches as Craig and Dave ride back northward through the valley, just a few kilometers out from the base of the hills. The others aren't far behind. Steve King drives up behind Brown and starts to set up his sound equipment. This is a real make-it-or-break-it point for the athletes. He'll stay here as long as he can. It matters.

The course official coming up on his motorcycle heralds the leaders' arrival. He pulls over and gives Steve Brown the bad news. He's written down the warnings and penalties he's assessed on a handheld notepad. He flips page after page, letting the sheer volume speak for itself. "It's been bad," he tells Steve. "The stop sign thing was the worst thing I've ever seen. Didn't hit the brakes or anything. Just went straight through. They knew it was there, too. A whole crowd of volunteers were there at it. Other than that, lots of drafting. These guys are out of control."

"Okay," Steve tells him. "We'll deal with it after we get to the finish line. Just stay on them." The official nods and motors off. He needs to get down the hill before the athletes. The last thing he wants is to present an obstacle to bikes hitting upwards of 45 mph. It's much more difficult to stop a 20-pound bike with hand-powered brakes than a 600-pound cruiser with hydraulics, especially when stopping is the last thing on the cyclist's mind.

Steve King keeps the music and the commentary going for the small audience as they wait for the leaders to make the summit. Minutes go by. The sun is warm and the air is rich with the scent of wildflowers growing on the side of the road. The winery's lawn and shade trees beckon to passersby to lie out a blanket and have a picnic. It's such a splendid place that Steve King's dance-pop music seems invasive.

A white bubble emerges from the pavement down the hill. It grows quickly into a full helmet, sitting on top of John Bergen's head. He's taken the lead. Or maybe not. Before the group is able to determine his identity, he's joined by Dave Matheson. Three other figures materialize before they're in full view. Christian, Inaki, and finally, Craig. From a distance, they conjure an image of gunfighters making their slow, grim walk to a final stand. Bergen is standing on his pedals, working like an abused animal. No one else knows it, but this is the end for him. His strategy today was to gamble all his chips on this climb. He envisioned a huge effort to make a clean break from the pack, then continue riding steady and extend the lead once he was safely out of their sight. Unfortunately, Christian Isakson had the same idea and went out hard as well. But he'd burned out his legs making up the time he lost after Steve King's intervention. He cracked a while ago, and now the only thing keeping him with the group is sheer force of will. The group bunched back up once the climb slowed Dave and Craig. When they saw Bergen make a go, everyone went right along with him. Bergen knows he'll still be able to race well, but he's no longer racing for first place. Now he has the descent on which to regroup mentally and physically. It will be a brief rest before he has to push on the pedals again. He has to decide how to pace himself for best results over the rest of the day. He starts to ease off, and Dave Matheson comes around.

More surprising is Craig's appearance as he gets over the hill. He's maybe 10 meters behind the pack, but the look on his face suggests that there's a bigger deficit underlying the physical distance. Though every bit as athletic as the others, he's the tallest, and therefore heaviest, of the bunch. He's felt every ounce of his weight on this climb. His eyes are wide in a vacant, primal stare. His jaw's gone slack. He stands on the pedals, but they turn so slowly it's almost as if they're pushing back against him. He's in hell. John Bergen's charge may not give him first place, but unless Craig recovers, he'll advance one notch in the standings.

Just a minute or two after Craig disappears, Alexey Panferov comes up the wall. He looks pretty beat himself. For all his determination, the combination of yesterday's fatigue and today's pace force him to give up the chase. Steve Brown looks at him with a half-knowing, half-admiring grin as he labors his bike onward. He's seen this scenario play out enough times to recognize it. "He was living the dream," he says to Tony after Alexey passes out of earshot.

The other participants follow after a short time. They also struggle up the wall, but with better humor. More than one rides in a zigzag pattern up the road in a search for a shallower, albeit longer, approach to the top. Peter Vaughan walks again, but he does it with a smile on his face.

They stay as long as they can, until Alexis finally has to leave and get to the next point along the road. Steve and Tony follow. You don't feel the descent as much in the vehicles, but it's there. Race volunteers have to take a few special precautions on the back roads to ensure the athletes' safety, one of which is to lay large sheets of plywood over a couple of cattle guards to prevent the bike wheels from binding up in them at 30 mph. Steve stops to check on the volunteers manning the site. They have to stay because cars rolling across it would turn the wood into splinters. He and Alexis stop to ask them how they're getting along, and they make him aware of a new problem he has to deal with. Stacy Shand has two crew vehicles. Worse, they're both driving slow on the course and one of them is unmarked.

Steve rolls his eyes upon hearing the news. He hasn't gotten 10 kilometers from the spot where he heard the litany of the morning's infractions. He catches the unmarked vehicle and asks the occupants what they think they're doing. Some athletes use multiple crew vehicles during Ultraman because they're participating in the event for charity or corporate sponsors and have a media crew join them to produce video of the endeavor. But they still have to be marked and must obey certain rules, one of which is that they cannot be used to provide aid to the athlete. It's just logistically impossible, not to mention unsafe, to allow so many cars to drive slowly along these roads.

It turns out that one member of Stacey's crew left Penticton after she finished the first day and stayed in another town. The crewmember thought she would be back in time to start the race this morning, but wound up arriving late and so is driving by herself to the end of the course. The only problem is that she's not sure where she's going, and the crew only has one map of the course, so she's stuck following everyone else instead of driving normally.

She may be stuck, but Steve reminds her flatly that all of this was explained at the rules briefing. She has to go. The same goes for tomorrow as well. So after Stacey finishes, her crew will have to shuttle the extra vehicle all the way back to Penticton and then bring the final crewmember back. It's a huge waste of time for the people who'll have a depleted athlete to take care of, but Steve doesn't budge on issues like this. "This is why the rules briefing is so long. This is why we ask over and over again, 'Do you understand everything we've said here?' It's not because we like to do it. It's because people don't listen. We talked about this explicitly. They have no excuse. They just didn't listen," he says.

"Actually," Alexis interjects, "Stacey's crew didn't even attend the brief." Steve throws his hands up in frustration. "Well, there ya go."

The situation addressed, they pile back in the cars in the hope that it will at least be 50 kilometers until the next crisis. They trek southward to the town of Keremeos. It's rural through this area, with very little traffic. The land is blanketed with golden meadows and fields, dotted with the occasional crystal blue lake.

Steve can't help but brood over the safety violations. He has good reason. If something disastrous were to happen, it could be the death of the race. "Triathlon Canada won't sanction Ultraman. Their whole focus is on Olympic distance triathlon. The organization is trying to grow interest and talent to win gold. So they're putting money and manpower toward larger races. We're too small in athlete numbers for them to bother with. On the plus side, that means they don't mandate how many course officials we have to put on the road, which on a course this long would be a *lot*." Thanks to the watchful volunteers, Steve has been able to catch just about everything today. But that's *un*official supervision; it wouldn't satisfy the bureaucracy of a national governing body. There's no telling what the combined expenses would be if the event were sanctioned. As it is, he's paying $2,000 to keep himself insured. Next year he's looking at requiring all the athletes to have their own personal health insurance policies to help make sure he's covered.

Steve and Tony pause in Keremeos to talk to the race volunteer making sure athletes don't make a wrong turn at a fork in the road. She says everyone is doing fine. Dave, John, Christian, and Inaki are still in the front, 150 kilometers into the course. Craig has struggled through a dark stretch since the wall, but he's coming out of it and has caught sight of the pack. The fork at Keremeos marks a turn northwest through a deep-cut valley, where the undulating hills of emerald and gold farmland give way to the dull gray of mining towns literally cut out of sheer cliffs. The towering walls of granite block out the sun, and the mountain range creates its own weather. The sun dims, clouds in the north darken, and the road leading to the finish in Princeton is a slight yet unmistakable uphill. The forecast is rough and nasty, with a chance of horrendous storms. There's no telling what will happen.

To emphasize the point, Dave Matheson suddenly decides that it's time for him to go. Just as Craig ties back into the pack, Dave comes off the leash. The road here is fairly consistent. There won't be another major climb until the end. Every inch that Dave opens up on them will require that much more effort from them to close the distance. It's now or never, and it's up to John Bergen in the No. 2 spot to make the call. He tries for a moment, then realizes that his legs are too burned out from the wall. He watches Dave drift farther ahead. Nor do Christian or Inaki take up the cause. But Craig's gained his second wind and isn't ready to give up yet. He goes by the other three men and gives chase.

It takes him another 25 kilometers, but he finally gets his claws into Dave just past the town of Hedley. The wind whips up and there are spots of drizzle, but it never gets worse than a threat of rain. The air chills in the shadow of the mountains and the country roads substitute rough chip seal for smooth pavement. Dave doesn't relent on the pace. Craig doesn't waver in his resolve to hang on. It is a physiological game of chicken—testing to see who'll step back from the brink first. The looks on their faces hold the answer: they'll break before they give up.

They finally come out of the deepest parts of the valley as they turn directly northward into the town of Princeton. Here they have to endure the demoralizing view of the finish line being set up for them in the local community center parking lot. The course isn't quite long enough to be a full Ultraman at this point, so they have to ride about 20 kilometers north of town before turning around for the home stretch. It's just steep enough to be tough. Dave is in front when they appear at the bottom of the hill. Then Craig passes him. They keep going, neck and neck, tooth and nail. About five minutes after they pass by, John and Christian pass through, about 30 seconds apart. Christian spent an hour and a half chasing John and Inaki and finally overtook them so quickly that he thought he'd make a clean escape. It's his second rookie mistake of the day. John knows the course and is saving up for the last bit of climbing at the end. Now that they're hitting it, he's reeled Christian back in and starts to slingshot by. They're out of sight before Inaki comes into view.

Dave and Craig approach the turnaround up ahead, where Steve Brown and Tony are scrambling to ensure they don't miss it. Alexis received a call from the volunteer who was supposed to mark the point and help guide athletes just before the first athletes went by. Somehow, she missed a turn and got lost. There's nothing out there to indicate the spot. With five guys in the hunt for the podium and possibly a record finish, a snafu like this could be disastrous. There was no time to figure out a better solution. Steve jumped in his car and raced ahead to the spot. He'll remain there until the volunteer can find her way back. It's been a long, by-the-skin-of-his-teeth day, and it's far from over.

Dave and Craig hit the turnaround. It's all downhill from here, but that doesn't mean they're going to coast. It's full throttle all the way to the line. Dave has been checking his watch intermittently as they climbed to this point, figuring they'll see their closest pursuers on the way down. He checks his watch again as they go by John and Christian, and figures they have about six minutes. *Don't let up now. There's still 84 kilometers left to run tomorrow. Craig still has a seven-minute lead and if John or Christian can run a pace 30 seconds faster per kilometer than him over that entire distance, they'll win. Keep going. Don't stop. Pedal. Pedal. Pedal.*

But once they pull off the road into the community center parking lot and hit the last 100 meters before the finish, Craig is still glued to him. It's been a hard day, and sprinting at this point won't purchase enough time to matter one iota. Better to enjoy the moment. Both men sit up and coast. They come across the line holding hands.

Then a minor tragedy. Christian gets a flat tire. John picks up time as a result, though he's already gained a few minutes by virtue of his experience and pacing. Inaki also passes him. After all that, Christian finishes fifth on account of a piece of punctured rubber. That's racing for you. He takes it in stride and brings it on in to the finish. All five men are in visibly greater pain than the day before. Craig is hardly as ginger getting in the ice raft this time. He'll do anything to dull the throbbing in his legs. John Bergen grimaces in pain as he gets off his bike, and has to lean against a truck in the parking lot for several minutes before he feels up to walking. Christian retreats into his own mind to hold out against the suffering, as if it's a bomb shelter against the nuclear winter hitting his muscles. He sits in the ice bath and takes it one moment at a time. *Breathe in. Breathe out.*

It takes them about 45 minutes in the ice water before they can bring themselves to get to the massage therapists. They go inside the community center to get worked over. The scene looks and sounds more like a trauma center this time. The slightest pressure on a calf muscle causes one man to jerk back and gasp in pain. Another has trouble even getting on the table. Everyone is hurting, and the therapy only hurts more. Yet it's necessary. If they don't do it, their joints won't even budge in the morning. So now, an hour after the racing is over, the enduring continues.

The physical suffering can't extinguish their good spirits, though. Together for the first substantial amount of time since the race began yesterday, the group trades vignettes from their day. John's forthright with everyone that he wanted to physically break them on the wall. Craig isn't bashful about his low ebb after going over the climb, and everyone joins Dave in laughing when he confesses to checking the time gap on the others.

The rival-bromance duality is so extreme it feels as if the banter were taken right out of *Top Gun*. It's like everything else about the landscape, the people, and the collective endeavor—so genuine that it's too good to be true. It seems inconceivable that these guys can flip the switch so quickly. One minute they're trying to drive each other into self-inflicted paralysis, the next they're hailing each other's accomplishments. The key to understanding it is to see the difference between Real Craig and Race Craig. He doesn't hold any grudge against the others, but there is a distinct change that overtakes him when it's time to race. Competition is his Dr. Jekyll elixir. Like all sports, triathlon is a form of recreation, a form of release. What better way to blow off steam for such a pleasant, kind man as Craig than to recreate himself as Mr. Hyde, an unapologetic racer who burns rubber with wild abandon?

Now returned to his usual, more tranquil self, he also postulates that the potion can be its own sort of disease. "I had no intention of going out that hard today. Never would have thought I'd race like that. But you see these guys go and you start to think about hanging with them. You get a spot of white line fever." He's referring to the Australian term for the change that comes over a player when he crosses onto the field of play. A 1975 American film bears the same title. Its protagonist is a truck driver pushed to fight a corrupt shipping company. His battle ends when he drives his own truck through the company's towering steel-and-glass sign, killing himself in the process. Both contexts seem applicable to the day's events. Craig is all smiles now, but seeing the way he's raced today makes you wonder if he'll hold anything back tomorrow, and what consequences it could hold for him.

Christian Isakson perhaps offers the best interpretation of their collective speculations and anxieties about tomorrow's final contest. "You know, the run tomorrow is going to be like opening your drawer and finding nothing in it but dirty underwear. You just gotta go with what you've got." Everyone here is close to the breaking point.

It was a dog-eat-dog day, but the bites are forgiven now that they're settled on the porch. Most of them, anyway. Steve Brown has yet to address the unsavory business of the time penalties. He's finally made it back to the community center after the lost volunteer made her way back to the turnaround. Now the unpleasant conversations begin as the men get off the tables and prepare to head to the local hotel.

When Steve tells John that he's being docked six minutes for blowing through the stop sign, he's sincerely contrite and also relieved that it's only six minutes. He knows that other races disqualify competitors for things like that. Thanks to the penalty, his lead on Christian for the day is reduced to just one minute. Inaki De La Parra has to work a little harder to keep calm. He's hit for both incidents at the stop sign, costing him 18 minutes overall and dropping him back to fifth place, 16 minutes behind Christian. All day he saw his hopes of placing in the top three slip away. Now the last flicker he was holding on to is snuffed out. He has no one but himself to blame, and he does. Harshly. "I totally slipped on that one. I knew what I was doing when I did it, but I just didn't stop. It was wrong, and I got what I deserved. I'm happy I'm not disqualified, but I'm kind of disappointed in myself. Tomorrow's going to be about racing well, doing the right things, and remembering what's important," he says.

"Harshly" also characterizes the way his mother accosts Steve Brown after she hears the news. Her tirade against him resounds with "How dare yous?" and accusatory language, as if he was a schoolyard bully who'd mugged her son. Steve doesn't protest or argue. He just calmly explains the situation and suggests that she should consult her son about things. But in his head, he's already calculating whether Inaki will ever be invited to another Ultraman event. He can sympathize with a mother's love for her child, but she's part of Inaki's crew, and this sort of behavior runs contrary to everything the race stands for. Jane has the same reaction as Steve when she finds out. Maybe that's just the way they do things in Mexico or in their family, but she won't have anyone come to Hawaii and treat *her* family like that.

The other athletes begin going by on their way up to the turnaround. Iona MacKenzie is the first woman to the finish line again, arriving at 10:11:53. She now holds a commanding 90-minute lead over her closest pursuers. Everyone starts to look at the white board in the officials' tent and count the names of people still out on the course as the last hour approaches. There are two remaining. Then Devon Kiernan arrives at 11:19:43. Now there's just one. Rory Bass only has 20 minutes and 17 seconds left to make it home.

A 47-year-old from Kelowna, Bass' first triathlon was in his hometown, the 1989 Mini-Apple Sprint. His slight paunch doesn't fit the mold of a stereotypical ultra endurance athlete and he admits he's never been a fast athlete, but he is one of the friendliest, funniest people out here this weekend. A machinist by trade, the twinkle in his eyes and kindness in his smile would be right at home in Santa's workshop. Like several others, he knows he's not the fittest and he's certainly not trying to break any speed records. He just wants to find out if he has what it takes to finish this thing. He's living a dream, taking the same roads and doing the same things that some of the most prolific athletes in the world are doing, and that few people in the world ever dare to do.

Anxious volunteers and athletes begin to turn to each other and ask how long ago he passed by the finish line on the way to the turnaround. It's 60 kilometers from the finish to the turnaround and back. It's a fast descent once he makes it up. But how fast can he get to the top? No one knows the answer, but any way you cut it, it's going to be close. Any athlete who hasn't left the scene is riveted in place now. No one has taken a DNF—yet. Making it all the way through day two with everyone still heading toward an official finish would be something really special. People start wringing their hands. The worry in their eyes intensifies as the clock continues its pitiless subtraction of the moments left to hope. They begin to whisper the timeless silent prayer known by sports fans everywhere. *Come on. Come on, Rory. You can do it. Almost there. Don't stop. Ride, Rory, ride.*

Rory hits the turnaround with time dwindling. He gets a fresh water bottle from his crew, then they take off to meet him farther down the way. They round a corner and go out of sight right as he hears the sudden, sickening hiss of air escaping rubber. *Not this, not now.* He looks down and watches as the underside of his tire splays out flat against the pavement. He got rid of his spare tube and air refill cartridge a while back to save weight on the climb, and now his cell phone isn't working. That's it. The hope seeps out of him like the air from the tire, and no one can hear him call for help.

"Do you need help?" It's a cyclist who just happened to be going up the hill as Rory came by. He heard the noise of the tire and stopped to check, a common courtesy within the fraternity of cyclists. Rory quickly explains his situation. The man nods and takes off at breakneck speed to tell Rory's crew. Rory starts walking the bike down the hill. At least he can make a little progress. By the time his wife and crew get back to him, they're nearly hysterical. They get a new tire on quickly then urge him to move. They stop alongside the road more frequently now, but something tells him it's not because they're worried about another mechanical mishap. As he comes by at one point he asks how much time he has.

"You've got— there's— *just ride!*"

Oh, God. That can't be good, he thinks.

He almost pedals harder going down than he did coming up. The crew vehicle goes by and he doesn't see them stop ahead. They must be headed to the finish line. He pours everything he has left into the pedals. He comes around the last bend like a meteor and begins easing up when he catches sight of the finish line, until he hears Steve King's voice on the speakers telling him there's no time to lose. He gets back to work and flies in. The crowd screams frantically until the last moment. Then come cheers and laughter and gasps of relief and tears of joy. As astonishing as the front of the race was today, it's the end that takes the cake.

The clock reads 11:58:06. He comes across the line with just one minute and 54 seconds to spare. The look on his face is one of disbelief as he dismounts the bike, almost as if he'd just watched the whole thing happen on television. It doesn't really hit him until his wife, Susan, tears streaming down her face, throws her arms around him and sobs. Finishing day two with everyone still racing toward an official finish is more than something special this year. It's a bona fide miracle. They never got to thank the guardian angel who rode to his rescue; the cyclist never comes back to check and see if Rory made it. He kept riding on his way, figuring that he'd just done what anyone else would do. It was no big deal, as far as he knew.

The finish line is torn down in due haste. The volunteers and crews are exhausted after a long day in the sun. The athletes are in even worse shape. There are plenty of strained muscles and cramps to go around. Everyone is used to that from their normal race regimens. But what really hits them is the fatigue—they're all just plain *tired*. The cumulative stress on the system will be visible tomorrow morning before they even start the run. The potential for mechanical hiccups during the bike phase of the race will be replaced by a loosening of the grip on one's emotions, cracks in the walls blocking out pain and discomfort, and a comingling of sensory inputs from the real world with figments of the imagination. The run is less a footrace than a mental one. The Ultraman course went into the pain zone long ago. The only thing left to go through is suffering, and it's waiting out there for everyone.

Some people suffer less than others. Later in the evening the volunteers and course officials hit a local pub for dinner. Two athletes, Alan MacPherson and Michael Brown of Canada, are having a couple of beers with their crews. Alan raises his glass to everyone he knows as he sees them come in. The Scotsman is much more subdued than he was during his raging fit on top of the Richter Pass the first day. That he's out downing brews this late the night before an 84 kilometer run is just another example of his ruggedness. Brown is every bit as hard—it's just that he likes to party hard. When he's not training for Ultraman and Iron-distance races (he's signed up for Challenge Penticton right after Ultraman), running a chain of Tilted Kilt franchises throughout Canada, and organizing and operating his own long-distance triathlon and a rugby tournament, there's nothing he likes more than kicking back for some beer and laughs with his friends. He's one of those "sleep when I'm dead" types, the kind of guy who simply can't sit still while there's an opportunity to do something else. A rugby player, solidly built and standing over six feet tall, he knows the run is going to hurt tomorrow. An extra hour of sleep isn't going to change that. Might as well eat, drink, and be merry. "Besides," he jokes, "it's a long run tomorrow. Gotta load up on those carbs!"

Everyone is back to the hotel and out soon enough. There's a chill in the air as the lights go out. It will persist into the morning. Located on the opposite side of the mountains forming Okanagan Valley's western wall, Princeton rests on the intersection of four different river valleys. They each dump into each other to form a large, bowl-like depression in the mountains. It lends to late sunrises and early sunsets, with voluminous fog banks spilling down the mountains and settling over the town around dusk, just like the one that has blanketed the town tonight, layering the vehicles in the parking lot with a satin finish of dew.

In contrast to Penticton's emerald hillsides and crystal lakes, Princeton is framed in granite and bark. It's a town of only 2,500 people. The pickup trucks outnumber the cars and SUVs. The buildings are older and the fashion is blue collar. The movie *First Blood* was filmed in the town of Hope, only 70 kilometers to the west. Thirty-one years later, Princeton still looks as if Sylvester Stallone could walk out of the mist at any moment, thumbing for a ride in his drab olive jacket. Everything about this place tells you that it's a mining and logging town. The Ultraman athletes stick out wearing their compression socks and shirts bearing endurance event logos.

Morning comes too early for everyone. It's only gotten colder during the night, forcing everyone to put on fleece and long pants over their running gear for the time being. Steve Brown has negotiated with a local diner to open at 5:00 AM so everyone can get some breakfast. The athletes and crews chow down on a buffet of eggs, coffee, toast, and bacon. It's a pretty sedate affair. You don't hear the animated conversation and laughter that marked the prerace breakfast. Everyone is still waiting for the coffee to wash the cobwebs out of their heads. Once it does, the energy that would otherwise be directed to humor will instead focus on the ordeal at hand. It's ironic. This is the moment they all came for: the genuine test of will. The previous two days were only the prelude. You don't know what you're made of until you push your mettle to the breaking point. Now they've arrived at that point where there's about as much anticipation and excitement as the Monday morning drive to work.

The run begins on Old Hedley Road, just east of town. The athletes assemble at the start line at 6:00 AM. It's so foggy that you can't see the town itself looking back downhill into the bowl; it's filled to the brim with clouds. The coffee is helping the athletes to manage smiles, but they're still quiet. Dave Matheson and Craig Percival share words of encouragement, as do Christian, John, and Inaki. There's not a lot of fanfare. Everyone knows what they're here to do. Best to get on with it. Steve Brown takes the microphone from Steve King, gives a final few words of encouragement, wishes everyone good luck, and sends them on their way.

The road is paved, but soon enough it will turn off onto dirt and gravel logging roads. The terrain saves the athletes a bit of the harsh impact on their joints, but it will also be more uneven and extremely steep in places. Worst of all, the steepest portions, exceeding 10 percent grade in parts, don't come until the last kilometers. It's a cool morning, and everyone starts out wearing either a light vest or a long-sleeve shirt. The sun is going to start heating things up, though. By 10:00 AM it will be very warm. And by noon it will be hot—and it will stay hot until most of the athletes finish. That's the biggest factor. Cramps and dehydration will be a constant problem. If untreated, heat exhaustion and other serious medical problems can ensue.

But for now, all is flat and cool—perfect conditions to let loose with a killer pace. The conditions are the ultra-distance equivalent of Odysseus' Sirens, luring them toward the rocks of their own physiological limitations.

There are other factors at play. This is going to be a long day no matter what, but the choice the top competitors have to make is how they want to spend it. Is it better to establish an early lead and gauge your effort by how well your pursuers keep up, or to hang back and let the man in front pace you, or to disregard everyone entirely and run "within yourself"? It comes back to the mental race. Ultimately, the body can only do so much, but where you are relative to others can have a significant impact on your emotional state. There's a delicate psychology at work to keep yourself believing there's a carrot dangling in front of you rather than sour grapes.

Inaki takes off like a spooked racehorse. He's got all the wrong things on his mind—the time penalty, his place in the standings, the belief that he can claw his way back into the top three. His plan is to establish an early lead and then add to it throughout the day. It is a daring plan, but perhaps that's what makes it so irresistible to him. A chemical engineer by education and an entrepreneur by trade, De La Parra spent five years as a professional *muay thai* kickboxer and grew up playing jai alai, a sport that resembles ninjas playing dodgeball with a golden snitch. He also drives in the occasional automotive race. His entire life is a high-wire act. It's worked for him so far, so why change now?

The rest of the leading men take time to warm up their legs and get into the swing of things. Michael Owen starts to pick up the pace first, finally feeling at home in his favorite discipline. Then Dave Matheson starts to build up a rhythm. John Bergen and Christian separate according to their respective views. John knows what lies ahead and has settled on racing the course instead of the men. Christian is less sure, and decides to be more conservative just in case. Craig remains steady. He's already getting a sense of how this will play out. He's got the lead but not the legs. Today is going to be a struggle. If he doesn't manage this right, it could fall completely apart.

Inaki's strategy looks shaky after the first 10 kilometers. Michael Owen, only 30 minutes behind Inaki in the overall standings, reels him in and threatens to pass at speed. Dave Matheson comes up next. Though he's not in sight, John Bergen isn't losing that much ground either. Inaki might have backed off by now if he'd built enough of a cushion, but with everyone still coming on he keeps pushing it. Worst of all, it's starting to warm up. After going by the organizers and volunteers, the runners hit their first significant hill of the day. Inaki immediately slows down, and Owen and Matheson blow by him. Craig passes the volunteers. He manages a smile, but just barely. He's found his suffering point.

The field stretches out over a wide distance again. Within two hours everyone is pretty much running by themselves, with only their respective crews to keep them company. Dave goes by Michael with a definitive pass and runs off into the lead all alone. He achieves another important goal, building a more-than-seven-minute lead on Craig. So long as he keeps it up, he's running to the winner's circle. Inaki is suddenly hobbled by cramps and has to abandon his gamble to walk and recover. As speed holds constant and distance is consistently reduced, the outcome of the race approaches mathematical certainty. Squeezed out of their role in the front, chaos and X-factors slide toward the back. At the four-plus-hour mark, they begin to play havoc with the best laid plans of crews and Ultramen.

Eight athletes run in what might be considered the "red zone." They're not in any immediate danger of missing the final cutoff time, but they can't afford any unexpected delays or to slow down. Some of them just aren't as well-trained runners as they are swimmers or cyclists, but for the most part their pace is a natural consequence of the accumulated abuse they've endured in the last two days. Lucy Ryan's feet swell and her good humor bottoms out. She has to stop for 30 minutes to put her feet up and get her head back to a place where she can continue. Peter Vaughan chugs along evenly. His beaming smile remains indefatigable, but it's nip and tuck.

Nick Mallett is not having the day he envisioned. His progress varies drastically from moment to moment. He's jogging, then he's walking, then he's sitting, then he's jogging again. His legs are cramping and he can't find a rhythm. A traditionalist who deigns to use ultra-expensive gear including compression garments or boutique endurance nutrition supplements, he stops to get into his crew vehicle at one point and wraps his thighs in gauze to shore them up against incapacitating spasms. It works well enough to keep him moving, but the best he can manage consistently is a quick march. He's slowly falling behind pace for the cutoff.

Bruce Schoenne is the first athlete to fall. The heat and exertion cause him to develop major stomach issues. He's too nauseous to keep food down, and without the calories he can't keep going. Last year he DNFed on the run in the same way. He's run well most of the way, and is in fact well within reach of making the finish line with time to spare even if he walks the rest of the course. But at 53, he worries that pushing it under such adverse conditions might lead to adverse complications. "Never know when the ticker has had enough," he says. "Better to live to fight another day." He packs it in, satisfied that one way or another, some day or another, he'll cross that last finish line in Penticton.

Six hours into it the leaders hit the last, bitter obstacle to the finish; the logging roads travel over the mountain at near insufferable grades, then spill down into town between 9 to 14 percent for more than a kilometer. It's utter torture to the legs, but it's the landmark they've been anticipating. With just an hour left, reports of Dave Matheson's position to the staff at the finish line set Steve King to mental arithmetic. If Dave feels good enough and keeps a full head of steam, he may break the course record.

The volunteers have gone all out for the finish line today. They've lined both sides of the approach to the finish with flags representing every country that's contributed an Ultraman finisher, 31 in all. The most recent additions represent athletes here today—Mexico for Inaki's finish in the UK last year, Israel for Shlomi Kot, and Russia for Alexey Panferov, all of them competing here today. The latter two have to finish if they want the flags to stick, though.

The turnout is huge. In addition to the folks who've been following the race during the past two days, those who couldn't get away from Penticton have returned. There are also a few extra friends and family members of various people who have come to "see what it's all about." Finally, there come the random gawkers, the people who hear the music and Steve King's voice, see all the flags and the Ultraman logo, and come closer. Then they see the distances underneath the logo on the finish line archway and wonder if what they're seeing is real. They ask someone in a race volunteer's T-shirt what's going on, and once they hear straight from someone's mouth that this isn't a joke, they turn to whoever they've come here with and say "Let's stick around for a bit. I want to see one of these guys finish." It's true. If you build it, people come.

Steve King keeps working the microphone as the crowd waits. There's no telling when Dave will show up, and when he does it will be around a blind corner less than 200 meters away. Steve has to maintain a steady flow of commentary in order to keep the volunteers and spectators from getting complacent. His improvisation borders on incantation. It's so smooth and measured that you're ready to believe that Dave will show up only when Steve announces it. One moment he's relating statistics from Canada to records held by other athletes at the Hawaiian and Welsh races, the next he's recapping highlights from Dave's race up to this point. There's no office jam-packed with ESPN interns feeding him info; it's all out of his head. He has notes, but he hardly looks at them. He's surrounded by a veritable jungle of facts and figures, and yet he swings from one end of it to the other like a sportscasting Tarzan.

Dave's crew vehicle comes around the corner. That's the cue. The voltage in the air kicks up another notch as they get out. Then Dave comes around the corner. Steve's voice gets a little louder and only slightly faster as Dave runs in, joined by his wife and crew. His former coach and friend, and the man who owns the course record for another few seconds, Kevin Cutjar, joins him. The crowd works itself into a frenzy as they go across the line together, seven abreast. Steve King hits him with the good news the moment he breaks through the archway. He's swum, biked, and run 514.5 kilometers in 21 hours, 47 minutes and 47 seconds. It's a new course record, and more than five minutes behind the fastest time ever recorded in an Ultraman.

It's a huge accomplishment, but the biggest thing resonating in Dave's ears is "finishing time." That's when it becomes real. It's over. He can stop running, stop ignoring all the things in his mind and body screaming at him, stop being strong. He hunches over and lets it all soak in—the pain, the joy, the gratitude, everything. His crew and friends huddle around him, holding him up in their embrace. After a few moments, they finally give way to allow Steve Brown to place the official finisher's medal around Dave's neck. He makes his way through the crowd, shaking hands and accepting words of congratulations with exceptional humility. Slowly but surely, he's once again making a beeline for the ice rafts.

Michael Owen is the second man to arrive, just more than 26 minutes behind Matheson. His total time is 23:44:41. He's turned the tables on the men who've been in front of him all weekend, but now he has to wait for them to arrive to find out if it's enough to lift him higher in the standings. John Bergen starts to answer the question only four minutes later. He comes in the same way as his predecessors, taking a crewmember's hand in each of his own. His face is stretched taut from exertion, pulling his lips away to reveal teeth clenched in defiance of the rebellion in his legs. Ignoring it doesn't halt its progress, though. Instead of a last, triumphant burst across the line, he staggers in pain. The legs refuse to go any farther, and he doubles over. His crew catches him, and they help him down to the ground on his back. He stays there for a minute or two before they grab his arms and help him to his feet. John gets his medal from Steve Brown and manages a brief smile while he puts an arm around one of his crewmembers. The look on his face communicates the anguish of his body and the depletion of his mind. For such a competitive-minded man, it may be worth it. He's almost exactly 30 minutes behind Dave, and with a cumulative time of 23:04:23, he's currently in second. He started the day five minutes behind Christian and nearly an hour behind Craig. Is it enough?

It is. Christian Isakson comes in 15 minutes after John, with a time of 23:16:26. He falls to third by a mere 12 minutes. But the outcome remains uncertain. Craig is still out there. John still has 39 minutes left to wait to see if the man who's been leading up to today can hold on to second place. Christian will have to keep waiting after that mark. They each retire to the ice boats, their anxiety over the outcome dulled by exhaustion. Other runners start to come in. Twenty-eight minutes into the waiting, Inaki De La Parra arrives. He's suffered mightily after his early sprint, but summons the panache to run across the line holding the Mexican flag outstretched over his head. He bounces through the chute as if he were making his appearance for a title bout. Thirty-eight minutes down and Shane Zindel, finishing his first Ultraman, runs in with his crew. Another 60 seconds tick away, and that's the race for John. He's finished in second place. Now it's just Christian left waiting. He's got 12 more minutes.

Alexey Panferov comes in, running with his son and streaming tears of joy. The celebration at the line drowns out the arrival of Craig's crew vehicle. He has just two minutes to get in. The third and final day is going to deliver a nail-biter after all. Craig rounds the corner looking terrible. The sun has beaten him to death. The clock ticks into the final minute separating him and Christian. If he wants to finish in the top three, he's got to go into himself and find one last push. It's just not there. It doesn't even look like he's aware of Steve King and the crowd going wild, trying to pull him in with the power of their collective voice. His stride is barely a jog as he comes down between the dual rows of flags. It's a struggle just to stand up, keep moving. The seconds continue to tick away and the crowd loses its mind, screaming for him to hurry as if he were being chased by some wild animal that can't cross the finish line. Still to no avail. He's not here. His head is bent down, his attention entirely focused on a small piece of paper in his hand. His lips move, but the words are indistinguishable. Then he brings it to his lips and goes to his knees, shuddering from muscle failure and emotional collapse. He's gone way past the brink. But he's one step past the finish line, and that's all it takes. He's completed Ultraman Canada in 23:16:20—six seconds faster than Christian Isakson, and good enough for third place overall.

Craig is in obvious pain. His crew asks for water and advises the nearest volunteers that he struggled with the heat all day. They start by dumping a few cups on his head and back to help him cool off, then offer him something to sip. After several minutes he comes to his knees but he has yet to get up. Through it all, he won't let go of the piece of paper in his hand. It's a photo of his children. There were several moments on the course today when he just wanted to quit and go home. The expense of his trip here and the time taken totally for himself rather than his family weighed on his conscience before the race even began. But the physical beating he took gradually wore down the walls of his resolve and magnified the feelings of guilt and despair. In the end, finishing Ultraman became the ultimate test of heart.

Craig's crew and a few extra volunteers help him to his feet. His face is twisted in agony. They hold him up by his underarms as he staggers to Steve and Alexis Brown. She puts the finisher's medal around his neck. Behind them is Dave Matheson, and it's his embrace that brings Craig back from the darkness he's plunged himself into. All the pain and misery suddenly melt away. First and third place simply don't have any meaning in this moment. What is most valuable is what they've found in each other. These two men had to swim, bike, and run 514.5 kilometers around British Columbia to find out how they'd finish in the individual standings. To discover what they have together, they had to go an immeasurable distance within themselves.

Craig marks the end of the day's first and most dramatic act. Volunteers and spectators get nearly a half-hour break before the next runners come in. Alan MacPherson, the tough-as-nails Scotsman, arrives at 9:09:15. Then Aaron Postema at 9:10:26. Then Greg Pelton. Stacey Shand is the first woman to arrive, at 9:27:39. She's now in the same situation as John Bergen and Christian Isakson before her. If Iona MacKenzie takes more than an hour and 28 minutes to finish, then Stacey's the winner. All she can do is wait and wonder.

Five athletes cross the line inside the 10-hour mark. Iona makes it home in 10:34:56, winning the overall race by 21 minutes. Kathleen Wood is the last woman to arrive, and the last person to finish in less than 11 hours. Four others come in before the cutoff. During that time Steve King announces that the run has claimed a second victim. Nick Mallett is out of the race. He's struggled against his body all afternoon, and would keep going but for the fact that he's reached the last checkpoint on the course eight minutes after the cutoff. The distance left before him and the remaining time to cover it make it all but certain he won't make it in less than 12 hours. It would take a miracle to overcome the deficit, and there's nothing approaching a miracle left in his legs. It will soon be too dark for him to continue safely. Though a DNF, he's still a participant for having come this far. He's been a part of this event, in this place, with these people. And that's all he ever needed.

Nick isn't the only one who finds catharsis. During a lull in the festivities, Inaki De La Parra pulls Steve Brown aside. He had no idea that his mother had complained to Steve about the penalty yesterday, and he became upset when he found out what she said. He explains that she didn't understand what the race was about. He assures Steve that he does get it, and explained it to her. He apologizes for the altercation, and says he wants to set things right. Steve assures him that the apology itself is enough to do so. It's more than just the apology, though. It's the fortitude it takes to step up and make it. Even an intangible thing like character can be measured by distance. It took a big man to make that short walk over to Steve. That's exactly the type of athlete who Jane and Steve like to see at their events.

All this emotion and drama might lead one to question the sincerity of it all. A cynic might observe that the weekend has produced more sappy moments than a Julia Roberts movie. But there's no denying the link between the physical distance and the spiritual upheavals. Steve Brown's daughter, Alexis, has been supervising events on the course all weekend thanks to the help of her husband, Hal. He's neither a big sports fan nor endurance enthusiast, but like Gerry Bockus in the early years in Kona, Hal has found his own kind of enjoyment in the event. It's a unique vacation weekend for him and Alexis, and he appreciates the spectacle of it all. Having observed the race as an outsider for years now, he has a special insight to the physical and emotional extremes. "You know, we signed up for a 10k run a while back. And I didn't train for it or anything, right? I just did it for fun. So I can get out there and just do an event like that pretty easily. I can fake it for 10k. But there's no way you can do something like this unless you totally commit to it. These people live and breathe this stuff. They have to. There's no other way. You can't fake this."

The festivities continue for some time, thanks in part to the small beer garden Steve Brown has set up with the help of a local brewery. The first can is on the house for athletes and volunteers. Most people are only too happy to buy subsequent rounds for their crews and compatriots. Lucy Ryan takes a seat inside an ice boat within the garden's confines, which are fenced in per local laws. She leans back, taking in the frigidness of the water, the totality of the weekend's adventures, and the cold beer in her hand. It all adds up to a satisfaction of unrivaled purity. Tied to the fence nearby is a sign made by one of the volunteers. It reads WHY 84.4? BECAUSE 85.5 WOULD BE CRAZY!

The endorphin-and-lager-induced euphoria can't last forever. By sundown, the top athletes have found new strength and acute awareness of pain such that they are encouraged to get to their hotel rooms, get a shower, and make for bed. The crews are also exhausted. They'll return to their accommodations, dump dirty bikes and smelly clothes all over the floor, shove everything to the side, and crash.

Ariane Allen didn't even wait to get home. She began to shiver within minutes of finishing and had trouble staying warm. Her crew wrapped her in a space blanket and tried offering her some food, but she was out cold almost immediately. All the music and laughter and shouting doesn't even register. Her husband and crew let her sleep, and when it finally comes time to go, they just carry her out. A shower and food can wait until she feels like getting around to it.

The park can't, however, and there is no rest yet for weary volunteers. Everything that was set up has to be torn down. All the empty pizza boxes have to be bagged and disposed of. The beer cans, too. The flags have to be taken down and wrapped up for next year. It all gets packed into a large moving truck, which Steve Brown will have to sort through in the next week. Cleaning, packing, sorting, and accounting. He'll chip away at it over time.

It will take quite a while before everything is settled. By then it will nearly be time to begin the preparations to haul it all back out for the 2014 event.

There are a few other hurdles between now and that time. He and Tony Horton will have to regroup on how to proceed with Ultraman Australia. They'll actually have a chance to do that soon enough. One member of the Ohana Loa board travels to Wales each year to observe the production of Ultraman United Kingdom, or UMUK, as everyone calls it. The rotation order makes this Steve's year to go see it once more, and Tony will go along for the ride again. This is a crucial event for both the UMUK organizers and Ultraman as a whole. The UK race is in danger of sinking, and it may take the hopes for further expansion races with it. Personal investments are also at stake. Jane has developed friendships with the UK organizers, but some of their transgressions have put those relationships on thin ice. There's a lot riding on this year's race making a good show.

chapter twelve

Chasing the Dragon

"I can't believe that having said what I said was interpreted as having been what I said when I said it, because I said it where I said it, when I said it, and who I said it to."

—Don King

"IN SUMMARY YOU CAN CALL IT A SHIT SHOW." That's how Steve Brown describes Ultraman United Kingdom 2013. He remarks on several administrative failures, lost athletes, inadvertent rules infractions, a shortage of course officials to keep athletes and crews in check, and two competitors hit by a car during the run. In his estimation, it is a disaster in race organization and a black eye for Ultraman's reputation as a whole. Tony Horton accompanied him as part of his initiative to get better acquainted with the race series, and left making the comment, "Now I know how *not* to run one of these things."

But Steve King, who also traveled to Wales to work as the race announcer, has a much different view. He recounts the selflessness of two race volunteers who were commended by the local police chief for stopping to help with a motorbike accident not associated with the race. Teams that got lost blamed themselves for being unfamiliar with how to use the route books. He wrote, "The ecstatic feelings and joy at the final finish line were expressed by all and again at the awards. Simon [Smith] was flexible and got the awards and meal put on early to make sure all could be present and again the athletes were delighted...it was another awesome Ultraman event in my opinion and Simon [and his] team deserve a lot of praise."

It's all a matter of how you see things, and an existential challenge of ultra endurance races is that no one can ever see everything. Even from halfway around the world, Jane and Sheryl have anxieties about what they see in photos, but more so because of what they *haven't* seen. In their exuberance to make this event memorable, a couple of relay teams have made custom race jerseys for themselves, complete with the Ultraman logo on it. Rules state that you have to pay a royalty fee to Ohana Loa if you intend to do that. They weren't aware of that condition because Simon failed to specify as much in his race information packet. Each team agrees to pay £500 for the rights; the money will be given to local charities.

Worse, Simon never sent Jane the paperwork showing that the event is insured. When pressed about the forms, Simon writes back to Sheryl that he's given hard copies to Steve to carry back. He tells her that his Internet connection isn't fast enough to scan and email them to her. But Steve Brown sends her another message saying that the forms have been filled out incorrectly. The coverage is only provided for Racing Quests, the company Simon set up to run Ultraman UK (commonly called UMUK). It does not cover Ohana Loa, LLC. Jane is displeased. Sheryl is furious.

Steve Brown emails Sheryl, writing that he has "some comments from athletes & crews as well which Simon is unaware of—issues about value for money," but he also says that it's difficult to straighten out how many athletes used the Ultraman logo because "no one here speaks English." Six of the eight athletes in arrears are from Spain or the Middle East. Steve and Tony leave before the awards dinner.

The entire Ohana Loa board is underwhelmed. In March, Simon wrote an email to Jane and Sheryl lamenting Ultraman UK's state of affairs. Low participation has caused financial losses since the first race in 2011. He had invested a significant amount of his personal cash to keep it going. At that time, he told them he was done. He offered to put the 2013 race on, then sell the equipment back to Ohana Loa to compensate for unpaid licensing fees he owed them. He wrote again in July to say that he was thinking of cancelling the event entirely. Not enough athletes had signed up and he didn't want to be bothered. He needed at least 10 registrants to break even. Because pulling the plug on the race so soon before it was due to occur would have caused a publicity issue for the Ultraman name, Jane and Sheryl told Simon to put the race on and that he could defer the licensing fee until the end of the year. All they could do was ask favors and offer consolations. There was nothing in their contract with Simon dictating that he *had* to put on an event.

Steve Brown was supposed to observe the race and see what could be done to salvage it. He came. He saw. And he gave up. A few weeks after the dust settles, Jane and Sheryl are ready to call it quits, too. David Cobb is so livid he has to leave the room when the subject comes up. He shouts from the other side of their house when he overhears Sheryl mention items that particularly set him off. "This whole thing has been an exercise in futility since day one," he says. And that's putting it nicely. Any way you look at it, UMUK is done for.

There are just as many explanations for the failure of UMUK as there are perspectives of how it was run, and together they produce a unique study of the life and death of endurance races. People who raced the inaugural event blame the foul weather. They say it scared people away the next year. Others posit that there are plenty of European athletes who live for extreme events who would flock to UMUK...if only they knew it existed. An equal number say that all those European athletes live on the continent, and that if the race had been in Spain or Germany then it would have filled up year after year. It could have at least done well enough to survive in southern Britain. But Wales? That doomed it.

The difficulty with these theories is that they ignore the one race that has survived all of those troubles and more—Hawaii. There have been a couple of years where the race didn't go ahead because there weren't enough registrants, but it always came back. Jane always shepherded it through the hard times. But if Jane's leadership in Hawaii has always provided the solution to every problem there, it leads to the uncomfortable possibility that Simon is the cause of every problem in Wales. Evidence to back that theory presents itself less than a week after UMUK. Not only is Simon inexplicably reinvigorated to keep up the good fight, he announces that registration for UMUK 2014 is open. Jane and Sheryl are shocked. They have not given Simon permission to start planning for next year's race. Nor do they have any intention of renewing his license. They tell him to retract his announcement, to which he responds angrily that they are "hurting the brand" by not helping him to capitalize on what he considers a successful race. No matter how many times they tell him, the runaway race and its rogue director just won't stop. If this keeps up, they'll have to sue him for misrepresentation and copyright infringement. Jane now faces an inconceivable prospect. She's going to wind up in court halfway around the world—over Ultraman, of all things. How did it come to this?

That story goes back four years to the 2010 Canadian Ultraman, when Simon Smith showed up to propose a new Ultraman event, much the same way Tony Horton did this year. It was the first time in 17 years that someone brought up expansion. It took everyone by surprise. The race roster for Canada filled up that year after gaining momentum over the previous three or four years, but it wasn't exactly exploding in popularity. After almost two decades, things were getting just good enough to believe it had become a reliable annual event. Yet growing a new race didn't seem reasonable in the immediate future. Ohana Loa, LLC was a company with a four-member board of directors, three of whom focused mainly on running the Hawaiian race and one who ran the Canadian one. They swapped emails and phone calls. There were no quarterly earnings reports or global strategy meetings. They had no established guidelines or procedures in place to assess Simon's proposal. They made it up as they went along. What they didn't realize was that Simon was doing the same thing.

Simon Smith got his introduction to Ultraman in 2007. A former soldier in the French Foreign Legion, he found that he'd gotten a little soft in civilian life. He started riding a bike to get the extra weight off. A friend named Richard Robinson asked him if he'd like to be part of a relay team for that year's Ultraman, and Simon agreed to ride the bike segments of the course. Richard performed the swim and the run. They had a fine time, finishing second in a field of three relay teams, the other two of which had three members to Richard and Simon's duo.

Sheryl remembers meeting him at that race. "He was a nice enough guy. But a character, for sure." Both men fell in love with the event. Simon proclaimed that he'd come back and make a solo attempt in 2008. He did not, but Richard finished solo in 2010, and Simon crewed for his former teammate. They later presented themselves to the Ohana Loa board as business partners in the UMUK enterprise.

There were immediate concerns. For one thing, both men were relatively new to the event and neither had worked as a race volunteer or seen the process from a director's point of view. But Jane's biggest source of apprehension was that neither of them had been to the Hawaiian race. They might have understood how to put a 320-mile race together, but did they understand how to organize an *Ultraman*? Though they had seen Canada, she still felt it was important for them to experience the spirit of the original thing.

Their presentation was encouraging, though. "Simon had an answer to every question," remembers Dave. That was because Simon had first gone to Steve Brown with the idea, and Steve helped to put the proposal together. That caused Sheryl to become uneasy when Simon discussed their list of potential sponsors for the event, including Peach City Runners. "I didn't understand why Steve would be a sponsor of the event. He was on the board, he was helping them, and he was also somehow going to be financially involved. It just felt like they were crossing lines."

The location and weather were concerns from the beginning, but the two Britons thought it was manageable. Despite everyone's reservations, there was a sense of excitement. After 20 years, this expansion signified that the race had successfully promoted its ideals. There were plenty of European athletes who wanted to take part in Ultraman. This would make it easier for them. There were challenges, but that was nothing new and it hadn't stopped them yet. After everything they'd been through and found a way to succeed, how could they say no to a pair of seemingly genuine guys? No one had a really good answer to that question, and the atmosphere of enthusiasm in the room during the presentation didn't lend to contemplating it at length. "Jane was ready to pull the trigger," Sheryl recalls. "Everyone wanted to make the big announcement in Canada. There was a lot of pressure to say yes." It was enough for them to grant Simon and Richard their blessing that day. Ultraman United Kingdom was announced at the awards dinner after the 2010 Canadian race.

The trouble began immediately. Right after the announcement, Simon decided to hand out a free race slot to Canadian finisher Dan Squiller. Sheryl flipped. "No one saw that coming. I was like, 'Oh fuck.' I mean, that's money he's not going to get on a new event, plus the fact that everyone starts to wonder if *they* can get a free slot. It was just downhill from there."

Downhill enough that Richard Robinson withdrew from the partnership within six months. Though he said at the time it was due to his wife's objections to the amount of time he was putting into the event, in retrospect Steve says that he's "never heard from him since." This was especially worrying because Robinson was the one with the actual money. Simon started looking for new options. He began more serious discussions with Steve Brown about buying a stake in the new company that would produce UMUK.

He eventually found another partner in Liam McElroy. However, Liam could not sign on to an executive position with another company because of his contract with his employer. The pair worked around that snag by putting Liam's wife, Sarah, on the paperwork as Simon's partner. The new company was called Racing Quests. Everything seemed to be okay. Simon even began talking about a new site for a second expansion race in Spain, and everyone at Ohana Loa found renewed enthusiasm. That was until Steve and Jane visited Europe to assess Simon's progress and perform the site inspection on the course in February 2011. Flaws in the board's disorganized approach to expansion began to show. There were disagreements over the required safety measures Simon was planning, as well as some roads that were deemed unsafe, causing the course to be rerouted. There were various other administrative holdups in registering the race, its logo, and characteristic distances for trademark in Great Britain. Then there was the matter of the plane tickets.

Among the few standing rules the board had written down about expansion races concerned travel and accommodation expenses for Ohana Loa staff coming to supervise events. Each year, one or two of the Hawaiian members—Jane, Sheryl, and Dave—flies out to Canada. They help in myriad ways, but officially it's to perform quality control. The race directors are on the hook for these expenses. Jane typically uses her frequent flier miles, accumulated from trips visiting relatives in Canada and California, as well as the occasional European vacation. She did the same for the 2011 Wales inspection, leaving Simon responsible for only Steve's airfare. At some point during the visit, while the group was in the middle of enjoying several pints of Welsh stout, Steve remarked that he was having so much fun that Simon didn't need to pay for his ticket. Simon took the joke literally. In fact, Steve had been anticipating the payment to help fund a European vacation with his wife. He was able to write the ticket off as a business expense, but it put a dent in the vacation and left him furious. It was about the same time that

Simon told him Liam and Sarah had bought into Racing Quests, and there was no more room for another partner. It did irreparable damage to their personal relationship.

All of this built up to the 2011 race, which Jane and Steve returned to the UK to watch. It looked good enough at the beginning. Twenty-nine athletes registered, three of whom had to drop out before the event began. Still, it was a prodigious field for an inaugural event. Steve was unimpressed with the other metrics, however. He constantly remarked on Simon's shortcomings and mistakes. Jane tried to mollify him, but he was insistent.

Meanwhile, Simon had other problems. Foul weather moved in on the morning of the swim, blowing so hard that the buoys marking the course drifted back toward the shore. Yet even with all the waves and rain, the athletes still logged some of the fastest swim times in Ultraman history, mainly because the course was short by nearly a kilometer. In a cringe-worthy moment, Simon was able to get a boat out in time to move the buoys back out for the athletes in the back of the pack.

The hits just kept on coming. National forestry rules prevented Simon from marking the bike and run courses, and road signs in Wales aren't the easiest to read. (The consonant-heavy dialect is something like a cross between Gaelic and Klingon.) Nor did the weather cooperate. Athletes got lost on several occasions.

In the end, 22 of the 26 participants who started the race were able to finish, many of them becoming devoted fans of the race. Sometimes, the harder something is, the more you appreciate accomplishing it.

But there was still more disappointment in store for Jane and Steve after the race. Once everything wrapped up in Wales, the trio went over to Spain to check out the racecourse Simon had been telling them about. What he'd called a garden spot turned out to be a minefield. Sections of the course weren't even paved. The Spanish government also presented significant obstacles of its own. The permitting and license fees for a race were astronomical. It was simply uneconomical. All this came as a surprise to Jane and Steve after what Simon had told them. It was another incident of reality failing to meet Simon's sales pitch, and the number of those occurrences was mounting.

Jane was willing to chalk up the mishaps to rookie mistakes. She and Steve compiled a list of necessary changes Simon would have to make. At that time, his license from Ohana Loa to organize an Ultraman race was only good on a year-to-year basis. If Simon could get the race running smoothly on all fronts after 2012, Ohana Loa would issue him a five-year license for the race. He had a lot of work to do. But not even Jane could overlook Simon's failure to produce a certificate of race insurance. She asked him to send it to her for her records as soon as he could. Simon assured her she'd get it in the mail. She never did.

The event improved in 2012, but things with Simon got worse. He never signed his agreement with Ohana Loa for the race. Nor did he provide proof of insurance again. Jane and Sheryl repeatedly asked him to send the necessary documents before the race. Each time Simon assured them that they were either at some stage in the approval process or on their way. When Sheryl and Jane finally came to Wales, he told them that he'd lost the paperwork somewhere in the trunk of his car. He had further bad news for them about the airfare: he couldn't pay it. Jane wound up putting hers on her frequent flier account. Sheryl's ticket came out of Ohana Loa funds. Simon was politely but explicitly reminded that these expenses were part of his agreement for the race, and that he'd have to start honoring his contract if he wanted to solidify UMUK's status.

Only 11 athletes registered for the 2012 race, one of whom dropped out before it even started. Nine finished, including Inaki De La Parra and Yasuko Miyazaki. Simon lost significant money on the deal. Jane remarked that things had improved since the inaugural year, but that Simon had to get the paperwork done. They decided to keep UMUK on probationary status and grant him another one-year license for the race.

This year, the task of looking in on UMUK fell to Steve. Though he didn't necessarily look forward to the trip, he didn't carry animosity with him. He went in hoping that Simon had finally gotten his act together. If things went bad, Tony would see the difference between a well-practiced operation like Canada and the kinds of races that can happen when you're not prepared. Then they'd spend a couple of weeks in London talking to some parties interested in taking over the UK Ultraman. If things went really bad, it would be a shit show.

In the immediate aftermath of the race, everyone back in Hawaii is at a loss to determine exactly what happened in Wales. As Winston Churchill once remarked, "a lie gets halfway around the world before the truth has a chance to get its pants on." Thanks to technology, rumors today spread immeasurably faster through the fiber-optic grapevine. Though Steve has trouble finding enough reception and resources to email a detailed assessment of the race, Simon writes a hasty message to Jane and Sheryl on Facebook:

> *Hi all, another year done all had a great time I think next year might be the break through year for UMUK. I plan to open the entries for next year and as long as the event breaks even go ahead if not any fee that has been taken will be refunded and the event put on ice for a year. I think this was the best solution steve and I came up with. The main thing all had a great time. Athletes and crews THEY ALL GOT IT!! ...Last but not least you were all missed this year by me and Rachel. Thank you for letting us be a small part of the family. I am sure our friend ship will always be there as we guide this FANTASTIC EVENT as it gets big and bigger love to you all. all things agrement will be with you via email and insurance will be with you today*

In other words, "Everything is great. The check is in the mail. Pay no attention to the man behind the curtain." He organizes his thoughts about as well as his races, which probably explains a lot. Sheryl detects the smoke screen on Simon's breath, assumes it means fire, and in characteristically prudent fashion douses him with cold water. After Simon sends the insurance certificate, she responds:

> *Hi Simon,*
> *Thanks for the insurance certificate...however, the license agreement was not attached. Please forward that again as soon as possible.*
> *Also, we must request that you not open applications for a 2014 event until we have had time to meet as a Board and discuss the 2013 event. No license agreement for 2014 will be issued until after that meeting. Prior to the 2013 event, you were quite adamant that this was your last year, so we need to have some discussions to decide what the future of the event will be.*
> *We will have a Board meeting quickly after Steve's return to Canada to determine the future of UMUK.*
> *Thank you,*
> *Board of Directors Ohana Loa Inc.*

In other words, "Ease off the gas pedal. I want to stop and think about this before I go any farther down this road with you." It hasn't exactly been a smooth ride up to this point. Now Steve is able to get a message out to Sheryl:

Hi Sheryl,

I just saw Simon's email in regard to opening next years applications - we should tell him to not do that until I have had a chance to give you guys a report. Also I am meeting this weekend with the other guys here in the UK to get their thoughts. Also we do not have an agreement in place with Simon - did he send you the agreement for 2013? I also have concerns about the insurance as I am not sure what he is saying is in fact the case.

By the way I think the event in the UK was a disaster. 4 of 8 got lost at some point, 2 guys hit by a car on the run (not serious but could have been). Ticker is not working and no markings on course is making it a nightmare for crews - Tony and I got lost twice and we didn't have an athlete to worry about. Have some comments from athletes & crews as well which Simon is unaware of - issues about value for money.

He is not prepared to rejig the event he thinks he has put in 3 years and now has it figured out. With no marshals there were violations all over the place from one rider have a pacer all of Day 1, drafting behind vehicles, and transporting an athlete in a vehicle to get them back on course after being lost - this event is a joke when it comes to rules.

We need to have a long discussion upon my return before we do anything - just make sure he doesn't open applications until then.

In other words, it was a shit show. Yet despite Sheryl's direct message and Steve's face-to-face conversations with him, Simon plows ahead with his plan for 2014 like the captain of the Titanic. The day after Sheryl tells him not to open registration for the next year's UMUK, he does exactly that. He makes the announcement on the Facebook page he's created for UMUK. Sheryl goes through the roof. Since Simon is undeterred by her warning shots, she goes for the nuclear option. First, she publicly comments on the post that "there are issues that need to be worked out with the event." That should be enough to make people wary of giving Simon money. Then she calls Jane, who messages Simon directly:

Simon, please do not put 2014 UMUK registration online yet. There has to be another Ohana Loa board meeting to review the 2013 event, and Steve has yet to return to Canada when we can do our conference call meeting. So glad all participants "got it"!

In other words, "Ultra Mom sees what you are doing, and she is most annoyed." Simon responds the next day:

Hi Guys, I did not know that there would another review. I thought thats what we did last year. I thought the only question was if We on this end were going to go again in 2014. We had a chat with Steve and Tony regarding us going ahead, We agreed that we would go ahead and open the event entries. If the event broke even, to do this it needs 10 entrants we would go ahead. If it has not got there by March next year then we would refund all entries, and maybe look at every other year. Apologies I thought you knew this, i did not know they had to report back to you. The event was great 100% fantastic feed back from both athletes and crews. Weather 21c - 25 sunny with alite montain mist on day2 bike for 2 hours or so. water temp was 17c. Ultraman remains very special to us all over here. The only problem we had was the logo…. As long as I do not have to use Family money to prop the event up We will be here. That is the only issue this end. We look forward to you guys being here next year for more ultraman smiles and stories

It's hard to tell what's going on with Simon at this point. His statements now are completely at odds with the events of the last seven months. Does he have no memory, or just a convenient one, or is he just plain lying? Steve gives a curt assessment when he responds to Simon:

Hi all, To be clear we did not agree to opening applications - that was Simon's plan of attack. I am not in a position to make those decisions and until the Board Meeting upon my return that decision cannot be finalized. As I said in Wales we have some concerns and those have not been addressed in full. I am still concerned about the insurance issue and I did not receive a copy of the License Agreement. There are other issues as well but the Board needs to have discussions before we proceed. I do have some feed back from Simon, that we need to consider before any decision is made.. Steve

In other words, "He's just plain lying."

Communication moves at a trickle after Steve's message. Simon is slow to respond, gives half answers, and seems to deliberately avoid acknowledging that he understands directions, even when explicitly told to. When asked about the collision between the car and the athletes on day 3, he flatly denies that anything happened. He says, "It was a near miss at the end of the day no one was hit."

Lefteris Paraskeuas has a much different version of events. The Greek athlete says that he and another participant were hit by a car less than five kilometers from the start line as they ran across an intersection. "As we were crossing the street...we noticed a car coming out of a side street on to the main road we were on. Thinking [the driver] had seen us, we carried on. She hit the [Spanish athlete] with her mirror and knocked him to the ground. I slammed onto her boot, pulling my right leg muscle in an attempt to avoid being hurt by the car. She slammed on the brakes and sat in amazement in her car while two hot blooded Mediterranean men had a word with her in all languages!"

Rumors begin filling the void left by real information. Word has it that some people are already starting to sign up for the 2014 race. This could present a crisis to Ohana Loa. One of the big draws of UMUK has been that it offers a qualifying slot for Hawaii. It's very plausible that anyone signing up for it would have Kona in mind. That means Simon is making money by falsely advertising that his race is associated with Ultraman, making Ohana Loa look like the bad guys when they turn down someone trying to get into Hawaii with a "qualification" from a bad race.

Not that Simon is actively advertising, as such. In that regard, the liability of his failure to promote UMUK to the broader endurance audience shifts from Racing Quests to Ultraman. Simon has three years of participants and word of mouth working for him. None of the athletes are aware of these behind-the-scenes dealings. In some respects, he's growing the race the way Curtis Tyler did. And without any clear-cut statement on the Racing Quests website, no one would know until it's too late.

Jane hounds Simon for two weeks. Finally he sends word implying that he will change the event's marketing and name sufficiently, to eliminate all possibility of mistaken identity. Even the website for Racing Quests is pulled offline to be retooled. Through it all, he maintains his own version of reality:

> *We have made it quiet clear from the start on the news page on the site and on the face book page we are no longer part of the ultraman world champion ship event or a qualifier. You have to be quite clear on that type of thing. we are still friends with Jane. It was our choice not to be part of ultraman group. It cost a small fortune to fly two board members over put them up in hotels for a week and part with 5 percent of gross we have dropped entry fees re logoed and have 15 solos and two relay teams so all good this end.*

No such statement disavowing association with Ultraman exists on the website. The rulebook for the "new" race still refers to it as "ultraman uk." The website itself continues to call the race "UMUK." When asked why the name hasn't been changed, Simon achieves a new level of denial:

> *who said UMUK anything do with ultraman it does not stand for ultraman*
> *No need to be confused ultraman uk past, (UMUK) future If you have seen the new web site and logo there can be no confusion. I am sure there will be a few slip ups with language in both camps the early days. what is that they say "two nations divided by a common language"*

He insists that UMUK no longer stands for "Ultraman United Kingdom." Instead, it's just "UMUK" now; a word without definition, spelled in all capitals for no reason. Sure, there's bound to be some confusion, but it can't be helped. Everyone will just have to make do. Move along, nothing else to see. He avoids answering further questions, but there are bigger issues involved than just this race. The question is quite literally "What's in a name?" In the case of a race series, it entails the legitimacy and legal standing of the whole enterprise.

Simon claims that Racing Quests, not Ohana Loa, owns the trademark logo of Ultraman in the United Kingdom and Spain. And while the logo might "be put in a drawer," it leads to complicated arguments over how carelessly the name "Ultraman" or its derivatives can be thrown around. Simon's walking on a narrow ledge. He's not waving a big flag with the word

The father of Ultraman, Curtis Tyler directed the first race in 1983.

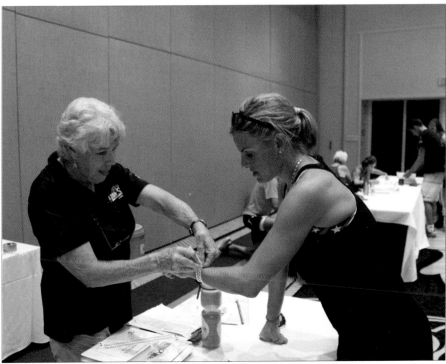

Jane Bockus, aka Ultra Mom, and Ironman champion Hillary Biscay.

Steve King has become a fixture at Ultraman, announcing the race and maintaining meticulous notes.

Australian Tony Horton and Ohana Loa, LLC board member Sheryl Cobb. Relations between the two were often strained.

Ultraman world champion Amber Monforte.

Steve Brown and Jane Bockus.

Alexandre Ribeiro and Miro Kregar celebrate at the finish of Ultraman Hawaii in 2012. The two competitors have become great friends and supporters.

Out on the course, an athlete's support crew is his or her lifeblood. Here, John Bergen gets much-needed hydration during Ultraman Canada 2013.

Craig Percival and Dave Matheson crossed the line together on Day 2 of Ultraman Canada 2013. By that point, they had become true friends.

Rory Bass greets and hugs his wife after crossing the Day 2 finish line with mere seconds to spare.

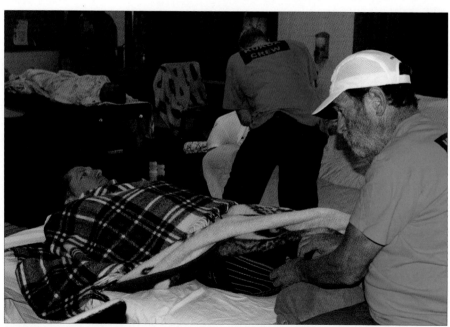

Volunteer massage therapists work on the athletes. It's an excruciating process for the competitors, but a necessary one if they hope to reach the finish.

Christian Isakson eases into an ice bath following his ride on Day 2.

The leaders head out for the 84.3km run on the final day.

Dave Matheson embraces his family after his record-breaking finish.

John Bergen reached the finish line with nothing left to give.

ULTRAMAN written on it, but he's conveniently ignoring an obligation to take down the one he planted in Wales three years ago. Regardless, Jane is seriously considering a legal fight. She's already begun gathering evidence to support her case. It's going to be an odd assortment of memorabilia showing that the name "UMUK" is in fact too closely implicated with "Ultraman United Kingdom" to be a credible distinction. Exhibit A in this peculiar gallery is a plush toy dragon. Everyone in the Ultraman community knows him at first sight. His name is UMUK. UMUK the dragon.

UMUK the dragon made his first appearance at UMUK the race in 2012, when Dave and Sheryl attended. The pair stayed in a local hostel with bunk beds. Because they left their dogs at home and the beds were too small to share, Sheryl had trouble sleeping. Dave bought Sheryl the stuffed dragon to have something to cuddle with. It somehow followed her to the lake the day before the race. She got the idea to take a picture of it looking down the way the athletes would swim. That was the beginning. Sheryl decided the dragon would become the race's mascot, which was fitting since the Welsh flag prominently features a large red dragon. UMUK was subsequently photographed throughout the weekend "helping" volunteers on different parts of the course. When they got back to Hawaii, Jane decided that the race there also needed a mascot. Sheryl bought a stuffed toy gecko and named it "GUS," which stands for "Gecko Ultraman Supreme." GUS and UMUK were photographed all over Hawaii during the 2012 Ultraman World Championships. They have been seen together frequently since then. At the end of the day, that little stuffed dragon may be the undoing of Simon's trademark charade. It will be hard for him to outrun the reputation that precedes it. Jane just has to chase down all those photos.

As much as some people hate the corporate mentality of bigger franchise races, there's no denying that it has its advantages. Ironman's bureaucracy may be slow on the relay with regard to individual athlete complaints, but it covers all the bases when it comes to contracts. True to its name, Ohana Loa tries to do business family style. Their latest adopted son has turned out to be a black sheep, though. Jane is not terribly worried. She figures that Simon can't possibly stay in business for more than two years at the rate he's going. But all that means is that they've dodged a bullet, much the same way Valerie did with the Bud Light crew and Julie Moss in 1982. If the quality of Simon's scheming matched the quantity of his lies, this could have ended very badly. It will have to wait for now. She has Hawaii to prepare for in less than 60 days. But just because UMUK isn't getting her immediate attention doesn't mean it's over.

chapter thirteen

Supply and Demand: Endless Possibilities

"A triathlon is nothing more than a complex operational structure. We have events in 17 countries all over the world. We have probably over 50,000 athletes competing in our events worldwide next year, and there's a whole process that goes along with that. About six months ago, I sat down with a group of other event-management people, and all of us were engineers."

—Ben Fertic, Former World Triathlon Corporation CEO

THERE IS AN OUTPOURING of emotional reactions once the greater community of athletes hears of the split between Ohana Loa and UMUK. Just about every athlete who's been to Simon's event declares moral support on the Facebook pages for both the UK race and the at-large Ultraman following. Most of them take his announcements at face value. Jane, Steve, and Sheryl decide to take the high road and avoid saying anything negative about Simon, even if it's true. This gives him a decided advantage in the messaging campaign, but Jane sees it as a short-lived victory. She predicts it won't take long for the truth to come out. In this, there's as much executive patience in her thought process as Ultra Mom–style forgiveness. She's been at this for 20 years. It's going to take a lot more than Simon to make her worry. Besides, things are looking a lot better at the next planned expansion site.

While Jane fights her battles with Simon, Consuela, and Trung Lively wrap up a weekend at Ironman Florida in Panama City. Sway finishes fifth in her age group, but even more impressive are the 25 athletes in her club who attend, 24 of whom finish. Appropriately enough, her coaching business is named "Tri With Sway—Endless Possibilities."

It's a good motto for a woman with a relentlessly cheerful outlook on life. It's also a good characterization of the results it brings. She and Trung took a big risk to raise a new Ultraman event from the ground up, but karma is paying off. She has an abundance of volunteers already signed up, and all 40 race slots were taken within three weeks of registration opening. It also seems the exceptional competition in Canada has given the Ultraman name a boost. She received between three to five requests about the race each day during Ultraman Canada. Since then, she's been getting between one to three a week. Despite a half dozen original registrants dropping out for various reasons, the wait list for slots in the 2014 race still has twice that many names on it. And that's not counting the people waiting to register for 2015.

UMUK now appears to be the exception to expansion rather than the rule. It was a rotten organization in a dreary location. But it wasn't the wrong race. Put an Ultraman in a place like Florida, under the qualified and genuine care of someone like Sway and Trung, and the magic is recaptured. If you build it, people will come. The only questions are how many do you want to build, and where and when? These are the things Jane has to worry about.

At present, the answers are "one," "Australia," and "2015." It looks as if Ultraman Florida will make enough noise to drown out the sound and fury coming from Wales. Tony Horton's Down Under operation will be an interesting addition. Australia is a deep well of triathlon talent and culture, and endurance races of all kinds are very popular there. Six of the last seven Ironman World Championships have gone to an Australian man, as well as two of the last four women's titles. Given its proximity to Hawaii and the allure of Kona, Tony could be sitting on an untapped vein of ultra endurance enthusiasts.

But what about beyond Australia? Six of the 40 Florida registrants come from Mexico and South American countries. Alexandre Ribeiro, the six-time Hawaii champ, comes from Brazil. Why not a race there? And continental Europe still beckons. Two Slovenians have done well in Ultraman, and Jure Robic, who won the Race Across America five times before his death in a cycling accident in 2010, is still hailed as a national hero in that country.

There are ultra-cycling races around Italy, France, and Austria. Greece holds the Spartathlon, a 150-mile running race between Athens and Sparta, which is held every year to celebrate the legendary run of Pheidippides, known as the first marathoner. The event draws about 300 participants every year, and the streets of Sparta fill with spectators at the end. Then again, Germany is always nice. The possibilities are endless.

So are the opinions. Tony Horton and Steve Brown are bursting at the seams to get new races cranked up. There's already been one race proposed, another one in the conceptual stages, and a third party waiting for its turn to start a franchise. People have caught the fever, and it's all Jane and Sheryl can do to keep things from boiling over.

The first idea for expansion was actually proposed a few years before the UK event. Cory Foulk teamed up with Alexandre Ribeiro to pitch Ultraman Brazil. It seemed ideal: perfect climate, a welcoming culture, and a pair of record holders and longtime participants putting the whole thing together. There was just one problem: Cory. His legend-in-his-own-mind outlook worried Jane and Sheryl. They thought he might make the race more about him than its principles or the athletes. Since then, Cory and Alexandre started a website for a race they call "UB515," indicating a triathlon with distances very similar to Ultraman. Cory still calls it Ultraman Brazil. It might become a problem, but first they have to get it off the ground.

Substantially more serious was Michael Brown's pitch for Ultraman New Zealand in 2012. He ran in the 2012 Hawaiian event and made his proposal at the same time as Consuela and Trung. Though Consuela and Trung won the bid for the 2014 event, Brown didn't exactly lose. The board told him that his New Zealand venture would have to wait until 2015. A man who puts as much energy into business as he does his racing, Brown had no interest in just letting the project sit for a year. He scrapped the idea and started planning a solo attempt to swim more than 100 miles in 2015. It was nothing personal, just business. Not everyone is able to let go, however. For them, Ultraman's growth *is* a personal thing. Nick Mallett is among them. He spends the last week in October scouting the Ultraman Australia course with Tony Horton. He'll have a significant role in the race going forward, but he's got eyes for further possibilities. Namely, Ultraman Thailand.

Next to Penticton during Ultraman week, Thailand is Mallett's favorite place in the world. He dreams of retiring there. Between a little work as a massage therapist, maybe another odd job, and a little profit from running a few endurance sports events, he thinks he'd get by. The country offers beautiful scenery, entertainment, and best of all it's dirt cheap. "I always said that the only way an Ultraman would be profitable is if you held it in a second- or third-world country and treated it like a superior destination race and charged US dollars. People will pay the same or more to go to an exotic or dangerous—perceived—country and do an event if they feel they are being looked after. You are also able to actually pay staff to look after aspects of the event in poorer countries. Happens all the time."

His problem, of course, is a matter of time. He knows that under the current system there's no hope of getting Ohana Loa's blessing for the event until at least 2016, and more than likely it will be 2017. In the meantime, he's already contacted officials with the International Ultra Triathlon Association (IUTA) about running a double- or triple-Iron-distance race in Thailand. Such races require athletes to race two Iron-distance triathlons back to back in a swim-bike-run, swim-bike-run format. They also differ from Ultraman in that they run continuously, rather than in stages. You can take a nap if you want, but the clock keeps ticking. There are all kinds of variations. Nick doesn't need Ohana Loa to run an officially licensed and widely promoted ultra endurance triathlon in Thailand. That's actually what makes him so worried about the future of Ultraman.

"Ultraman will expand, but sadly it is now becoming an expensive event all around, and I think it will end up being a niche event while the double-Iron and triple-Iron format will grow just like it is [doing] in Europe now. There is a new double scheduled for Oregon in July next year and it won't cost anywhere near the money Ultraman does.

"The Hawaii connection [his way of referring to Jane, Sheryl, and Dave] needs to bring their attitude into the next phase of Ultraman and decide if they want to expand or not. This idea of wanting to expand but only allowing one a year at the most is silly. If they want to keep it a race for their buddies then awesome, but they need to either move ahead and be the standard race series around the world or risk losing the prestige of the name because 10 other races just like theirs have popped up," he says.

Nick has been a bit of a crusader on this front. He's intervened in two cases in which organizers in Mexico and Brazil attempted to co-opt the Ultraman brand name to promote knock-off races. In Mexico it was "Ultra-Tri-Man."

The Brazilian race outright proclaimed itself to be Ultraman Brazil and was even put together by Brazilian athletes who'd participated in Canada and Hawaii. Thanks to Nick, Ohana Loa was able to peacefully negotiate with the organizers to shut down their operation. But there's nothing they can do about UB515 if it gets off the ground. Nor can they challenge the 2013 "Hyperman" ultra-triathlon in Hong Kong, because its run course is 100 km instead of the standard 84.4 km double marathon. Amazingly, the organizers have been so bold as to advertise the race directly on the Ultraman Facebook page.

Wherever opportunities exist, opportunists crop up. Mallett fears that Jane is "a little slow on the realization that she needs to protect" Ultraman from those opportunists because she's "still caught up in the touchy-feely side of the event." He thinks Steve Brown's business-oriented view of things better positions him to deal with the emerging issues. In his estimation, Sheryl and Dave strike the right balance between the two. As one of the most dedicated athletes in the entire Ultraman family, Mallett believes Dave and Sheryl's primary challenges as they gradually assume responsibility from Jane will be reducing the cost of the races and striking the right balance with the expanding crop of race directors to facilitate growth. His views are shaped by personal experience. He's always gone to Penticton rather than Kona because hotel, food, and vehicle costs for a Hawaiian race are prohibitively expensive. By contrast, a double- or triple-Iron race makes numerous laps on a shorter course, precluding the need for a crew. That's why he's racing the 2014 Florida double-Iron instead of Ultraman Florida, which takes place the week before.

While Mallett may be right about their foremost obstacles, Sheryl and Dave may also find myriad small problems pile up to create tough hurdles. They've ably navigated the occasional small dispute with Steve Brown, negotiations with Tony Horton, and appear to have Simon Smith well in hand, but in every case they've had the advantage of Jane being the one in front. A decision with the Ultra Mom seal of approval is as good as the word of Ultra Mom herself. But on the day that Jane is no longer there to approve, ownership of decisions will fall wholly on Sheryl and Dave. They may find people are more willing to voice objections at that point.

It's no secret, based on their demonstrated approaches to running the Hawaiian event, that Sheryl is *not* Jane. They also diverge in attitudes on how the greater Ultraman series should grow. Jane has always been welcoming and enthusiastic. Sheryl is much more cautious, especially in the wake of the UMUK fiasco. "As we mentioned to Steve, just because we are limiting it to one a year, it doesn't mean we have to add one *every* year," she says. From her point of view, new proposals will have to meet a set of criteria, some of which are unquantifiable. There will need to be a large enough demand among the athletes and the prospective organizer will need to have the necessary resources, but they will also have to demonstrate they've internalized the Ultraman ethos and a sincere commitment to growing the aloha spirit, not just putting on a race. They want someone with a head for business and a heart of gold. Someone like Consuela Lively.

The problem is people like that just don't fall out of the sky. But Sheryl would rather spend years waiting to see one eagle than to let cowbirds roost in the nest. She's seen the consequences of that. "It's the influx of the Ironman mentality into the Ultraman events that I am referring to.... There are those that seek Ultraman because they want a difference in the experience and environment and those that seek it because it is just longer. It is the second group that would love to see expansion everywhere and then it would just be a long Ironman to them, and they are comfortable in that environment.

"One other thing on the draw of [Ultraman Hawaii] is that it provides an opportunity for the athletes that aren't fast enough to qualify for [Ironman] Kona to race in Hawaii. One athlete is a perfect example and that was actually his quote after UMC 2012, 'Now I am finally qualified to race in Kona.' The reality of it is that it is just a long triathlon with some naps in the middle. I, for one, just don't want to see it become the corporate monstrosity that is WTC. You have to remember, I work in the Ironman race office [for] three days during race week. I have seen the 'monstrosity' personally. I spoke to John Collins at Ironman and thanked him for telling Jane to keep it invitational. Really helps us weed out the real jerks."

For Dave and Sheryl, it's all about maintaining the family atmosphere and ensuring the emphasis of the values on which the race was founded. Not everyone else sees it that way, but most aren't willing to say so. Nick Mallett has no such reservations. For as much as he loves the event and the friends it's given him, he calls the spiritual aspects of the Hawaiian event "happy-clappy" and "overly sentimental." While Jane and others believe they're spreading a cultural dynamic native to Hawaii, Nick contends that few if any buy into it all that much. For the most part, people play along because that's the way the event is. There's no doubt he loves this race, but standing in a circle and holding hands is a bit overboard. Several athletes feel the same way. Nick isn't into the spirituality, and he doesn't see a way to justify the expense of going to Hawaii.

The Beckers and Wang are really into it and they do see the justification. Like Sheryl says, Hawaii is by invitation only. They can bring in whomever they like. The qualification criteria are just there to serve as a filter. They're just one way to help weed out jerks. That doesn't mean there aren't other ways. Under the rules, "eenie, meenie, minie, moe" is an acceptable method. This has the uncomfortable consequence of seeming arbitrary and, depending on who gets in and who doesn't, nepotistic. That's what has some people worried about Sheryl taking over for Jane. It was okay for Sheryl to be the heavy-handed one, so long as she was Jane's right hand. But now that the bad cop stands to become the chief executive, people are wary that the Ultraman family could turn into something more like a police state.

The problem begins much earlier in the process than getting into the Hawaiian race. You have to qualify for the qualifier by first completing an Iron-distance event. This usually translates to "Ironman." It stands to reason that someone would first run an Ironman before an Ultraman, but the problem is that the candidate pool has a definite culture. To say that the typical Ironman athlete is an overachiever is an understatement. People look at their times. They train to perform. In other words, Ironman is a meritocracy.

Ultraman plays by totally different rules: it really isn't whether you win or lose, but how you play the game. Some Ironman athletes aren't sure how to respond to that. They've come to believe that winning is an indication that you're playing the game well. Sheryl might think some of those people are jerks who need to be weeded; they might think Ultraman is unfair and opaque. It's a culture clash where people disagree on the fundamental definitions of what's important in sport. Dave characterizes the dynamic with his typical mixture of salt and sage. He says there's a popular bumper sticker that best summarizes the Hawaiian mantra: WE DON'T GIVE A SHIT HOW YOU DO IT ON THE MAINLAND.

"You can't just come out here and buy a piece of land," he says of people who come to the islands looking to build retreat mansions. "People come out here with lots of money and run into walls when they find out that money isn't the most important thing here."

Sheryl observes the flip side of the cultural dynamic: "People come from California and get angry that it's not California. You have to be able to let go of where you came from to live here." But holding to those ideas while trying to expand their race elsewhere may prove a little naive. With Ultraman Florida open for business, Ohana Loa now has *two* races on the mainland. That leaves them more vulnerable to the possibility that people on the mainland don't give a shit how they do things in Hawaii.

Sheryl insists that you don't just come to Hawaii to race, though. You really have to be prepared to embrace the whole thing. No one knows that better than her. A native Californian, Sheryl moved to Hawaii in 1992 to build a new life after her old one had fallen apart. She used to be a competitive water-skier, but an accident wrecked her ankle in the late '80s. Not long afterward, a close friend was killed in an auto accident. She finally decided to get away from it all and start over. She joined the Keauhou Canoe Club in 1995 and began paddling for fun. By 1996 she was racing in the six-man and long-distance events. That was how she first got wrapped up in Ultraman.

Sheryl met Jane in 1994, while volunteering at local races. Their relationship grew closer as they raced together. It wasn't long before Jane approached Sheryl for help with Ultraman. "She knew that I had worked races before, but I was also a single young woman with nothing to do for Thanksgiving." She laughs, knowing Jane targeted her because she had no good excuse to get out of it. So 1996 was her indoctrination into Ultraman.

Like everyone's first time, it was a little chaotic. Jane first planned for Sheryl to work as support crew for two Guatemalan athletes, but at the last minute they received the news that their coach had been killed and decided to return home for the funeral. Jane brought Sheryl into her own vehicle as an assistant. Soon after they began the ascent up Kilauea, they came upon an athlete experiencing difficulty. He was dehydrated and his legs were cramping. Worse, he'd somehow managed to get on the course with only one person working as his support crew (rules state athletes must have at least two support crewmembers). Sheryl got out and worked on his legs a bit and the cramps subsided. He took off on the bike and the crewman asked Jane if he could take Sheryl on as a second crewmember. The athlete might not make it otherwise. She agreed and switched vehicles. It turned out to be a fortuitous turn of events for the beleaguered athlete. On day two he got off his bike and propped himself against a rail on the side of the road along the Hamakua Coast, about two-thirds of the way to the stage finish. "We got out of the car and he started telling us he had seen Elvis, then he almost fell backward. We caught him before he went over the edge. He looked at me for a moment and then said, 'You don't look like Elvis,'" she remembers. Somehow, they managed to get him back on the bike and over the Kohala Mountains. He struggled all through the next day, ultimately taking 11 and a half hours to complete the double marathon. Still, it counted as an official finish.

And that was how Sheryl Cobb saved Cory Foulk's first Ultraman.

The two bonded over that experience so much that she asked if he'd room with her in a new place she'd found in 1997. She also worked as his crew again that year. Playing things a little too fast and loose, once again Cory failed to get a second crewmember by race day. He also forgot to secure a support vehicle. That left Sheryl driving in her own car for the weekend. It wouldn't have been so bad except that the driver's side door almost literally fell off on the first day. She had to tape it in place and use a trash bag to cover the window. There was a torrential downpour that lasted the first two days of the race. "So every time he needed help, I had to get in and out of the car *Dukes of Hazzard* style, with the rain pouring on me," she says.

A retired Air Force intelligence sergeant, Dave Cobb stayed in Honolulu after he got out of the service, except for a brief stint in Spokane. He got into triathlon after his first marriage soured. He spent so much time training to get over the broken relationship that he finished in the top five at nearly every race he entered. Dave's first time crewing at Ultraman was in 1995, and he came back in 1998. He reconnected with Sheryl earlier that year when she asked if he'd help some athletes she'd met in Special Olympics who were living on Oahu. The two young men had the potential to qualify for the half marathon. The problem was that they had to run with someone else and their parents weren't able to keep up the necessary pace themselves. He trained with them for several weeks and they qualified. That November he came out and he and Sheryl crewed for separate athletes. He'd recently broken up with his girlfriend and the two hit it off. It soon became clear to everyone who knew them that it was a serious romance. He found a job in Kona in 1999 and moved in with Sheryl. Then he moved out again.

While it was obvious to everyone else, Dave and Sheryl wanted to make sure. Dave has a ponytail, goatee, and a penchant for crude jokes. He likes to tell people that "redneck" is his first language. Sheryl's wardrobe includes no end of board shorts with patterns of wildly colored hibiscus on them. Her trademark move is to stick her tongue out at any camera pointed at her, and that's usually how photos of her show up on Ultraman's official website.

During the race the cab of their pickup truck looks like a tsunami dumped the contents of a bike shop and an office building in it; it's filled with binders, pens, clipboards, laptop computers, hex wrenches, and assorted athletic gear and snack foods. The bed hosts their two dogs, the necessary food and water for them, and more race supplies. Altogether they look like the happiest couple of beach bums on the planet. That carefree appearance belies the exceptional pragmatism life's hard knocks have taught them to use in approaching big decisions. There was no big fight or event that caused Dave to leave. He just wanted to make sure he was settling with, and not for, Sheryl. Sheryl was in no rush to get married either. "I knew he'd been married twice before," she says with a smile. "If he needed to make sure he was sure, that was fine by me."

Sheryl and Dave balance their refusal to suffer fools with phenomenal patience and compassion. They also have a solid understanding of the Ironman community, seeing it at its most extreme from the inside out. But understanding how things can go bad isn't the same as knowing how to make them go right. Even with the rules helping them to weed out the "jerks," there's still the growing bumper crop of real McCoys to build races for. And though Sheryl and Dave might slow expansion down to one race every three or four years, that still means the number of qualifiers for Hawaii will double within 10 years and conceivably triple during their tenure as chief executives of Ohana Loa. That brings them back to the core dilemma. There are endless reasons why a person might want to participate in an Ultraman, but in the end probability says everyone wants to go to Hawaii. There's an inevitable math problem involved. You can't have 41 qualifiers when the race for which everyone is trying to qualify only has 40 slots. "And that is a concept that we as a board have been pondering for some time," Sheryl says. "[We] haven't determined how we will approach it. But with Ultraman Florida being early in the year, it may become an issue as quickly as next year."

In fact, it's already become an issue. Some of the most loyal Ultraman athletes look askew at how the only time you hear "Ultraman Hawaii" anymore is in conversations between athletes and volunteers. On official websites, news releases, and most memorabilia and merchandise, it's the Ultraman World Championships. Tracey McQuair has won the women's event at both Ultraman Canada and Ultraman UK, but not Hawaii. She raced there in 2012, coming in fourth behind Amber Monforte, Kathy Winkler, and Yasuko Miyazaki. She doesn't for a moment dispute Amber's dominance in the women's field. But she thinks that Ultraman suffers from a fixed site for the World Championships. The veterans all keep going back to Hawaii, and the other races are left to newcomers. To her mind, this creates the need for a filter. McQuair thinks that the most competitive athletes would race the other events if the world championship title was rotated between them.

It's not an unprecedented idea. Just as Ohana Loa is contending with these sorts of issues, World Triathlon Corporation announces that the world championship for its half-Iron distance 70.3–branded events will begin rotating in 2014. For years, WTC has struggled to keep its own Kona championship qualifiers stocked with top-flight professional athletes. To the extent possible, the athletes most favored to win that race compete as little as possible to stay fresh for the big event. Instead of breaking themselves down at multiple races trying for relatively small cash purses, they instead put all their eggs in the Kona basket and compete only enough to maintain fitness and their credentials as professionals. World champions used to stay almost completely out of the spotlight until it was time to defend their title.

This created a PR problem for WTC. So they instituted the Kona Points Rankings system, in which final standings in different races were given a points value, and then an athlete's total at the end of the season would determine if he or she qualified for one of the pro slots. Its 70.3-mile races were added to the points system to encourage athletes to make appearances at those events. The company put on the additional requirement that all athletes, regardless of their finish in Kona, had to complete one 140.6-mile race between world championship races to ensure athletes didn't rack up points while dodging the longer races.

This had humorous consequences. Less than a month after she wins the 2013 Ironman World Championship in Kona, professional triathlete Mirinda Carfrae is spotted walking on the Ironman Florida marathon course. She finishes in 24th place, only four spots from dead last. They said she had to race, but no one said how fast. No matter what type of system you institute, it will always have systemic flaws. Maybe Carfrae makes it look like a joke, but at least WTC gets what it wants: pros showing up to races and engaging the public. But WTC gives no signal that the Ironman championship will move away from Hawaii, and no industry insider is willing to bet it will. There's too much history and mystique wrapped up in the place now. The first three rules in business are location, location, location. Ironman stumbled onto the goose that laid golden eggs when it landed in Kona. Not that it's without consequences. Geography dictates that Kona will always be an exclusive location. If you want to get into the Ironman, you have to be fast. If you want to get into Ultraman, you've got to be genuine.

Similarly, Sheryl has no intention of rotating the title. It's not so much a business decision for her as a personal one. "I don't think [rotating the World Championships] is something we will consider. UMFL is already full, so no need to help them. The World Championships will always be in Hawaii as far as I am concerned since this is the original and longest running. No need to move it as far as I can tell," she says.

All of this leads to a more fundamental question: Why even have a world championship race to begin with? Vito Bialla bestowed the label on the race during his two-year tenure. It was part of his broader strategy to make it a for-profit venture. The idea of a world championship has a sense of gravitas and allure. Who wouldn't love to take a penalty kick in Old Trafford or hoist the Stanley Cup?

Though Bialla's attempt to go big went belly-up, the name stuck. No one really gave it much thought. Maybe they should have. Alexandre Ribeiro is a sponsored professional. Christian Isakson is bringing some sponsors with him to Hawaii this year, as will a few others. Hillary Biscay is doing interviews with the triathlon press about her return to the event. A big part of the journey documented in Rich Roll's best-selling book, *Finding Ultra*, is about competing in Ultraman. ESPY winner Jason Lester has partially built his reputation on finishing the event, which he has parlayed into his own race-organizing business, putting on events like the Epic5. But no one ever talks about Canada or Wales or Florida. As much as Sheryl hates the idea of Ultraman becoming a WTC-style "corporate monster," imitating the Ironman model with a world championship and a qualifier system may leave Ultraman open to that prospect.

Making that slope even more slippery are the unacknowledged, dollar-sign shaped gates everyone must pass through on the way to Ultraman Hawaii. Athletes strongly depend on family members and local enthusiasts to volunteer as crew, which defrays some expenses. But vehicles, gas, food, and airfare add up to a hefty sum. And then you have to consider that many athletes stay in Hawaii for the two weeks around the race. Michael Brown estimates that his total bill was about $15,000 (Canadian) to race in Hawaii, while he spends about $8,500 to race Canada.

There are more than a few people at every race who can write a check for the whole thing, but people like Amber, Hillary, and Christian Isakson count their pennies to make their budget. The entry fee is currently $1,600, and it may have to increase again based on local expenses. However, there are more financial considerations than outside expenses. Just as with Ultraman UK, Ohana Loa requires expansion race directors to pay the travel costs of one board member to come and observe the race each year. Both Hawaii and Canada also throw a catered prerace breakfast and a postrace awards banquet. Jane rents a large conference room at the Kona Sheraton. It's humble compared to the Mardi Gras atmosphere the day after Ironman wraps up, but by 1980s Ultraman standards it's an elegant affair. Back then, the postrace banquet was a potluck dinner in a local public park. Sheryl and Dave don't see that as a possibility anymore. With 40 athletes, their crews, families, and dozens of race volunteers, the group is just too unwieldy to organize everyone to bring enough food to feed the entire group. Even the meal at the day-three finish line is catered these days. In its own way, Ultraman has gotten a little more corporate and monstrous over the years. Monsters don't manage themselves, and cages cost money.

Again, people differ on how to fix this. The Cobbs compare expanding the race series to driving a car at night. You can't go faster than your headlights and brakes will allow. More enthusiastic athletes want to set course for the second star to the right and drive straight on till morning. But whether it's expanding the number of races or managing the prices of existing ones, Dave and Sheryl face the same underlying problem. They're not Jane. Jane has always been Ultra Mom. Sheryl wears the badge of the bad cop, and she's going to wear it so long as there are people racing the event who remember her that way. Sheryl readily admits it was a deliberate decision to assume that role. The question now is whether she can transition into a new role just as deliberately. Time is on her side. Jane doesn't anticipate giving up the race in the near future. Sheryl has a lot of convincing to do, though. Tony Horton and Nick Mallett worry that Sheryl is too controlling to let them put the Australian race together. Cory Foulk says she's had it in for him ever since she married Dave. Others think she shows Cory favoritism. Ultraman is a small community. It has small-town drama.

Ironically, the most objective member of the cast may be the one who Sheryl turned away. Michael Brown tempers his hard-charging business acumen with all the humility and pleasantness of Jane. He's also, like Sheryl, an unabashed pragmatist. His personality is augmented by the fact that he has experience running a race. In 2009, he bought the Great White North Triathlon from its owner. Brown threw himself into the event, boosting its popularity by pulling in new sponsors and advertising. Brown's only financial goal for the race is to have enough profit from it to defray his Ultraman fees. If there's anything more than that, he puts the money back into the race to keep registration fees low for the athletes. Occasionally, he doles out slots to athletes he knows can't afford to pay those fees. One of them was Jeff Simons, an up-and-coming athlete who wound up winning the event. He used the prize money to boost his career and finish third in the Ironman 70.3 World Championships in 2011. Simons' girlfriend worked on Brown's support crew during Ultraman this year.

Brown's pubs and rugby tournaments are much more lucrative operations. He puts on the race for fun. Then again, that's why he runs every business he does. He likes to joke that he loved playing rugby, so he runs a tournament; he loves to drink and eat, so he runs pubs; and when he found out he loved triathlon, he started running his own. Then he fell in love with Ultraman, so it was just natural to try and run one of those, too. But even a country the size of Canada isn't big enough for two Ultraman races. He got an idea. "They love ultra-racing in New Zealand," he says. "They have these coast-to-coast races there where you run, kayak, and mountain bike. The Speight beer company gives a ton of money to sponsor that race. New Zealand sponsorship deals are crazy."

The combination of popularity and money made it an ideal location in his mind. And it didn't take him long to find high rollers willing to back an Ultraman. When he presented his plan to Jane and the Ohana Loa board in Hawaii in 2012, he guaranteed that the entire thing was financially secure. He paid them $3,000 that day. (The fee was mandatory for a race proposal. Ohana Loa uses it to file for copyright and trademark requests for the Ultraman logo and name in the country of the proposed race—another lesson learned from experiences with Simon Smith.)

Michael went the extra mile to show his commitment. "I was willing to put $60,000 in a bank account for the race. Even if only one person signed up, they'd get all their money," he says. He didn't stop there. Michael is nothing if not an enthusiast. Prior to his arrival, he'd already secured support from several high-level endurance officials and organizers in New Zealand. The head of the country's ultra-running association had signed on to work as run course captain, and the bike course director was the organizer of numerous long-distance cycling events. Even Scott Molina, the only athlete ever to win both the Ironman and Ultraman World Championships—and a New Zealand native—was on board. Michael also wanted to make New Zealand as much a holistic cultural experience as Hawaii. "We had this plan to get New Zealand Maori warriors to come out and do a tribal dance before the race start," he says.

It sounded like a slam dunk. But in the end, Michael thinks his enthusiasm worked against him. "I even had polo shirts made up with ULTRAMAN NEW ZEALAND written on them for the presentation. I think they saw Consuela and Trung as these really down-to-earth people, and then I came in there hard-charging with some money and it really intimidated them. They also asked me how I felt about another race 'in the southern hemisphere.' I told them that I'd heard about Tony's idea for Australia and that I knew Tony. I thought it was wrong to set us up as competitors, and I told them that I could see Tony and I working together and that we could make ours the busiest two Ultraman races. But I don't think they liked it. I told them that I was already planning to go on a vacation trip to New Zealand in February, and that I'd like to do some planning while I was there so I wanted to know if this thing was a go ahead of time. And they just never got back to me," he recalls. He stayed in contact with the board for several months, emailing them in December to tell them that a large company had shown strong interest in sponsoring the event and was prepared to sign a letter of commitment. For the first time, an Ultraman event stood to have legitimate financial and local support. Yet there was no response from Jane or Sheryl.

Michael finally got his answer through a post on the Ultraman Facebook page announcing the new Florida race while he was traveling with a rugby team. He was disappointed that he hadn't received the courtesy of an advance notice, and told Steve Brown as much in an email. Steve wrote back to apologize for the board's failure to notify him, and copied Jane and Sheryl on the message. Neither woman provided a further response.

Eventually, he did get a message saying that Ohana Loa was interested in putting on an Ultraman in New Zealand—in 2015. It was a failure to launch in Mike's view. He wrote back to the board, telling them that he was scrapping the idea of association. "I mean, they wanted me to wait for two years," he says. "I've got stuff ready to go *now*, and they just want me to sit on it? What was I supposed to tell the sponsors? No one in business puts something like that on ice for two years. And I had a kid on the way and a bunch of bars to run. I can't just sit still. I'd rather be making things happen. I've been in business a long time. And I've learned in business that if you don't feel right about something, it's probably better to walk away sometimes. And I didn't have a good feeling."

While the choice between Michael and Consuela was difficult, the criteria and methods by which the board went about making it are odd. There are consequences to eschewing the behavior of a corporate monster. Why was there such worry about putting two races so close to each other in a region of the world that is so enthusiastic about endurance racing, but little concern about staging a second race in North America? Jane feels that Florida is much more accessible to Mexican and South American athletes, which will hopefully make up for any entrants it loses to Canada. But competition is a two-way street. There are three Canadians signed up for the Florida race. There are also 21 Americans, and while most of them hail from Florida, there are a few coming in from places like Colorado and Oregon, which are decidedly closer to Penticton. Steve Brown has had enough registrants in the past few years that he's had to turn away nearly 10 applicants every year. Everyone on the board also believes that because the Canadian race happens in August and the Florida race is scheduled for the last weekend in February, athletes would have enough time to compete in both if they so chose. Yet given the damage to the body and the wallet, it's debatable if that's a realistic expectation.

In the end, the board's choice came down to one underlying issue. Consuela is hosting an event literally in her backyard, and Mike was almost halfway around the world from his proposed location. "It would have made a great destination race, and we're sure it would have filled," says Sheryl. "But we were really hesitant about Mike trying to plan an event from so far away. Sway and Trung were ready to go. They had the body of volunteers ready to make it happen," Sheryl says. These predominantly come from athletes in Consuela's triathlon club. They're people she knows well and sees on a daily basis. Though Mike's contacts were arguably more experienced, the board viewed them *only* as contacts. "These were people Mike had networked with online," Sheryl remembers. "He didn't have a personal relationship [with them]. So he was going to depend on people he didn't really know to do a lot of the legwork for him, and I was really hesitant about that. Simon Smith lived in London and could drive to Wales, and it was still all screwed up. I was really worried that Mike wouldn't be able to react to situations that cropped up." Mike's done well with his bars, races, and rugby tournaments this far, but in the end it wasn't a risk they were willing to take. It's a matter of divergent philosophies. Mike believes in effective delegation of responsibility; Jane and Sheryl believe in the personal touch.

Insisting on the personal touch was actually the reason word didn't get back to Mike. For all their drawbacks, corporate monsters do have some evolutionary advantages, such as clearly defined responsibilities among the staff. The board decided two weeks after Mike and Consuela made their proposals. What wasn't agreed upon was whose job it was to actually inform Mike and Consuela. "This is one of the issues we have as a board," says Sheryl. "After the meeting, no one volunteered to send the message to them. And when no one volunteers to do something, no one does it. And if someone does volunteer to do something, it's either me or Dave volunteering and we wind up doing all the work of the board." This is the price Sheryl pays for being Jane's right hand. She's always the go-to woman, but sometimes she gets used a little like a crutch. Jane's daughter and granddaughters came to visit shortly afterward, and Steve's mother and father became ill, requiring him to see them on urgent notice. Then the holidays happened and the business of notification just got lost in the mix. Sheryl sent Mike an email the day before she made the announcement, but he didn't get it before the social-media announcement. It further aggravated Sheryl when Steve apologized to Mike. "The way he wrote his email, it was like he was saying that he was sorry for what happened but he also thought 'the board' should apologize. And my immediate reaction was, 'Gee, Steve. Aren't you part of the board? Why can't you apologize on its behalf?' It was like he didn't want to assume any responsibility. So I let his message stand as the board's collective apology."

Mike harbors no hard feelings over it. Ironically, the same business-centric outlook that might have turned Sheryl off to him is also what makes him the most copacetic of all the people who ever tried to get involved in running an Ultraman race. For him, Ultraman New Zealand was just a business deal that didn't work out. He still loves the race and what it means to him. It's for that reason his misgivings about the future of Ultraman sound the most reasonable.

"These people were supposed to be my partners and they weren't responding," he says. "To be fair, they never said they weren't willing to do it. They just said they wanted to wait two years. It just wasn't working. I like them. They're good people. They're just not businesspeople. There's an element of business in races. And a rule of business is that if you don't evolve, you get left behind. You don't have to lose the tradition of Ultraman, but there's nothing wrong with making money. And if you make money, there's nothing wrong with putting it back into your race so your race is better. If you're satisfied with what you have, you're inviting mediocrity. You should always want to improve, to evolve.

"Someone is going to come along with some dough, and put together some ultra-distance triathlons, because that's what's next. Thirty years ago, there were only 15 people doing Ironman. Today there are hundreds of thousands. And out of that number there's a large group of people looking for the next thing."

Mike's disdain for mediocrity echoes Valerie Silk's determined pursuit of excellence. Ironman made evolutionary leaps and bounds under her watch, but what it evolved into is what some today call a corporate monster. Therein lies the question. Is the monster only one of endless possible outcomes of the pursuit of excellence, or is it the only inevitable consequence of success in following a business model? Sheryl doesn't want to find out. But her decisions and views are shaped more by how she believes Ultraman should do business rather than how it shouldn't. Ohana Loa doesn't have reams of company policy memos, and that leads to goofs like the expansion notification, and sometimes even debacles like UMUK. What it does have are unspoken rules that Jane has developed through years of experience and which Sheryl and Dave hold as sacrosanct. Sheryl summarizes the Ultraman "corporate philosophy" with the kind of poetic bluntness you'd expect from John Wayne in a cowboy movie.

"I've never been impressed by money," she says. "Sixty thousand dollars is great, but it doesn't buy crews and paddlers. I've always believed that our races have to draw a lot of local support, and that the races should give back to the community." To make her point, she talks about going to have breakfast at Lava Java, a favorite coffee shop close to the Kona pier, with Amber Monforte and Martin Raymond, both of whom arrived early in advance of the 2013 race. "Just sitting there eating breakfast with them, someone overhears the conversation about the race and asks if we need volunteers. And just like that, I've got one more paddler for the swim. That's how it works here, and that's how we want it to work at our other races." It's a pretty ambitious idea considering they're well aware that no place in the world works the way Hawaii does.

Money certainly would help, though. While Ultraman stabilized financially after 2001, it's still not on what you'd call a rock-solid foundation. As the race series expands, the Cobbs' to-do list as board members grows while they maintain the responsibilities as primary operators of the Hawaii race. They love to do it, but they also have to work at regular jobs to pay their bills. Man can't live on bread alone, but he does need the bread. Dave occasionally comments that he'd love for the race to make enough money so he and Sheryl could work on it full-time.

Sheryl herself remarks that their own work lives figure heavily into Ultraman's expansion. Ohana Loa requires board members to travel to all the races, and there are only so many weeks a year that one or the other of them can get away from their day jobs. Even with Jane and Steve covering some of the events, the addition of Australia already approaches the limit of how much ground the four can cover. So long as they keep the field limited to 40 athletes and the race series to four events, there will be a severe limit on the possibilities. The primary solution up to this point has been to raise the entry fee. It was $1,600 for this year's race. Though the registration fee alone is already double that of an Ironman race, an $8,000 to $10,000 race effort is still manageable for a wide variety of athletes. It's more difficult for some than others, but those who are genuinely committed enough find a way to do it. Even as costs rise, Sheryl is confident they won't lose participants.

"You know, NBC is broadcasting its Ironman show this weekend, and Jane and Dave and I never watch it," she says. "You know why? Because it just looks so foreign to us. The way they present it on television is nothing like what we experience. Besides, we were *there*. I don't need to see it again. I guarantee you that 99 percent of the people who were there watch it just to see if they got on NBC." That's the thing about yuppies to her. "They want to be seen. And nobody sees our race. We don't get the ego culture because we're not highlighting ourselves. When we get together and have breakfast with our athletes, we don't ask each other about how many miles we've run or what diet we're on. We don't talk about sports at all. Our friendship is deeper than that. That's what makes this special."

Special enough in her mind that she doesn't worry about Mike Brown's predictions of competing race series. "I'm sure other people will build other races. They already are. Let them. Other races will have the distance, but they still won't be Ultraman. Some people do our race, and then another event like a double-Iron and we never see them again because they decide they like that format. Others do the other events and come back because they decide they like what we have," she says. In other words, they don't view themselves as a business. They're an incorporated group of caretakers. That which is to be taken care of always comes before the corporation. And they do things the way they do because that's how they keep the people that they want to keep. Some things are meant to evolve; Ultraman is meant to stay the same.

The catch is that, as much as Sheryl may dislike it, Mike is right about a few things. Florida changes things. Australia will change things. That Sheryl isn't the same as Jane already does and will continue to change things. Sustainment, growth, competition, predators, and maybe one or two parasites—it's a jungle out there, and there's no limit to the new dilemmas that might crop up. The same week that she finds a new support kayaker during her breakfast, Sheryl discovers that Cory Foulk is ramping things up on his UB515 Brazilian race. He's running afoul of Jane's good graces and perhaps copyright law, too. The name is different, but the distances and rulebook are straight rip-offs of Ultraman, right down to the emphasis on "Aloha, ohana, and kokua." On top of that, Steve Brown and Tony Horton are also coming in for the race to discuss developments with Australia. Steve has been talking about a new expansion race in Europe again. He's afraid the Simon Smith blight will spread.

There are endless possibilities to face. How is Sheryl going to deal with all of them? "I don't know the answers right now," she says.

chapter fourteen

Bleeding Deacons
and Minotaurs

"You spend a good piece of your life gripping a baseball and in the end it turns out that it was the other way around all the time."

—*Jim Bouton*

CORY FOULK GETS ONLY 150 MILES into the Race Around Ireland before he quits. He breaks every night to sleep instead of riding through the dark like the other participants, which means he falls behind by 75 miles each day and almost assures he won't finish before the time cutoff. But even in daylight the weather is cold and rainy, and on the third day he decides to pack it in instead of putting up with the misery.

Since the 2012 Ultraman, all he has on his race résumé is a DNF in the Hawaii swim and a DNF in an ultra-cycling event. Sheryl denies his application for Ultraman 2013. He's going to miss his shot at setting a record, as well as the race's 30th anniversary. He has no one but himself to blame for the position he's in, but he's going to blame everyone else anyway. He first says that he wants to regroup and try Ireland again because the race is "impossibly hard," a statement that's backed by the previous year's result of only three finishers out of a field that began with 13. But then he later claims he's angry with the organizers for extending the time cutoff by an extra 12 hours, which allowed a total of seven participants to finish in official time.

"That is such a letdown," he complains by email. "I had thought I had found an event that rose above that type of thing, and was truly a difficult test. To start expanding cut-offs so everyone gets an award bothers me. It is like having 500 walkers in the Leadville 100 - like they do today. Why not call it a walk, instead of a run? It used to be 40 people who could run that far. Now RAI is the same as all of the other feel good events - I have to find something else." He doesn't explain why the time extension makes the event less challenging.

Ultraman suddenly turns into sour grapes for him as well. "I think am going to do the UMWC on my own. they already have my money, they can keep it. I will just do the race without the banquet and other stuff. Their hard and fast rule about 'having to have completed an Ultraman event to be able to compete in the [world championships]' is BS. Dene Sturm never did an Ultraman and they let her in even after they are full this year. Wendy Minor [a longtime Ultraman volunteer who raced the event in 2010] never did an Ultraman and they let her in. So they make the rules up and enforce them how they want and since I am not a friend of Gary [Wang] I am out. I will just start doing the race on my own, it is less BS anyway."

What's ironic is that a handful of the Ultraman faithful outside of Hawaii think that it's Cory you have to be friends with in order to stay in the good graces of Jane and the Cobbs. It's an aspect of his natural ability to generate mystique. He's been around for so long that he's almost an institution within Ultraman, and he does little to discourage the propagation of that idea. The problem is that he's bought into it himself.

Cory digs in on the Dene issue. "The rules are the rules, and I had no trouble with not being allowed in because they were following the rules. One thing you learn about scofflaws like me—we know the penalty and usually have no trouble when breaking a rule, getting caught and having to pay. However, immediately after telling me that they couldn't allow me in because of the rules, they dropped the rule about having to finish an Ultraman and allowed Dene in. Rules are either rules or they aren't is all I am saying. why bother having them if it is all discretionary? Just say 'hey, it is entirely up to us to decide if we want you in and leave it at that.' Yes, Dene does qualify on the volunteer count. I wish her the best, she is a nice person doing a triathlon change of life thing," he writes.

He wants to say that it's about how the rules were applied to others, but really this is about him. It's an extreme change of tone from a man who holds a semilegendary reputation in both Ironman and Ultraman culture as a tie-dyed Loki. The bitterness and anger he displays is the antithesis of a philosophy he's promoted in the context of his entrant biography on the Ultraman webpage, which hasn't changed in years:

> Entering Ultraman because: Of the two iterations of "old timers" in triathlon—"elder statesman" or "bleeding deacon," I strive for the first. My task is to introduce new people to our sport while participating with as much grace as I can muster. To hold the oral history of this sport and pass it on.

He holds a lot of history. He also holds a place in it. One of his most legendary feats in Ironman history is recounted again in the pages of *Triathlete* magazine's September 2013 issue. He's a luminary among both Ironman and Ultraman's old guard. That's what makes it so odd. Now that he has accumulated such a wealth of accomplishments and notoriety, he seems to be the most sullen. He's playing out the fate of the original Ironman pros: the old racehorse in the autumn of his years, snorting at the track from behind his pasture fence. His differences with Jane and Sheryl stem from a point of view that doesn't entirely square up with reality. He talks repeatedly about the internecine politics of Ultraman and Gary Wang's influence over the system. It's somewhat a consequence of a madcap life spent living by his own rules—most of which are made up to suit whatever situation he finds himself in.

Foulk was born in 1958 in Boulder, Colorado. He was an exceptional athlete and student from an early age. From the high school swim and soccer teams to spending free time on his dirt bike and playing "bicycle hockey" with friends in the winter, he was always looking for new ways to entertain and challenge himself. He was selected to attend the United States Air Force Academy in Colorado Springs. But what was not accounted for in his academic and athletic honors was his resentment of authority. The Air Force and Cadet Foulk quickly realized that they fit together like the proverbial square peg and round hole.

He quit after his first year and enrolled at the University of Colorado in Boulder, where he earned a double major in molecular biology and aerospace engineering. Despite his course load, he found time for outdoor recreation. He worked as a lifeguard at the Boulder Reservoir, raced bikes, and skied whenever the opportunity presented itself. But it was at the Mile High Marathon in Denver where he found his lifelong passion for endurance sports. After trying to keep pace with the race leaders for the initial miles—with relatively little training—he stubbornly held on to finish in agony. He spent the next few days in bed. It was a point of departure. Endurance racing was the life for him.

Instead of getting into a profession more in line with his academic focus, Foulk traveled to San Diego in 1979 and took work as a sailing instructor. San Diego was a landmark in the early endurance racing movement. The climate allowed for year-round racing, and the open-minded culture accommodated people exploring new distances and race formats. Foulk's neighbor and running partner had a daughter with something of a wild streak. After a drunk-driving incident kept her from graduating high school on time, her father sent her to a convent in Kona to tame her ways. Cory was one of the few people the girl knew well enough to reach out to, so she began writing letters to him. Maybe it was her descriptions of Hawaii's natural beauty that captivated his imagination, or perhaps the desperation of her captivity garnered his sympathy. Either way, Cory's ultimate decision to move to Hawaii was propelled by his characteristic spontaneity. He quit his job at the sailing outfit, bought a one-way ticket, and with little more than his surfboard and a hundred dollars to his name, got on a plane to Hawaii.

The airline charged him an extra 15 dollars to fly the surfboard, landing him in Kona with 85 bucks. He spent his first night in Hawaii sleeping in some bushes near the King Kamehameha Hotel. The next morning he went for a run and discovered a tree house behind a recently burned-down home on Ali'i Drive. The plumbing still worked well enough for him to shower under the garden hose and the tree house was more than adequate shelter. With housekeeping set up, he went into town and found employment as a deck hand for a glass-bottom boat tour company. He had no rent, a job, and still a few months before he had to start paying back his student loans. "I was 20 years and 10 months old, and the world was out there," he remembers. "Wow." Having secured the foundations of his new life, he turned his attention to his original goal. From his Neverland tree fort, Peter Pan drew his plans to rescue Wendy from the convent.

That required gaining the confidence of a nun he remembers as Sister Victor. Armed with his talent for self-deprecating humor and his positive outlook on life, he earned her trust and convinced her to let the girl out of the convent on weekdays to help him at his job. After she proved herself trustworthy and Cory wrote to her father in California, Sister Victor allowed her to take a job at the local Kentucky Fried Chicken. The story played out as happily as it could given the free-spirited nature of its protagonists. "She turned 18 and was free from the convent. We took up as roommates and lovers and really had a good time for a year or so. Then she took off to Australia to surf and I focused on working and running mostly," he remembers.

Though everlasting romance didn't blossom in the tree house, Cory discovered the same intoxicating love of the island that keeps so many Kona visitors from leaving. He moved into more traditional quarters, started working with a company that caught tropical fish, and immersed himself in the native and athletic cultures. He also started working as a draftsman on the side, working over designs for local businesses. People who saw his work encouraged him to take the exam to become a licensed architect. Without any formal education, Foulk passed the multiday exam on his first try. Throughout all of this, he continued to train and race as a swimmer, cyclist, and runner. Yet he still hadn't competed in a triathlon.

That changed when Ironman came to town in 1981. Foulk gladly volunteered when his running club solicited help in manning an aid station. He watched throughout the day as the parade of oddballs and athletes streamed past. Scott Tinley finished third that day. He was beaten by John Howard, a three-time Olympic cyclist (1968, 1972, 1976). The next year Howard would go on to finish second in the Great American Bike Race, pedaling from Santa Monica to the Empire State Building in just more than 10 days. In 1985 he set a land speed record of 152.2 miles per hour by pedaling directly behind a car on the salt flats of Utah. But as extraordinary as people like Tinley and Howard were, the icons of counterculture impressed Cory the most. In a 2011 interview with Timothy Carlson on triathlon website Slowtwitch.com, he reminisced on one particular moment that drew him toward the sport.

> It was 2am and you could hear a song by The Knack coming out of the darkness. Sure enough, this guy rides in from Hawi on a bicycle with a boom box in the front basket carrying a five pack of beer and a pack of Marlboros.... It was some younger guy who got off, had a smoke, chatted us up, drank a beer and rode off.... I don't know if this guy even finished the run or if it mattered to him. I think back in those times it was just about participating. It wasn't 'God I've got to finish hell or high water because I told everyone I would!' It

was just a couple of wing nuts who showed up on a Saturday to do something they had never done before. I really liked the whole group it attracted.

Two summers would pass before he finally entered his first triathlon, the Keauhou half Ironman, in 1983. He raced several other off-distance, off-brand, and off-kilter events. Some of his favorite races were run by Scott Tinley. The best came at a relay triathlon. Foulk remembers that Tinley's habit was to write down the race rules on a piece of paper shortly before the start. At this particular event, the rules said that the athlete performing the bike or run segment of the race had to wait until their teammate doing the previous event tagged them before starting. As the race started, one team's swimmer stepped back from the water as the others plunged in. He asked Tinley, "The rules don't say we have to finish before we tag our teammates, right?" Tinley looked at his paper and confessed to having created the loophole. The other teams watched in dismay as the swimmer and his cohorts quickly tagged each other and went off to finish their respective events simultaneously. By then, the other swimmers were too far out to hear their friends shouting at them to come back.

The same sort of hijinks ensued at other races. Foulk and others routinely turned signs in the wrong direction on various courses, though knowing such tricks were played many of the athletes often deliberately went in the opposite direction the signs indicated. This was the type of crazy, seat-of-your-pants environment Cory grew up in, and he loved it. The 1980s and early 1990s were the formative years for both the sport and that first generation of athletes. As anarchic races nurtured his own antiauthoritarian nature, Ironman and other events became more rigid, formalizing their rules and strengthening the corporate structures that had come to own them. A clash of institution and individual was inevitable. And it was that one-man revolt that made Cory famous. The spark occurred during the 1995 Hawaiian Ironman. Cory stopped during the bike leg to help another athlete change a flat tire. A course official pulled up and threatened to disqualify him for breaking rules forbidding giving outside aid to others. He remembers coming back to the transition area and suddenly noticing how things had changed. "There was a lot of 'rah rah' you can do it, with hyper music and stuff. It was a lot different from the original vibe," he says. The memories stuck with him. At another race the next year he got into a discussion with athletes complaining about how expensive racing gear had become. The idea for Foulk's protest was born: he would race the Ironman on a $20 budget. His bike would be a junked-up Schwinn beach cruiser he pulled from a Dumpster. He spray-painted it like a hippie wagon and brought it to the race.

Course officials were speechless when he brought the bike to registration. First they told him that he couldn't have a bike with a kickstand. But then they found that the width of the cruiser's tires kept him from putting it in the special racks used to hold athletes' bikes while they swim and run, so they told him to put the kickstand back on. Weighing three times as much as any other bike on the course, Cory had a hard go of it but still made the cutoff with less than 10 minutes to spare. To stay underbudget, he skipped buying shoes and ran the marathon barefoot.

It was the bike gag that got all the attention, though. The local press ate it up. WTC officials were apoplectic. Cory demonstrated that Ironman's original counterculture was still very much alive and able to rear its head. In response, WTC redoubled its efforts to tie the beast down. The next year they made two new rules for the race: athletes had to wear shoes and could not ride beach cruisers. This was a competitive event with professional racers and television coverage. A bunch of kooks on beach cruisers upstaging that image hurt the brand. Cory claims he was banned from the event, but there is no evidence that he was. It's a small, unnecessary embellishment to an already amazing story. But that's Cory for you. As exceptional as the true story is, he has a habit of adding just a pinch of exaggeration to it.

That was more than 15 years ago. Cory hasn't had any spectacular adventures in Ironman since. There's been the Ultraman streak, but that's largely occurred outside the spotlight. And now even that may be at an end. It's up to Cory. He seems to have other ideas, though. His conspiracy theories about Gary Wang, Jane, and the Cobbs reach new levels of intrigue. Cory says that Ironman isn't fringe enough. The more he talks, the more it sounds like he believes Ultraman has become as commercial as Ironman. He'll "bandit" the race—meaning he'll compete alongside the others without registering— or otherwise finish Ultraman unofficially just so Gary Wang "will have an asterisk beside his name" on the record for most finishes in history. It's an odd belief, considering David Cobb is the one who maintains the records on the official website and would have no reason to insert the caveat. But that oddity aligns well with Cory's favorite claims about his racing career. He brags often about the number of races from which he's been banned, and how he entered anyway under the pseudonym Duke Raoul, directly referring to Hunter S. Thompson's *Fear and Loathing in Las Vegas* alter ego, Raoul Duke. Normally, people who engage in the practice of "banditing" races do not bother to register. Foulk's choice to do so, and to use such an obvious name, simultaneously exhibits his disdain for what he considers dim-witted authorities and his outsized view of himself.

Now he seeks to take that vision even further. Beyond taking an unsanctioned role in this year's Ultraman, he's starting the UB515 race. He's even trying to get Curtis Tyler to join him and put his official stamp of approval on the race as having "the true spirit" of the race he created. It's no longer enough for Cory to be the hero in his own movie. Feeling as though his discipleship to Ultraman has been betrayed, he wants to start his own religion.

Strangely, the one taking the most punishment in Cory's Ultra-manifesto is the one most sympathetic to his circumstances. Gary Wang couldn't care less about the record for most finishes. Between his 45 years and the demanding pace of his job, he'll be happy if he can just finish without incident and qualify to race next year. Even if he didn't, he'd probably come back and crew for someone. When he starts hearing the things Cory has said about him, he downplays it. "You have to understand, Cory has not always had a happy life. He gets like this sometimes, and he always gets better. This won't last, and when it's over we'll go for a run or something," Wang says. The way he says it sounds routine, as if he's explaining the plot of a movie he's seen a thousand times. Maybe he has. He doesn't offer many details. He doesn't want to say anything insensitive about his friend, and the conversation turns elsewhere.

Cory's not the first to go this route. After he retired from Ironman racing in 2007, three-time champion Peter Reid dropped off the radar completely. His three championships came with a horrible toll of self-imposed seclusion, doubt, and bouts of depression. He was supposed to board a plane to Kona for the Ironman championships as part of a publicity appearance for a sponsor on the day when he suddenly disappeared. He resurfaced two years later, working as a bush pilot on the western fringe of Vancouver Island. The vanishing act had been necessary for him to sort himself out and start anew.

None of this would have surprised former Ironman champ Scott Tinley. After he left professional racing, his own sense of despair drove him to study the phenomenon of depression among retired professional athletes. The effort lasted eight years and produced a dissertation and a book. He still couldn't find a way to go back to Kona until a few more years had passed. When San Diego Chargers Hall of Famer Junior Seau committed suicide in 2012, Tinley wrote a piece in *Sports Illustrated* that spoke from both academia and the heart. Of himself, he writes, "Navigating in the rear-view mirror, I now realize that I retired too late, too tired. And while I left professional sports in 1999 at 42 years old with nearly 100 career victories, two World Ironman Championships, and enough money to last two years, I still had no idea how hard it would be to become a regular guy."

There are other variations on the trend. Nick Mallet carries a significant amount of angst against the state of contemporary triathlon culture and business. It's common knowledge in the Ultraman community that you don't get him started about World Triathlon Corporation's management of the Ironman brand. He is one of the most frequent posters on the online forum for Slowtwitch, and his conversations regularly turn into lengthy, wide-ranging indictments of just about anyone that makes money through their involvement with the sport. In person and in any other conversation, Nick is a nice guy, but when it comes to the business side of triathlon, he can't hold back. Most people can relate to the joke that "the older I get, the better I was." For some, however, the older they get, the worse everything around them is. You can love a sport, but some people get into trouble by thinking it loves them back more than it really does. They imagine a kind of monogamy developing. And then one day they find out that it's been having an affair with a couple of dozen other guys all along. At first they get jealous of each other. Then ultimately they grow sour about the infidelity. Nick keeps things online, (mostly) polite, and strictly on-topic. But Cory is talking about engaging in extreme and highly inappropriate behavior in the real world. The elder statesman may well become the bleeding deacon. If Cory continues down this road, he risks winding up like the Cowman.

The Cowman is perhaps the most iconic version of this oft-repeated parable. Like Cory, he was a self-styled marauder and even somewhat of a legend in the endurance world, albeit more so in his own mind than anywhere else. His real name is Ken Shirk, but the name by which everyone knows him is "Cowman." Cowman A-Moo-Ha, to be exact, a consequence of his habit to wear a helmet with horns mounted on it while he races. Like the Ironman

The competitors gather before the Ultraman World Championships in Hawaii in 2013.

Alexandre Ribeiro and Miro Kregar, two of the favorites, played up their friendly rivalry.

Minutes before the swim on Day 1, Hillary Biscay and Amber Monforte prepare to hit the water.

The sun rises as the athletes begin the 6.2 mile swim.

Hillary Biscay became the first woman to ever lead the entire Ultraman field out of the water; moments later she tore off on her bike for the second stage.

Ken Shirk, better known as Cowman, greeted Alexandre Ribeiro after the swim.

Christian Isakson stumbled out of the water and up the beach, where his family sprang into action.

The athletes gather to begin the 90-mile ride on Day 2.

Hillary Biscay widens her lead.

Miro Kregar (top) manages a smile as he attempts to open up a lead on Alexandre Ribeiro (bottom), but his rival was in hot pursuit.

Hillary Biscay began the run on Day 3 looking to prove something to herself and her competitors.

Alexandre Ribeiro and Miro Kregar run side by side.

Hillary Biscay claims her first Ultraman World Championship.

Emotions pour out as Miro Kregar crosses the finish line.

The two champions.

itself, Shirk's idiosyncrasies earned him a small degree of immortality in Barry McDermott's fateful 1979 *Sports Illustrated* piece:

> Now, on a spooky morning on Oahu, the competitors contemplated the start of this year's Iron Man contest. Ahead were hours promising pain, mental anguish and significant physical danger. John Dunbar arrived at the starting line wearing a Superman costume sewn by the sister of one of his support crew. Also present was "Cowman," 34, a bearded 6'3" individual weighing 215 pounds who competes in distance runs while wearing "caveman pants" and a buffalo hat made of fake fur with two large cow horns protruding from it. Another fellow had on a football helmet.

The cow horns originally had nothing to do with endurance racing. It was not an attempt to create a brand or marketable identity. It wasn't even a tough-guy stunt. They were just...*there*. In the 1970s Shirk was bouncing around Lake Tahoe as an itinerant construction worker. As the United States approached its bicentennial, he prepared to celebrate in the most ostentatious exercise of liberty possible. He planned to strip naked; paint himself red, white, and blue; and run straight down the main street of his hometown. As he tells the story, he was on his way to buy fireworks when he saw the horns in an outdoor sporting goods store. He bought them on the spot. It was the only thing he wore on his bicentennial jog. For whatever reason, he got such a rush from the stunt that he began running in actual races. And wherever he competed, the horns went with him.

With that extreme sense of originality brewing under the buffalo-skin hat, Shirk grew into one of the great pioneers of American ultra-distance racing. He was just the third man to attempt and the second to finish the Tevis Cup 100-mile horse race on foot, in 1976. The publicity of his feat drew a field of 14 runners the next year. Soon after, the runners stopped competing alongside the horseback riders and ran their own race, known today as the Western States 100. It is one of the most prestigious ultra endurance events in the world and a favorite of Amber Monforte and Gary Wang, among others. It's so popular that today's athletes can only get in by a lottery entry system. Cowman, however, has a lifetime invitation to come back whenever he chooses.

Back then, Cowman never thought about becoming a legend in the ultra endurance hall of fame. There was no such thing. Western States was so fringe that it was difficult even to characterize it as counterculture or subculture. The population didn't seem to justify it. Not even the athletes really knew what to think of it. Cowman ran frequently. He competed in marathons on a monthly basis. But he wouldn't have called his regimen "training." He didn't execute meticulous plans to build his fitness leading up to events the way high-tech Olympians do today. It wasn't possible in a world where your next event might not be invented yet. Women had yet to gain entry to the major marathons. Ironman was still a few years away from being conceived, and when it was it would be considered off the charts of human possibility. Like his fellow endurance explorers, Cowman just did whatever came along that interested him. In between, he worked construction jobs in Tahoe and participated in the counterculture in whatever way struck him.

What struck him next was the Ironman. He traveled to Honolulu for that second race in 1979 and established permanent residency in Kona in 1981 when the race moved there. He got a construction job working on the Royal Sea Cliff hotel and lived the life of a free spirit, experimenting liberally with endurance races, marijuana, and people's patience. Through his connections in Ironman he heard about the new event being created in Hawaii. He signed up for the first Ultraman.

According to official records, Cowman competed in Ultraman 10 more times. He competed in the race every year until 1989 (except for 1987, when the race did not take place), at which point he went on an unexplained hiatus until his return in 1997. He was never able to accomplish an official finish again, though he tried five times—most recently in 2003. He's slowed down but he hasn't quit. He ran the 2012 Big Island International Marathon in just under six and a half hours and his most recent triathlon finish was in 2008 at the Honu Half Ironman. There's just one problem: Cowman isn't supposed to be able to get into any races. Part of his notoriety is that he actually has been banned from Ironman. He joins Lance Armstrong on the very short list of people ever to receive a permanent ban from competing in events sanctioned by USA Triathlon. If there is such a thing as an antihero in the endurance sports world, it's Cowman.

Through every event at every distance, over the mountains and through the waves, through the darkest nights and hottest days, the horns went with him.

It just became his thing, and as the participation numbers at Ironman grew so did his notoriety. The name Ken Shirk faded into obscurity and Cowman rose to institutional status in the Ironman and Hawaiian communities. He added "A-Moo-Ha" as a last name to demonstrate his solidarity with the Hawaiian principle of aloha.

But that which endeared him to the athletes and islanders made him a pariah to race organizers. It came down to the same combination that made him famous: the horns and the athletes. Ironman drew an increasing number of participants each year. And as the numbers increased, so did the crowding on the bike course. People began to worry about the potential dangers of a guy with giant cow horns riding in proximity to other cyclists on very windy roads. They asked Ken to take off the horns. He refused. For him, it wasn't about being iconic. It went to something much deeper, reaching all the way back to that first stark-naked run down Main Street.

To Ironman and USA Triathlon officials, it was mostly about safety, but there were also feelings of resentment toward his theatrics. By the 1990s the private equity investors at World Triathlon Corporation were intent on marketing a particular lifestyle to coincide with their brand. With his long, unruly beard and his choice of cotton T-shirts over contemporary synthetic materials, and those trademark horns, Cowman looked and played the part of an athlete from Ironman's formative years. To WTC, it was a liability to have someone around whose personality ran against the grain of the new image it wanted to sell. To Cowman, it was a battle between the establishment and the freedom to express one's rugged individualism. In his mind, the horns weren't so much representative of himself as they were his right to be who he was. If they could tell him to take off the horns, they could also tell him to remove the decorations he put on the T-shirts he raced in, which usually bore messages of love and hope for people in various forms of distress throughout the world. One company's pettiness is another man's principle. The conflict was a melodramatic comedy of egos.

Cowman probably fired the first shot. Sometime in the 1990s Ironman course officials told him that he would be disqualified from the race if he wore the horns. He did and he was—but he still continued to the finish line. Whether it was because of his blatant violation the year before or a failure to qualify isn't certain, but he definitely was not placed on the start list for the following year's race. Not that it stopped him. Cowman jumped into the middle of the swim from a hidden location and joined the race anyway. When he finished the swim, he returned to his spot on the sideline where he'd stashed his bike. He leapt on and went down the road with the rest of the competitors. He wore his cow horns from the moment he hit the water until he finally exited the course somewhere short of the official finish line. So began Cowman's second career as the Ironman bandit.

Banditing is a well-known and harshly viewed practice in endurance racing. In 2011, Peter Sagal, host of NPR game show *Wait, Wait... Don't Tell Me!*, jumped into the middle of the Chicago Marathon as an unregistered participant. Sagal was shocked when the endurance community demonized him overnight after writing about his caper in *Runner's World*. The biggest gripe most participants have isn't that bandits ruin the party by crashing it with overwhelming numbers, though they fear that it could encourage such behavior until the number of unofficial racers overwhelm resources. It's a matter of principle more than anything else. A bandit jumps into a race and takes water and food from aid stations that other people have paid for. A dozen or so "free-riders" don't strain the supply, but the act of taking without paying breaks faith with their fellow athletes. Banditing is essentially a form of cheating.

Cowman drew scorn from Ironman and USAT officials, but uniquely not from the actual athletes. To many, it was worth it to allow Cowman to break the rules in order for Ironman to have an unofficial mascot. He had become the race's equivalent to the Chicago Cubs' Harry Caray or the New York Jets' Fireman Ed—a character whose personality and antics made him far more visible than any outsized costume. He had more than just moral support. Though he carried enough water and food to provide for himself through most of the Ironman course, it was common practice among the local volunteers to give him anything he needed along the way. All of this only served to encourage his quixotic perspective: he was fighting the good fight against an oppressive corporate monolith, and the people had made him their champion. He was leading a revolution.

The Ironman officials were not to be outmaneuvered. They ratcheted up their complaints to Charlie Crawford, USA Triathlon commissioner of officials and former head referee at Ironman Hawaii. Exasperated with the constant back-and-forth, he finally served Cowman with papers in 2002 banning him not just from Ironman, but all USAT-sanctioned events. It was pretty anticlimactic as far as final showdowns go. Crawford spotted Cowman in the transition area mingling with the athletes and asked Peter Bourne, a competitor and volunteer in both Ironman and Ultraman who knew Cowman, to accompany him to help mediate in case an argument erupted. The two walked up to Cowman and Crawford brusquely shoved the paperwork into Cowman's hands. According to Bourne, Cowman simply read over the forms, then handed them back without a word and walked off.

He bandited the race again that year. And the next year. And the year after that. Cowman runs in the Ironman World Championships every year.

Nothing has changed. He's still a mainstay on the Ironman Hawaii course. He still runs the local marathons as an official participant and bandits the local triathlons. Because he's so well known no one bothers to stop him. There have been other changes, though. Now in his seventies, Cowman's health has taken a turn for the worse. He has some circulation problems, which lead to swelling in one of his legs. They've slowed him down a bit.

Additionally, his demeanor has changed dramatically. Mostly positive in interviews and in public in the past, he now goes through gloomy bouts of anger and paranoia. He appeared at the swim finish for the 2012 Ultraman for a few hours, but left after the first half dozen contestants exited the water. During that time he recorded the activity around the area with a hand held digital camera and spoke briefly to a few people. Asked about his life and thoughts on Ultraman, he broke into a lengthy oratory about the current state of Ironman and Ultraman. He called Ironman "a corporation that wants everyone to buy into their way" and said that Jane Bockus had turned Ultraman into a similar entity. They were party to a greater conspiracy whose membership and aims he couldn't articulate. He gradually began to mistake his audience's inability to understand him as dissenting opinion and abandoned the monologue. If you're not with Cowman, you're part of the problem.

Ironically, one of the most incisive observations of the rise and fall of Cowman comes from Cory. He remembers running against Ken back in the early days when he was still in his prime: "[In h]is early years he was really a special talent and spirit, but his idea of never training, smoking pot, and relying on the inner spirit led to not finishing anything. I got to see all of these guys like him turn middle aged and suddenly stop making cutoffs and so on. Not because they were injured or what have you, but because they did not honor the events they were in enough to train for them."

Perhaps the attitude was a final, inevitable manifestation of a change that occurred long ago. When he first donned the horns, Ken Shirk had only meant for them to express the idea of individuality and the wild abandon so often mistaken for craziness that is the lifeblood of ultra endurance. They were never an integral part of him until he decided that they were. For all the fame associated with the role of Cowman, there was a time when the actor and the character were easily distinguishable. Now he has trouble keeping the two separate. He talks about writing a book about his life. It's evident in the way he reconstructs history that he believes his life and legacy are defined by his rebellion against the structure of Ironman and Ultraman. But the tone of his voice betrays his doubt that it was worth anything and a fear that no one will remember.

Cory can still back out of his plans. He's told no one about his intention to bandit. And after a streak like his, maybe a year off is just what he needs. After Ireland, he can just tell everyone it's been an off year. No one would think less of him. He'd be missed, in fact. But something about his tone says he won't. Maybe he doesn't believe he can or he doesn't know how. Or maybe it's something even he doesn't understand, or would admit to even if he did.

After the harangue he lobbed toward Jane in the presence of others at the 2012 race, Ken was remarkably demure when he approached her to ask for a ticket to the postrace banquet, just as he does every year. And, just as she has every time he's asked her, Jane granted his request. Such charity is characteristic of her, but there's more to it than that. There's nothing to be gained by taking a crippled bull by the horns. "He's harmless," she says. "Besides, it's not going to break the bank to let him in the banquet."

In this case, her graciousness is accompanied by pity. "This is all he has."

chapter fifteen

Lava, Java, and Drama

If all the year were playing holidays
To sport would be as tedious as to work.

—William Shakespeare

November 22, 2013. Chris Draper's bike is broken. Really broken. He pulls it out of its case after arriving in Kona to find that the airline baggage handlers managed to crack the frame's top tube. This is not something he can fix with duct tape and a can of WD-40. The bike is made of carbon fiber, a sophisticated material used in everything from Ferraris to fighter jets. It starts out as thin filaments, gets woven into the shape you want, and is then baked solid in a kiln. The advantage is that it's very strong for its weight. The disadvantage is that it's susceptible to impact and very expensive. It is possible to repair the break, but it requires a skilled hand.

He puts an SOS message on the Ultraman Facebook page, asking if anyone knows of a repairman on the island. Jane does. The man believes he can remedy the issue, but he'll have to see it firsthand before he's sure. Chris schedules an appointment to meet with the repairman and shows up at his place on time. After waiting a while, the guy finally sends a text message reading, "In the mountains, will be late coming down. How about we do it tomorrow?"

Keeping his good humor, Chris relays this development to the Facebook group that's asking how things are going. Hillary Biscay immediately responds, "Island time!" It's a well-known phenomenon to those who have been to Kona that the locals don't exactly live and die by the clock. After all, there's no reason to rush when you're already in paradise. For the average local or vacationer, it's an ideal pace. But it can get a little aggravating if you're trying to organize or get ready for one of the toughest endurance races in the world. Hillary has yet to fly, and offers to bring an extra bike with her if he needs one. To his credit, Chris holds onto his cool. Twenty-four nervous hours later, the bike is road-worthy again.

The week before Ultraman is anarchic comedy at its finest. Whether the athletes arrive in Kona a few days before the event, as is Alexandre Ribeiro's habit, or several weeks beforehand, like athletes from the more frigid climes, very few of them make any real progress in the way of race prep. How can you justify spending time on bike maintenance and assembling supplies for three days of endurance racing when you can be swimming with dolphins or viewing active lava flows? For the snowbirds, the month has been well spent on getting serious outdoor training miles. But at this point long hours spent training will do more harm than good. This is the time to let the body rest and rebuild. They start "tapering," or reducing the intensity and length of their workouts. It's still pretty intense by normal standards—mile-long swims and 50-mile bike rides—but it's all relative. Still, an Ultraman athlete in repose is a rare species in this endurance-friendly environment. It's not impossible to catch one if you know where to look, though. The prime viewing area is a little restaurant right on Ali'i Drive in sight of the Kona Pier called Lava Java.

More than just a coffee shop, as the name implies, Lava Java is also an all-hours grill and bistro. Since its establishment in 1994, its location and cuisine have made it a landmark in the triathlon culture. This is your first time at Ironman? You've *got* to go to Lava Java at least once. Where should we rally for the group ride? Let's just start from Lava Java. Want to get your photo taken with some of the top pros? Lava Java. From Sheboygan to Stockholm, it is to triathlon what "the Bat" is to Yankee Stadium.

Amber Monforte and her husband, Ryan, passively scan the dinner menu at an outdoor table the Sunday before Ultraman. They're more interested in the sunset. The clouds prevent the magical green flash effect that sometimes occurs, but the red and purple hues are no less enchanting. After six years eating here between Ironman and Ultraman, they pretty much have the menu memorized anyway. They were here this morning for breakfast after a group swim with some of the other athletes. Yet they still ask for a little more time when the waitress makes her first pass. There's no rush, and there might be something they haven't tried yet. In a way, that's sort of what this entire trip is about. They're not running out of time to get ready for a third title defense, because Amber hasn't come to defend her title. The question has been hanging for a few months, but now she answers it openly.

"I'm not going to win this race." There's no doubt she's at peace with the reality. It's not about Hillary, or burnout from doing this three years in a row. It just isn't in the cards this time. She's swum, biked, and run past every twist of fate life has thrown at her over the past three years. Now they've finally caught up with her. "We did everything the books say you shouldn't do in the first year of marriage," she says with a laugh. "We moved to a new place, we changed jobs, we bought a house. And when you're the new kid on a hospital nursing staff, you go straight to the bottom on the scheduling priority. So you know what that means: *night shift*."

The topsy-turvy scheduling put their first year of marriage on a semi-chance-encounter basis. They were mostly in sync, but there were a couple of weeks when they'd go without spending quality time together for days on end. It also made sleep and training difficult for Amber, especially as winter approached. "I was basically going to work and coming home in the dark. I never saw the sun." Not being able to adjust to the rhythm was what put her thyroid out of whack. Though she didn't tell anyone, as late as September she really hadn't planned on coming to Hawaii. It was physically impossible. There was also the assumption that they'd never be able to get the time off together for the trip. But then medications helped Amber bounce back and a sympathetic supervisor made a convenient oversight in the scheduling system to grant them the vacation time. "This will probably never happen again," they were told. "Go."

So here she is once more, getting ready to do Ultraman like she'll never come back again. For some, that would mean a wild, against-all-odds attempt at a fourth win. Not for Amber. She's fought the tough battles and won the heroic victories. She'd do it again if she could, but having been there and done that she knows exactly what it takes. It's measured in miles and hours, and she doesn't have it. She'd love to go head-to-head with Hillary if she could, but trying when she's not sufficiently trained for it would be unfulfilling. It's time to find something else on the menu. If she's not going to be at the front or moving as fast, there will be more company, more time to take in the natural wonders of the course, and less urgency distracting her from them. The woman who's done nearly everything on this course will finally do the one thing she hasn't: soak it in.

Hillary, by contrast, is wound tight. She; her husband, Maik; and friend Marilyn land on Monday evening and opt out of sunset viewing to hit the local pool for a swim to work out the stress and stiffness of a day's travel. After that, it's down to business— getting everything ready for the weekend. Registration is Wednesday afternoon, allowing them little time to grab all the necessary supplies and get things arranged. For all Hillary knows, Amber is bringing her *A* game. But even that's not the foremost thought on her mind. She's thinking about 2010. She's thinking about the course, about all the things that went wrong, all the mistakes she made. This entire week will be spent checking and double-checking shopping lists, equipment, and plans. She doesn't need to win. What she needs is a great race. She talks about taking what the course dishes out without having it demolish her, but she couches it in terms of her own performance: "I'll be satisfied if I can go out there, stay in control and on top of my game. I want to be mentally *there* through the whole thing." She's not here to get even with the mountains or the lava fields. This is about settling a score with herself. Hillary's race is a contest between old wounds and new hopes, winner take all.

Christian Isakson is in the same boat as Hillary. He, Rhonda, Ian, and his daughter Evelyn get in from Portland on Tuesday morning. The preponderance of their afternoon is consumed by the task of consuming. The whole family is starving. Thankfully, Christian has heard from the other athletes about this great little restaurant on Ali'i Drive within sight of the pier. They take the same outdoor table that Ryan and Amber did two nights before. The kids are understandably excited to see the beach. Rhonda looks excited by a hammock between two palm trees. Christian is aware of their needs. He just can't help himself. He talks a mile a minute about getting to meet Alexandre Ribeiro and Miro Kregar. Ever since he decided to come to this race he's been reading up on the two titans. He's a bit starstruck. Rhonda finally tells him that he needs to get in gear if they're going to make the grocery store for supplies before hitting the hotel.

As for the titans, they don't even act like they're in a race. Miro has been going on exceptionally long rides all over the island with some of the other

European athletes. He pops up randomly all over town, always on his bike. He rides by Lava Java without stopping. Alexandre hasn't even arrived yet. He'll get in later on Tuesday, the same time as Jose Poinciano, his support crew leader for each of his last eight Ultraman endeavors. The two have been friends ever since they were in the same youth running club in Rio de Janeiro. With their combined experience and the intimate bond they share, race prep will only take a few hours. No sweat.

Dene Sturm is sweating enough for everyone. She and her boyfriend, Doug, worked out a 12-page checklist months ago, but she's still feeling anxious about details. She's been so on edge that she broke out in hives the week before the event. Just one more thing to worry about. The checklist is almost counterproductive to its own objective. Instead of making Dene agonize less over missing a crucial step, she's now constantly asking Doug what the next item to address is. Maybe there was no way to stop it at all. She doesn't realize it, but Doug has everything under control, including a few secret plans.

Jane, Sheryl, and Dave barely have enough time to catch their breath. Things are no less chaotic for them, and the pressure to bring order to it all is much greater. The reason the athletes can afford to stay relaxed is that the organizers and volunteers do much more of the worrying for them than they could possibly imagine. Registration happens on Wednesday, which gives Jane just 48 hours to turn an empty banquet hall at the Kona Sheraton into a streamlined processing station for 36 ultra athletes and their crews. Then there's the prerace breakfast and safety briefing on Thursday. Then the gun goes off at 6:30 AM on Friday. After that, chaos becomes a road show. But it'll go nowhere if Jane can't get the engine started. Not that she's worried. She's more of a pro at this than Alexandre.

Many people think that Jane has throttled back in recent years to let Sheryl and Dave do the heavy lifting for Ultraman Hawaii. In truth, she's so practiced at things that she gets everything arranged without anyone noticing. She doesn't have to give up volunteering with the local Lavaman triathlon the week beforehand, or her morning water jogging classes, or paddling with the canoe club, or the Thanksgiving luncheon the canoe club throws every year. She's in more places at once than Batman. People just don't notice because she doesn't make a big show out of it. Case in point: consider her chosen location for her meeting with several key race volunteers on Monday morning. She prefers to have coffee with Bill and Cindy Armer at Huggo's on the Rocks, which is down the street from Lava Java on the shoreline side of the road. Jane likes Huggo's better because it's not as crowded. There won't be dozens of athletes and crewmembers interrupting her to say hello. She works faster behind the scenes.

There are an overwhelming number of issues to address. No small amount of them have been generated by the Kona Sheraton. Jane has enough bones to pick with them to assemble a complete T-Rex skeleton. It started with the Lavaman Triathlon last week, for which Jane and Sheryl volunteered. The resort has been operating under bankruptcy for two years, and was recently placed under new management in an effort to turn things around. The new management strategy has been to raise existing fees and invent new ones. For the Lavaman registration the volunteers brought in coffee containers from Starbucks. The Sheraton charged a $250 "corkage" fee for them to serve from them. Then came the postrace lunches they provided to the athletes at the finish. Jane calls it like she sees it. "Twenty bucks for a soggy sandwich and some chips." They're charging her $30 a plate for the Ultraman prerace breakfast and $50 for the awards banquet. That's in addition to the $500 fee for the banquet hall. And all of this had to be *re*negotiated after they raised the rates from the original agreement.

There have also been a significant number of no-shows for rooms Jane has reserved. One athlete bailed and took his crew with him—the equivalent of 30 room-nights. Because no one called to cancel, the Sheraton is holding Jane liable for the fees. It's very difficult to get Jane perturbed, but she is beyond perturbed this time. She's definitely not reserving rooms for people next year. She may not even use the Sheraton.

Then there's the matter of support crews. Jane typically recruits local volunteers to work as paddlers and support crew each year. What starts as an ultra endurance matchmaking service usually deteriorates into something resembling a clown car smashing into the headquarters of an online dating website. Bill Conner lost his entire crew in a single night due to job requirements and sudden illness. But Juan Craveri suddenly had to cancel his participation in this year's event. Too easy. Juan's volunteer crew gets transferred over to Bill. That just leaves Jane with volunteers to find for Miro Kregar. She receives word that he's found one or two on his own.

Maybe that's why he's been riding his bike all over town. In any case, it's not uncommon for her to dig up a few willing volunteers in the last 12 hours before the race starts. She has 48 hours now, so why worry?

More urgent is the task of getting race equipment together. Much of it comes from Ironman. Diana Biertsch, the race director for Ironman Hawaii, has always been gracious enough to let Jane use a few items for Ultraman, including the flags representing the athletes' home countries and some French barriers to line the finish chute each day. The race clock and timing system come from elsewhere. Right now, the clock is being repaired and the components are in various places. She asks Bill and Cindy if they can help with that one. She'll try to get the sound system that Steve King will use for announcing duties, but she may need Bill to grab that as well. It will depend on how long it takes her to get the signed permits from the county and city of Kona to set up the finish lines in Kona, at the top of the volcano, and in Hawi.

Beyond that, she takes only a few moments to go over the schedule of setting up and tearing down the start and finish line on the first day. Bill's got it covered. He's been doing it for years. His official title is start and finish line coordinator, but he prefers the one he authored: "director of all the things nobody else wants to do." It will be his job to set up the tents and equipment at the finish line each day, get the generators going, and then start making food for incoming athletes. Once the last person is across the line, he'll head up a crew of four or five people to tear it all back down and pack it into a 16-foot moving truck. He's a pro at it. Jane doesn't belabor details. The whole meeting takes about 30 minutes, and then it's off to take care of an assortment of pending issues, including the leis.

Jane gives the traditional flower necklaces of Hawaii to each Ultraman finisher as they cross the line on the final day. She ordered them from Costco earlier in the week. She gets an unwelcome surprise when she goes over to pick them up, though. The small crown flowers used to connect the larger orchids in the chain are made of plastic. "I can't believe this," she exclaims as she inspects a couple of samples to be sure it's been done in all of them. "There's no way I'm going to buy leis with plastic crown flowers!" She tells the store manager to cancel her order, then drives out to the local farms near the airport. She finds a place with a sign out front saying that it makes leis.

The "establishment" is a disheveled concrete house with a 1968 Mustang under the carport that looks as if it just rolled off the line. Next to the car is a glass-front refrigerator with leis in plastic bags on one shelf and a cash box on another. A sign says $1 EACH. The guy who answers the door looks like he just got home from working the last Grateful Dead tour, but he says for $180 he can get 36 leis together by Sunday afternoon. Jane cuts him a check. The whole adventure takes about 45 minutes. It's time she could have spent doing other things, but she'll be damned if she's going to have plastic crown flowers in the leis at Ultraman.

It seems the only person in the Ultraman community who can sit still right now is Gary Wang. This is his 13th consecutive Ultraman. In all those years, he's finished third twice, fifth twice, fourth once, and a couple more times in the top 10. The most amazing thing is that he's never *not* finished. Suzy Degazon has as many finishes, but she also has three DNFs. Cory Foulk has finished once more than Gary, and he's got four DNFs. Yoshihiro Chijimatsu is the all-time record holder with 14 finishes. But even he could not finish the infamous 2000 event, when 19 athletes—more than half the field—was wiped out on the first day. That was the year before Gary's first go at it. He keeps finding a way to defy the odds time after time. Maybe that's why he's so relaxed. Or maybe it's the other way around.

He splits his time during the week hanging out with the other athletes he's made friends with over the years and staring intently at his laptop over at Lava Java. He's actually quite busy, keeping up with his job while on vacation in addition to some other projects within the ultra-distance community. He holds a PhD in physics and works in fiber optics, but he's a computer whiz to boot. He applies that talent to his passion for ultra-distance. On Tuesday of race week, he's creating an application to be embedded on the Ultraman website that will aggregate all posts from Twitter using the hashtag #ultramanlive. It will give all the athletes and support crews a way to update the greater Ultraman community trying to keep up with the event.

When he's not doing that, he spends time combing the results pages of ultra endurance running events around the entire United States and inputting them to a website he created called Real Endurance. In December he'll come out with a yearly report on the fastest 50-, 100-, and 150-mile runs of the year, and update the list of all-time fastest records in those categories if any new times qualify. It's a gigantic data crunch, and because races post results using different formats he has to input much of it by hand. He tries to put two to three hours toward the task each week. He uses Ultraman week to catch up on whatever is left to do before the end of the year. He sees it as part of his concept of Ultraman's meaning. This is a retreat. It's his time to commune with the sport.

"The times are important," he says. "There's a story behind every finish time. They're the history of the sport. And if we don't record them and keep them, then we lose that history. We need to track our progress—not just as individuals, but as a group. It shows that we're all getting better together. It's a shared experience. It's a recognition thing, too. A person goes out there and does something exceptional. They don't want acknowledgment, but it's nice. It reinforces and encourages them. It's not really different from cheering them at the finish line, if you think about it."

As far out on the periphery of the mainstream as ultra endurance sports might be, they still operate on the same cultural plane. From discussion forums and news sites to race registration and results, the ultra racing frontiersmen are increasingly moving onto the suburban sprawl of the Internet. The athletes are so spread out and so busy that the only plausible way they can watch and cheer friends at events is online. Ironman went that way years ago. Even with the yearly NBC special recounting the race, WTC set up a live streaming broadcast over the Internet. No one knew if fans would sit and watch all nine hours of the professional competition, but it actually turned out to be extremely popular. Today, several races outside of the World Championships are broadcast online through Ironman Live. Extreme distance cycling races such as the Race Across America and the Race Around Ireland have bought into live GPS tracking. The Western States 100-mile race has also begun broadcasting live updates from the checkpoints along the course. Technology has made it easier, but actually doing it requires someone to understand why it's important to invest the time and money. It brings the mountain to Mohammed, if you think about it. That's what Gary does. He spends a lot of time thinking about things like this.

And perhaps his philosophical side is the secret to his unbroken string of completions here. Many of the athletes talk about the necessity of "staying inside yourself" when going around this course. Thoughts of where you are in the standings, what your overall time is, winds and steep hills, and even pain are distractions that can wreck your day. You have to be patient with all the things that hit you. Some people can ignore them, others absorb them. But the key to success is not letting them pull you out of "the zone." It's the equivalent of hitting 18-foot putts on a rainy day or continuing a three-point streak through halftime in a basketball game. Doing it so consistently requires a deeply meditative approach. That's exactly what this is for Gary. He's widely recognized as a special soul among the Hawaii participants. This is about the only triathlon he does each year. When he finishes with Ultraman, he stashes his bike with all the race equipment in Jane's storage unit. Then he goes back to running. His sport isn't triathlon; it's ultra.

"I tell people this is my vacation. I call this my retreat. I come to slow down and reflect on the year. Ultraman offers the additional opportunity to look at yourself. It opens you up, brings out your true personality. Triathlon is too competitive for me. Everything is a competition, even your *stuff*. I don't like the constant comparing. There's no ego in ultra."

Someone else who's being very thoughtful on Tuesday night is Steve King. He's back to announce, and this time his wife, Jean, is here to go around the island with him. He's hard at work refining his notes and records on all the athletes. Like Gary, he's a true philosopher of ultra distance. Few people have studied or written about—let alone experienced firsthand—ultra racing to the degree he has. Asking him the whys and wherefores of ultra is like assisting on an open-heart surgery of the sport. His passion and wisdom won't just reveal it to you; he'll get you to touch it.

But with just three days before the race it's mostly numbers he's focusing on. His rationale mirrors Gary's. One of his favorite sayings is, "It's not about the time, but the time you have getting the time." This is the second full day he's worked from a dining room table in a condo he's sharing with other race volunteers. Wednesday brings registration. He'll be sitting at the last station in the Keauhou Sheraton conference center, waiting to conduct a final prerace interview with each athlete just to make sure he's got the whole story.

Steve Brown and Tony Horton arrive separately on Tuesday. On Thanksgiving Day they head down to the Keauhou Canoe Club's potluck lunch. They wind up having several laughs with Gerry Bockus, who doesn't show the slightest sign of his typical Ultraman-week grumpiness. Steve and Tony anticipate a much more relaxed week, too. After the Wales experience, Tony's looking forward to shadowing the supervisors of a more efficient, less contentious operation. Steve is here to play tour guide for Tony, which will be a nice break from crewing as he's done the last two years. But, as always, there's an underlying business impulse for his actions. The Ohana Loa board has scheduled its first in-person meeting since last year after the event wraps up.

That's when things will become uncomfortable for him again. The last few months have rattled him. He fears Simon Smith poses a threat to Ultraman with his unrepentant use of the UMUK name and overtures of a UMS race in Spain. For the last few weeks he's been none too subtle in telling Jane that he believes the schedule for Ultraman Australia ought to be bumped up. In his view, the questions of how to deal with the pace of change in the ultra community and the emergence of triathlons styled after Ultraman have brought his philosophical differences with the other board members into stark relief. It's no longer possible to paper over or skirt around them. He's going to get it all off his chest at one time.

"Look at it from Tony's perspective. He's going to make a down payment for $3,000 to the board this weekend for Ultraman Australia, and then they're going to make him wait 18 months. Does that seem right to expect that of him? It's time to face the fact that this is a business. That's the way it was set up. That's the way it has to run. And it has to make money. And I don't mean it has to make millions, but it's got to make enough to be sustainable. The way we are running this right now, it is *not* sustainable."

He's put serious thought into it. He starts talking about Ultraman from a standpoint as deeply philosophical as Gary Wang, but it's a philosophy with a business flavor. "We need to reorganize it," Steve continues. "There are all these little functions that need to be centralized. Doing so would cut costs. Another thing: Is there a succession plan in the event Jane stops running the Hawaii event or Ohana Loa entirely? I know that Alexis will take over for me when I stop running things in Canada. They need to have the same kind of security with things here. We need an expansion plan, too.

"The market is there, but more importantly we need to expand to protect the brand. Look at this catastrophe with Simon. He's basically giving us the finger calling his race UMUK, and we look like a bunch of chumps with our fingers up our butts, unable to stop him. We need to get an expansion race into Spain to cut him off.

"We also need to establish rules that clearly define how we can take a race director's license away. Look at how things worked with Penticton. There was a definitive line between when it stopped being Ironman Canada and when it became Challenge Penticton. And we need better coordination between those expansions. This time last year, I had 30 people registered for Ultraman Canada. This year I only have 15. I notice that Florida has filled up with a lot of South American athletes. I used to get a lot of those in Canada. But Consuela has a wait list 20 people long. I emailed her to ask if she'd refer them to the Canadian registration, but never even got a response back. How do you like that for cooperation between race directors?"

That segues into his most radical idea yet. "We have a husband and wife who help with the Hawaii race and the guy who runs the Canadian race advising the owner. Does that sound like a board of directors? What we really have is a management advisory group. Nobody on the 'board' has any stock in the company."

To that end, he thinks the "management advisory group" ought to be expanded to include the race directors. After all, they all have a significant amount of money and risk invested in the well-being of the entire series, not to mention the World Championships. All this leads to some pretty heavy reading between the lines. Steve doesn't say he thinks the board in its present state should be dissolved, but he doesn't say it shouldn't be either. And when it comes to the topic of risk, he's discussing things in terms of finance. There's a very subtle yet critical nuance in that. Steve, Tony, and Consuela have all sunk major cash into putting their races together. Jane has probably outspent all of them over the last 20 years keeping Hawaii going. But Sheryl and Dave have not. Granted, they've put more into this than anyone had a right to ask of them. But what's the value of blood, sweat, and tears in Steve's system of accounting? He doesn't say. Whatever the case, if the advisory group were to allow the other race directors in, the Cobbs' voting bloc would suddenly become a minority and Steve would gain the added support of Tony. Consuela hasn't been around long enough to express enough opinions to know which way she swings on these issues, so she could be a potential ally as well.

It looks like the universe is ready to cooperate with Jane when the sun rises on Wednesday morning. Tables in the Sheraton conference center pop up. T-shirts and computers and volunteers all appear in the correct places at the appointed hour. The athletes find their way in. It's still two days before the big dance, but the band is playing in rhythm. Cory Foulk even shows up and helps Peter and Katy Bourne set up the tables in the conference center. He'll take one of the race volunteers to the hospital that night when they appear to develop an infection in a cut on their leg. Cory is suddenly back to being an elder statesman. He doesn't say anything about banditing the race. Maybe he's changed his mind.

Registration works in two phases. The first-timers come in the morning, followed by the veterans after lunch. Dene Sturm is among the first and most eager registrants. She's a little nervous and very excited. This is her first tangible experience of the event, the moment when it changes from "I am going to do Ultraman" to "I am actually doing Ultraman." It's a dream that's coming true right before her very eyes—and that dream is going to get wilder than she expects. Doug acts suspiciously throughout registration. He keeps telling Dene to go sit with the equipment and drink water to stay hydrated. What he's really trying to do is to keep her from seeing him pay for an extra person on the crew at every waypoint in the registration line.

Later that evening, as Dene begins to let her anxiety get the better of her again over support vehicle packing and preparations, Doug tells her that someone has shipped Chris Draper a bike frame to replace the one that was broken, and that Chris asked him to go to the FedEx terminal at the Kona airport to pick it up. Dene nearly explodes. She doesn't understand why Draper's own crew isn't picking it up. Doug says they're "busy." Overwhelmed by everything going on around her, she insists on going with him. "You are *not* leaving me here with all of this!" They get in the van and go, but things only get more frustrating to her when Doug drives right past the FedEx warehouse even after she tells him the turn is coming up. He blankly responds that they'll just turn around at the passenger terminal. As they go by the passenger pickup area, he points to an older gentleman standing by the curb. "Hey, that guy looks like he needs a ride. You think we should pick him up?" Dene can't believe her eyes.

"Dad!" she beams. Her father has come all the way out from Montana to serve on her support crew. He's just one of dozens of parents who come to support their children at this event, crazy as they may think it is. Some do it because they want to understand what it's all about. Some do it because they're inspired and awestruck to see their offspring accomplish such a feat. But all of them talk about how much they love their kids.

Registration is a family affair for the Isaksons as well. Rhonda and the kids join Christian, looking like they just came off the beach. They're working as much relaxation and enjoyment as possible around the preparations they have to make. Christian is turning up the intensity, though. He was distracted and excited when he first got to town, but a night's rest and entering the registration area transform him. Now he's got his game face on. It looks like it was carved into him. He hasn't had enough time since Canada to change his strategy. For the most part, he'll run the same plays as he did there. The biggest alteration is in his nutrition. He primarily drinks plain water when he races and eats premade meals of things like chicken, avocado, and rice as opposed to the typical endurance sport nutritional products.

He says that the biggest mistake athletes make is to mix their fuel with their hydration. A legion of companies hawking bars, drinks, gels, shakes, powders, and potions have emerged since Gatorade and PowerBar first hit the market in the early 1980s. They're all primarily composed of high fructose corn syrup and salt—designed to pump as many calories and vital electrolytes back into the system as the athletes burn or sweat them away. People at the Iron distance can manage on this, but Ultramen can't live on sugar alone. The duration of their effort causes the body to burn fat stores at a tremendous rate while on the road, and regardless of how fast it's digested, eating the bars all day eventually reminds them what it was like to eat all the Halloween candy right after coming home from trick-or-treating. Because the event goes all day for three straight days, the athletes can't afford to skip lunch on the road and just gulp extra junk food. That's why Christian does everything homemade.

He's not alone. Gary Wang normally boils a bag of potatoes before the start and eats them throughout the event. Hillary Biscay and Rusty Carter keep themselves sustained on strictly vegan diets. Stacey Shand's approach is a departure from what you'd expect of a health-conscious athlete. Her favorite snack is the kind of beef jerky sticks you can pick up at the local convenience store. There are different strokes for different folks, but everyone keeps soft drinks handy—in case they need unexpectedly go into caloric debt and need an emergency injection of sugar. And, of course, to keep their heads in the game, every support crew vehicle has a couple of cans of Red Bull or similar super-caffeinated elixir.

Christian's major concern is portion size. He says he probably ate too much at various times during Ultraman Canada, leaving him feeling as if there was a brick in his stomach. He has watched every YouTube video of Alexandre Ribeiro he can find, trying to discern any secrets. "I'd love to know what he eats. But I know we both set our bikes up the same way, with just one bottle instead of two," Christian says. Isakson's relationship with Ribeiro is a combination of starstruck fan and challenger waiting in the shadows. He idolizes Alex, but he also wants to beat him. More than anything, he wants to race with him, get to know him, and earn his respect. That would be Christian's dream out here.

Registration for previous finishers is more of a social hour. They don't have any questions about procedures or schedules. It's just more family reunion time for them. Alexandre Ribeiro finally makes an appearance. Miro Kregar comes in shortly afterward and soon the pair are talking as if they'd seen each other just yesterday. Hillary comes in just before Amber and they catch up. There's still a difference between them. Hillary gets through registration at a pretty quick pace. Once they're done, she spends a few moments to say hello to other athletes and then she and her group are out the door. Her anxiety is starting to sink in, and her coping mechanism is to do something productive. Get home. Get ready. Amber, on the other hand, is in no hurry whatsoever. She visits with everyone along the line, and she lies down on the floor to nap while she awaits her turn at Steve King's table for her brief prerace interview.

Jane is able to snag a final support crewmember for Miro. Erin Stephens is a 24-year-old runner and Olympic hopeful who heard about the Ultraman through friends. She mentioned that the idea of crewing sounded neat. That was enough to get someone to make a phone call. The next thing she knew, she was talking to Jane about her weekend plans. She meets Miro for the first time at registration. He introduces her to his friend and crew chief, Grega Ziore, also from Slovenia. It's a short conversation. Where they'll meet at the race start and what she ought to bring with her is about all the detail they get into. She leaves feeling like it will be okay. Miro seems like a nice enough guy, and looks pretty athletic. No one tells her that he's one of the fastest people here.

Christian comes back for the veteran registration session after his family leaves, just for the chance to meet Alex. He stands off in a corner for a while until it seems like there's a free moment, then comes and introduces himself. "I just wanted to meet you and shake your hand," he says. Ribeiro tells him good luck and even offers some advice: "This is your first time? Remember, respect this course. It's *three days*. Don't push it too hard the first or second day. Be patient and stay strong."

Christian departs with mixed emotions. "I get what he's saying. I mean, he's done this so many times. I absorb everything he says. I'm not sure if he knows what I'm capable of, though. I mean, why should he know anything about me? It's okay. I'll show 'em what I've got when we get on the course." Maybe Alex doesn't know Christian. Or maybe Christian doesn't know what he doesn't know. The course will fill in the blanks soon enough.

That's what's on Hillary Biscay's mind on Wednesday night. She talks about all the potential factors that could influence things over the weekend. "There's nothing else you can do. Just get in the water and see what happens," she says. For all its entropy, ultra racing has a way of aligning itself. It accommodated Jane at registration. But it also positioned itself against Hillary out in the lava fields in 2010. Three years distant, that race still casts a long shadow.

Some people disparage ultra-distance competitions because more "truly elite" athletes like Hillary don't come out. According to them, winners like David Matheson and Alexandre Ribeiro are paper tigers. But Amber's win over Hillary shows that isn't necessarily the case. Other races have demonstrated the same thing. Jonathan Boyer was the first American to compete in the Tour de France and later won the 1985 Race Across America, but he didn't have an easy go of it and no one else of that caliber has ever attempted it since. Similarly, there are few if any notable Kenyan ultra-marathoners.

Hillary's 2010 experience indicates why. Even though professional athletes cover as many miles during their weekly training as their traditional-distance counterparts, they follow a completely different method. They take breaks and spend as much of their downtime as possible resting. They strategize their race schedule for the year well in advance, sometimes even following five-year plans to an ultimate world championship or Olympic goal. They scrutinize each course and time the ebb and flow of their physiology to peak at each race. Then they immediately go through recovery procedures and rest for at least a few weeks before they train vigorously again. Even with her unique reputation among Ironman pros for going the distance, Hillary remembers that her body "wasn't right" for months after Ultraman. Professional athletes' bodies are as sophisticated as a particle accelerator. The drawback is that they also come with equally precise tolerance levels. By contrast, the ultras are built like tanks. Their physiological framework isn't geared for the same speed, but they can plow through mountains of punishment and keep going. They're two distinct groups within the same species. It's very difficult to train to do both well. Failing carries significant penalties and just competing excludes the possibility of earning any prize money for months afterward. In other words, ultra racing is scary to professional athletes. Hillary is unique for more than just her physical attributes. She's one of the rare ones to have the guts to try.

Or maybe it's just that she's decided there are other things in life to be afraid of. Over dinner she talks about other physiological concerns far beyond the three-day journey around the island. At 35, she's in the last few years of her athletic career. She also hears the sound of the biological clock ticking. "I'd like to have a kid," she says. She's unsure about child*ren*. She's considering adopting. The look on Maik's face doesn't betray any opinion. Whatever happens, she is acutely aware that she will radically change her entire life in the next few years. There's no guarantee that something like Ultraman will be in the cards for her again. Hillary came to Ultraman in 2010 because it was something she wanted to do. She's back this time because it's something she *has* to do. And on the eve of giving it one more shot, she's hinting that it's now or never.

Thursday morning is the prerace breakfast. Everyone gathers for their $30-a-plate buffet meal, which isn't bad. Sheryl Cobb likes to joke that she and Dave call Thanksgiving "Bacon Day," and the group probably consumes enough pork for a luau. After an introduction from Steve King and a few pleasantries from Jane Bockus, the tone changes from family reunion to stockholders meeting. Sheryl goes to the podium, which can only mean one thing: it's finally time to get down to business. The course overview. The rules review. The penalty system review. Over the next 90 minutes, Sheryl,

Dave, and the course officials take turns at the podium explaining to the athletes in excruciating detail that there's a right way, a wrong way, and the Ultraman way.

Sheryl closes the segment the way she does every year: "Everyone here understands the rules, right? Okay. Everyone here knows, so listen carefully. This. Is. Your. Warning. Once the race starts, if you get caught doing something wrong, you can't say, 'I didn't know' or ask for a warning. This is it. Screw up and you're going to get a penalty." Everyone disappears afterward. The athletes spend the rest of their day with their feet up or sleeping. Jane, Sheryl, and Dave run a few errands, but it's relatively quiet even for them. The vehicles are already packed. The hours slowly tick by. The island awaits.

It's still dark on Friday morning when everyone begins assembling at the Kailua pier. Nothing is the right color in these moments between not-night and not-day, as if Mother Nature rolled out of bed and went straight to work slapping paint on the canvas. The pier is awash in the tangerine hues cast by the local street lamps, accented by the faint traces of orange behind the mountains. The normally crystal blue water ripples, wavering between the obsidian of the depths and the silver of the sky. Steve King starts pumping the discotheque beats and welcomes everyone to the event, awakening locals and vacationers alike. Unlike Canada's more secluded water entry, the swim start here is surrounded by hotel buildings. A few hotel guests step out onto the balconies of their rooms at the King Kamehameha hotel to see what all the noise is about.

Amber's happy to get started. Dene is *super* excited, but that's Dene. Hillary just wants the wait to be over. The sooner they can jump in, the better. Lucy Ryan is of the mind that the sooner she can get *out* of the water, the better. She is not a particularly fast swimmer and just wants to get out fast enough to give her enough time to get up the volcano. Beth Brewster, a coach and outdoor adventure guide from Canada, has it even worse. She watched *Jaws* when she was eight years old, and has been terrified of sharks ever since. The biggest challenge of her day will be to keep herself together. That's part of why she's here. She doesn't want to look back on her life and say she didn't do this event because she was afraid of sharks. Miro Kregar is relaxed. Alexandre Ribeiro is all smiles, the ever-confident rock star champ going out in a ball of fire—win, lose, or draw. Christian Isakson still has the cigar Indian look on. Gary Wang looks as if he is just going for a relaxing swim.

The haunting trumpet of a conch shell suddenly reverberates across the early dawn sky. This is it. The athletes wade out into the bay and splash around excitedly. For all the anxiety and aggravation it took to get to this point, the real drama begins now. Steve King leads the crowd of support crews, friends, family, and well-wishers in a final 10-second countdown. And then they're off.

chapter sixteen

The Wild Blue Washing Machine

"A lot of people run a race to see who is fastest. I run to see who has the most guts, who can punish himself into exhausting pace, and then at the end, punish himself even more."

—Steve Prefontaine

THE FIRST DAY IS INARGUABLY the most brutal of the Ultraman World Championships course, and possibly of any of the Ultraman courses. It takes the most difficult terrain of Canada and mixes it with the harshest conditions of Wales. It demands the utmost physical output and dishes out the maximum punishment. Between the water conditions at the beginning and the climb up the volcano at the end, you really have to race smart if you're going to achieve your goals.

At the outset, the swim looks like a saltwater version of its Canadian cousin. It's smooth sailing for the first half of the course. There's minimal chop at 6:30 in the morning and sighting toward the outcropping of rock on the near edge of Keauhou Bay is a piece of cake even in the dim light. It's a straight shot all the way down, then a 90-degree turn around the buoy leaves just 200 yards to the beach. Once the sun comes up the athletes are treated to a perfect view all the way to the sea floor, where they can see any number of coral reefs, fish, and even the occasional dolphin. The problem is that there's more than tropical fish beneath the surface, and it's not all good.

First come the jellyfish. Three days before the start, a local swim club event is canceled after a legion of small box jellyfish drift into Kailua Bay. Unfortunately, there's never a way to know when they'll show up. In past years athletes have had their weekends ruined by these creatures alone. Some have even gone into anaphylactic shock from the stings. Most people simply get a painful mark that looks like a narrow rope burn. Everyone at Ultraman makes a clean getaway this year, but the worst is still to come.

It's deceptively easy to the uninitiated. What they don't realize is that time is their enemy. When she spoke of her DNF in 2012, Suzy Degazon said that it was primarily the harsh conditions in the water that produced an insurmountable delay. "I just spent so much time and energy getting tossed around out there near Keauhou Bay. It was like swimming in a washing machine." It's a good analogy for any year. The machine gets turned on the moment the athletes take off. By 8:00 AM, the drum is full and it's time to start agitating. A strong northward current develops, running out of Keauhou Bay. The fastest swimmers hit strong resistance from the four-mile mark onward.

Amber describes it like hitting an invisible wall. "You're going along, and suddenly you realize that you've been staring down at the same patch of coral for about 10 minutes, and you know—*Oh boy, here it comes*. The only thing you can do is push extra hard." Even world-class swimmers like Marty Raymond and Hillary Biscay have to step it up a notch, not exactly the easiest demand to meet. The slower swimmers are really in for it.

By 9:30 conditions are in full spin cycle. It will suck more energy and more time away from the athletes as they push even harder and gain less distance. If that isn't bad enough, the wind also picks up later in the morning, increasing the surface chop. The rolling and pitching plays havoc with the athletes' rhythm and breathing. Even getting nutrition and hydration off their support kayaks becomes challenging. After they've taken in water and food, the waves can cause seasickness bad enough to make them vomit. It's a knife that cuts twice. The slower you go now, the slower you'll go later.

Therein lies the strategic fork in the road. You either start out hard and fast and gamble that you'll bypass the worst of the rough water with enough left in the tank for the bike, or you reserve your strength and gamble that you'll have enough time left to get from the beach to the volcano. However you place your bet, the outcome still depends on permutations farther along the course. The weather ascending the volcano is equally mercurial. The conditions are always challenging. But when it's bad, it's *really* bad. In 2000, an unheard-of 18 athletes failed to complete the first day because of the currents. Seven of them didn't even make it to Keauhou Bay. The rest took so long getting out of the water that they didn't make it to the top of the volcano in time. As the group works its way down the coast today, the washing machine looks like it's working at industrial strength.

Hillary goes out like a torpedo. She leads the entire pack, even surging ahead of Marty. If she wasn't so sick, she might be happy about it. The rough water starts hitting early this year, and all the pitching around turns her stomach. Amber is more than 20 minutes back and feeling the same way. Christian Isakson fares much worse. He's fallen way off the back of the men's pack and is getting slower. What started as mild queasiness turns into full-blown projectile vomiting into the water. He empties his stomach and continues to dry heave. He's nearly 45 minutes behind the men's leader and 10 back of Ribeiro and Kregar. That will screw with his mind later. Right now, all he wants is to get out of the water.

It goes even worse for six other athletes. Stacey Shand and Lucy Ryan fall way behind, and they're as tough as they come. Kathleen Wood is likewise an accomplished multi-Ironman finisher who did well in Canada this year. Antonio Nascimento punched his ticket here by way of UMUK, giving him extra bona fides. Duncan Cairns was here in 2012 and DNFed on the swim. He spent the year focusing on his swimming so he could overcome this. Yet the water is pushing them all farther back in their battle against the clock, putting them on a projected pace of more than four and a half hours.

Hillary arrives in Keauhou Bay 17 minutes off her record-setting performance in 2010, but she's still done something extraordinary. She manages a smile when Steve King announces that she's the first woman ever to lead the entire field out of the water. The truth comes out once she gets over to the grassy beach area where the crews and cycling gear await. "Oh my God, that was fucking terrible," she says. She groans as her crew helps her tear off her wet suit and get her cycling gear on. Candor is good. From this point onward, positive psychology and self-affirmation go out the window. Crews meet their athletes on the beach like trauma teams rushing critical patients from the ambulance to the ER. Lots of moving parts have to come together quickly. More than encouragement, the athletes need sunscreen and treatment for any injuries they might have developed, whether it be a jellyfish sting or a sore shoulder. Athletes who try to be tough and crews that try to be delicate fight a losing battle.

Hillary continues to talk about what she just went through. It's valuable information, because it gets the crew up to speed on her physical experience as well as how she's processing it mentally. Maik and Marilyn need as much insight into her state of mind as possible. It's a necessary jumping-off point to gauge how they'll manage her pain and outlook for the rest of the day. A support crew can make lots of mistakes during an ultra endurance race. Things like forgetting spare socks or getting the athlete lost on the course are forgivable. Losing awareness of one's emotional and physical condition are lethal. You think your athlete is doing fine, and then suddenly he or she breaks down for some reason. Now you're stuck trying to help an irrational, despondent person solve a problem after you've confessed you don't even know what the problem is.

Mentally, Hillary is in a good place. But her stomach issues persist once she's back on terra firma. It's a little unsettling to be so queasy this early, but all she can do is press on and find out what fate has in store for her. Between that and the exhilaration of getting on her bike, a smile takes hold of her as she begins turning the cranks.

What Hillary doesn't know is that several of the other athletes are experiencing the same nausea as they arrive on the beach. Some just feel bad. Others have spent an hour or more puking in the water. They're physically weak and way behind on hydration and nutrition. Tim Sheeper, a 50-year-old businessman from California, comes out 10 minutes behind Hillary. The last time he came here, in 2007, he finished in third place, less than 14 minutes behind Ribeiro. Today he gets onto the bike 29 minutes ahead of Ribeiro, almost exactly the same deficit as back then. Sergio Meniconi and Marty Raymond come next. Then another surprise: Kurt Madden, the winner of the first Ultraman, runs onto shore just ahead of the three-hour mark and in fifth place. Anyone who wrote him off due to his age is going to have to readjust his view. He's a factor.

The competitors keep arriving in a steady stream, about three minutes apart from each other. That leaves Madden roughly 22 minutes behind Hillary and 12 behind Sheeper. The intervals keep the transition area a fairly tranquil scene.

Shortly after Madden gets under way a familiar face rolls down the hill on his bike. He looks pretty much the same he did last year, wearing the same helmet with makeshift cow horns affixed and bike shorts; the smell makes you wonder if he's washed them in the year since. The Cowman is here to watch the race again. He spends a couple of hours chatting with anyone who'll say hi to him. Compared to the odor, his disposition is greatly improved since 2012. He speaks fondly of Jane and Ultraman. He obliges happily when folks ask to get their picture taken with him. And when he goes to Jane to ask for a wristband that will let him into the awards banquet dinner, his face looks a little brighter. Like always, Jane gives him one. He lingers on for some time, taking videos and cheering people on. However he expresses it, he will always love Ultraman. Till death do them part.

Someone else is coming out and expressing their love today, albeit not in the same way as Cowman. Steve Brown comes back to the start after helping to drive a few volunteers out to positions on the course. On the way in he runs into none other than Cory Foulk. After all his goodwill gestures earlier this week, Cory is making good on his pledge to bandit the race. When Steve stopped to talk to him he was already approaching Captain Cook. He claims he swum seven miles earlier in the day. There's no way to know if he's telling the truth. Jane plays it close to the chest when she hears the news. The expression on her face darkens just enough to tell that she's irritated. How much is anyone's guess.

Amber is the seventh person out of the water. Ryan runs alongside her from the finish line over to her bike, where her dad is waiting. The first words out of her mouth are, "How far ahead is Hillary?" If she's relaxing this year, there's no sign of it right now. She's not much farther behind Hillary than she was in 2010. Depending on how their respective stomach issues resolve themselves, they could end the day right on top of each other. Miro and Alexandre step onto the beach about five minutes after Amber and less than a minute apart from each other. Tim Sheeper has about a 30-minute lead on them, but this is nothing new to them; neither man is a swimming specialist. Their racing strategy is a savvy application of the old adage, "I've never lost, I've just been a little behind when the road ended." The swim is only 6.2 miles of water. That still leaves *all* of the road to race on, and there's asphalt akimbo to recoup a 30-minute deficit. These old lions have stalked too many quarries on this island to be anxious right now. If anything, it's Sheeper who may be running scared.

Christian Isakson half jogs, half stumbles from the beach to the area onto the grass, where his family has laid out his bike and gear. He looks like Jonas after the whale spit him out. "I threw everything up. My stomach is totally empty. Oh, I feel terrible," he moans. The more he talks about it, the more his family and support crew realize how bad off he is. But at least he's talking. They move like clockwork, Rhonda and the children grabbing beach towels in unison and holding them up in front of themselves as they encircle Christian so he can get out of his Speedo and into his cycling shorts. It's the triathlon equivalent of Superman ducking into a phone booth. This time, though, Superman is suffering the effects of kryptonite. Christian walks uphill to the bike start area with his hand over his abdomen. During his prerace interview with Steve King, he mentioned that one of the keys to success in this type of event is "getting comfortable with being uncomfortable." He's about to find out how uncomfortable he can get. The course is starting to fill in the blanks.

The arrivals keep coming, about three to five minutes apart. Beth Brewster leaves the fear of sharks behind her after struggling for three hours and 52 minutes in the water. Gary Wang is the last person out in less than four hours. After that, the intervals get ominously longer: 4:05, 4:18, 4:30, 4:44. Dene Sturm and Lucy Ryan both arrive looking worse for the wear. It takes Dene a little while to get reacquainted with standing on dry land, but the grin never leaves her face. She's eventually on her way and having fun. Lucy, by contrast, looks wrecked. She is miserable and sick to the point that she's doubting how this will to end. But there's only one way to find out. Her family walks her up to the bike start after a long break and then she's off and rolling. Stacey Shand is the first person in after the five-hour mark. Experience and conventional wisdom say that she has her back against the wall. She'll have to have a great day on the bike today to make the cutoff.

Jane and Sheryl stay until nearly every athlete is on the road, then it's time for them to join the race. They get in a minivan filled with race equipment and binders and take off down the road to get to the finish line before the first athletes arrive. From Keauhou Bay they jolt up the hill leading to the Mamalahoa Highway. It's a two-mile climb so steep that they pass one athlete who exited the swim 10 minutes before they left. From that point on all they have to do is follow the winding, two-lane route to the top of the volcano. The challenge is beating the front-runners. Sheryl negotiates this road on a daily basis, commuting from her home with David approximately 30 miles south of Kona. She knows every spot where the double yellow lines give way to passing zones almost by heart, and takes advantage of them now with a precision rivaling Sebastian Vettel. She calls it "driving like a local."

The difference between residents and visitors is noticeable. At times the asphalt corkscrews between sheer jungle mountainsides and precipitous cliffs like something in a Dr. Seuss landscape. Vacationers alternate between timidly rounding the curves and blundering into the oncoming lane while rubbernecking the various coffee plantations and local shops. Sheryl finds a path through all of them. Jane watches for the cyclists and goes through their names as they pass by. It helps them gauge how far through the pack they've gone and how far ahead the leader is.

It looks as if they've worked through most of the field by the time they reach South Point, only 45 miles away from the finish line. Though Hillary and Tim Sheeper have been on the road for more than three hours, they haven't made as much progress as one might expect. While the top guys in Canada all knocked out the first day's bike in less than four and a half hours, that time would mark a course record here. This course is much more challenging. The Hawaiian route profile stands in stark contrast to the generally flat one through the glacier valleys of Penticton and Osoyoos. From Keauhou to South Point it's a series of rolling hills with successively higher crests. After that, the road straightens out into more gradual climbs. It gets tricky again with curves around South Point, then turns northeast toward the volcano.

Like the swim, it's in the final miles that the bike gets difficult. Going around South Point, Jane and Sheryl see clouds pouring down rain on the ocean to the west. The sky is getting dark to the northeast along the volcano approach as well. The wind begins pitching the deciduous trees around, the leaves fluttering off of them like a child blowing the seeds off a dandelion. They pass another cyclist who looks to be wrestling with his mount like a sea captain trying to hold his ship's wheel steady in a typhoon. It forces the realization of just how sequestered from the outside world you are inside a vehicle. Sealed inside 4,000 pounds of climate-controlled air and stow-and-go seating isn't altogether different from being on a submarine. You can see what's happening outside, but you're totally cut off from feeling its magnitude, let alone what it's doing to the athletes. People talk about the spectator experience, but it always bears the inherent qualification that it's the very nature of spectators to be detached from the athletic experience. You see the look on his face and the tension in his arms, but you can't feel his anxiety and frustration as the wind tries to wrestle him to the ground like a wild animal. We are always disconnected as spectators. Teddy Roosevelt was right: the man in the arena has a special dominion in this world. Whether he feels victory or triumph, at least he feels it. The rest of us are just watching.

Turning toward the volcano has its benefits and drawbacks. The wind is no longer blowing across the cyclists and threatening to push them off the road. Instead, it's straight into their faces, forcing them to claw for every inch of ground on the ascent. Tim Sheeper takes the lead at the bottom, but surprisingly not by much. He gets about 10 to 15 minutes ahead of Hillary. She's hung on amazingly well, considering she spent the first 90 minutes trying to get her stomach to go along for the ride. Behind her are Madden and Ribeiro. The first and defending champions are riding extremely close, but Madden is losing ground to Sheeper while Ribeiro seems to be gaining. Miro Kregar is another 20 minutes behind. Behind Kregar, Christian Isakson burns hot and gathers a full head of steam. The stomach issues never stopped for him. He eats when he can, pukes when he has to. If any man in the arena is feeling it today, it's him.

Amber goes through a rough patch, too. Ryan puts on an impromptu roadside fashion show to lift her spirits. He grabs whatever is handy, including one of her bikini tops stuffed with a couple of avocados. It works. She laughs. Farther back, Doug is doing the same thing for Dene. But unlike Ryan's ad hoc compositions, Doug incorporated his costumes into the checklist for the event. His outfit is much more elaborate: green bodysuit with a pink Speedo and wig, set off by giant sunglasses that would be at home on stage with Lady Gaga. But he still gets outdone in the offbeat category by another sideshow. Tim and Hillary pass Cory Foulk as they reach the base of the volcano.

It's hard to tell what to make of him at first. True to what he calls "old-school fashion," he's wearing nothing but a Speedo, cycling shoes, light rain jacket, and a pair of shades. He's not even wearing a helmet. Jane and Sheryl pull over to talk to a couple of support crews parked on the side of the road, and he stops to say hi when he rolls up. Up close, his appearance is a little unnerving. He traditionally rides up and down the lava fields in just his Speedo with a light coat of sunscreen, giving him the dark tan you'd expect to see on a competitive bodybuilder. He seems even darker than he was last year, though. He flashes everyone a Hollywood-white smile as he says hello, but there's something unstable behind the grin. He takes his sunglasses off, revealing a decided pink tinge in the whites of his eyes. Duke Raoul is on some kind of trip; his fear and loathing fueled by imagination and energy drinks.

Jane greets him and then asks him why he isn't wearing a helmet. "I didn't want to look like an athlete," he says. Shay Bintliff, an emergency room doctor who is volunteering as the race medic, presses him about the safety issues. Cory starts debating with her about research on the relative safety of bike helmets, but finally cuts her off when she gets to his earphones. "You know what? I didn't come here for this," he says. With that, he rides off. Sheryl and Jane get under way again shortly thereafter. At a couple of turn points manned by race volunteers they give people the heads up that Cory is coming through. They might not like what he's doing, but he's still part of the family. They'll do their best to keep him safe, even if he doesn't care.

The finish line looks more like a scene from Macbeth than stereotypical Hawaii by the time they arrive. At 4,000 feet above sea level the jungle gives way to evergreen forests and the sky is gray to the horizon in every direction. There's a light, steady drizzle that occasionally gets interrupted by downpours. Rain jackets and fleece vests come out. Steve King has the music pumping and Bill Armer rolls out the first batch of hot dogs for hungry volunteers and athletes. They don't have long to wait.

Tim Sheeper reaches the top first. He beats Hillary in by just fewer than 21 minutes. He's exhausted from the effort but jazzed by the result. Celebration and rumination will have to wait, though. His support crew drove in a few minutes ahead of his arrival, and now start grabbing him and his gear up, working like the deck crew of an aircraft carrier. One takes his bike. Another hands him a jacket and something to eat. They bombard him with questions: Is he hungry? Is he hurt? What can they get him? What does he want to do next? He's limited on options. Other than the Kilauea Military Camp, where everyone will spend the night, this isn't the most happening place. The biggest constraint is his physical condition. His body is starving for calories, and unless he gets somewhere warm fast, his muscles will seize up in the cold. He's in the crew vehicle and off to his room at the camp in no time.

Hillary is just as happy with her result, though she tempers it with perspective. "It went really well. Let's not get too excited, though. It's still just the first day," she says. Instead of immediately getting in the van and speeding to the camp, she opts to change into some dry clothes and hang out for a few minutes.

Alexandre Ribeiro breezes in nine minutes after her. They briefly congratulate each other and then get on with business. Alex's crew is even faster with their pit-stop routine than Tim or Hillary's. Jose Poinciano has been doing this so long he can go through the motions with his eyes closed. Not that he tries. He fusses over Alex like an overbearing mother. "Come on, we need to get you out of the rain. You need to eat. Come, sit over here," he says. Alex relinquishes himself to his crew. He knows that the best way to help everyone at times like this is to let everyone help him. An amazing and somewhat disturbing transformation takes place. Invincible as he looks in motion, he appears timid and even a bit fragile once he's off the bike. And as strenuous as the 96.2 miles getting here were, the sudden stop at the end is the biggest shock to the system. His body keeps running like he's pushing at max capacity even though he's standing still.

While they're going, the athletes generate so much body heat that they barely need any protective clothing. Their bodies continue to dissipate heat to restore normalcy to the core temperature after they stop. But the cold air and water on their skin continues to suck the heat out of them after the body's thermostat reaches a happy place. Now the body must try to generate heat again. It pulls them in opposite directions. Hypothermia has been observed in marathon runners on days better than this. Jose issues a few more directives in Portuguese. Alex gets into the van and they're off.

Kurt Madden rides in seven minutes after Alex. In 30 years, he has only added 25 minutes to his swim time. His bike leg can't be compared to the 1983 race because the course has changed dramatically, but finishing just behind Alex and a little ahead of Miro isn't shabby. He comes across the line in good shape, wearing a bike jersey with a giant *M* on the front. It's a custom design he had made for himself. Tim Sheeper did the same thing, with an altered Superman logo on the front and the words TEAM SHEEPER on the shoulders.

Those athletes who can afford it spend big bucks to put together their own jerseys and support crew T-shirts. For guys like Ribeiro and Kregar, it goes with the territory of being a professional sponsored athlete. Hillary's racing shorts and jerseys are all made by Smash, an apparel company she started with a friend. But for most others the accessorizing is a vanity project. For as much as they train and sacrifice to get here, they want to look good in the photos. This is as close to being a professional athlete as some of them will ever get. The "team me" apparel gets them a little closer. It's really not different than attending your favorite team's fantasy camp. The price tag is about the same, too. Custom cycling kit companies require minimum orders of five to 10 sets and charge between $80 to $130 for each pair of shorts or jersey. It's no small deal, but the people who do it typically get the wear out of them. It's a common sight at the Ironman championships, as well. Athletes who devote a significant portion of their lives to this sport bind their identity to it. There are countless personal blogs, websites, and social media accounts on which people describe themselves as "triathlete, husband, parent..." The clothes are just another extension of their compulsion to wear their hearts on their sleeves.

Miro comes in with 9:02:53 expired on the clock. He's nearly 43 minutes behind Sheeper, and 13 behind Ribeiro. Not bad, but he'll have some work to do the next couple of days if he wants to win. He and his crew move faster than Ribeiro, disappearing just before Christian Isakson comes in seven minutes later. Christian's pulled off a miracle to push through the pain and starvation caused by his stomach issues today, but at tremendous cost. He hands his bike off to Rhonda and steps over to the grass to vomit. He walks around for a minute, then returns to the grass and vomits again. He groans, crawls on his hands and knees farther into the grass, and vomits again. It starts drizzling rain again, and he stays there in the cold, wet grass. And vomits.

"This was the darkest day of my life. All I thought about was a Bible verse I read this morning from Job: 'Now prepare to answer Me like a man,'" he says. He dry heaves. With his stomach empty again, he can stand up. Rhonda gently puts a hand on his back and looks at him. The look on her face says she's never seen him like this before. Ian starts to tear up a little at the sight. Christian has pushed himself so far over the edge that the cold and the soreness in his legs are distant concerns. All athletes talk about those times when they have to "dig deep." To get here and keep himself in the race, Christian bore deep into his mind and soul. The spiritual and physiological carnage of that is going to stick with him for a while.

How much further down he can go before he hits bottom is questionable, and maybe even cause for concern. He is a man of profound faith and passion. He's a rare breed: one of those who can run themselves to death—or at least the emergency room. The title "extreme athlete" isn't a marketing gimmick with them. They're the real thing. Support crews have to be more familiar with the in-flight safety procedures when getting on board with them, because they don't pay attention to turbulence or the fuel gauge. After he eats a few bites of bread and gets some water, the family gingerly helps him into the van. He's shivering and ready for sleep.

The rain picks up as more people arrive. Amber is the 12th person in. It took her a full hour longer to make the bike leg compared to last year. With 9:45:50 showing on the clock, she's more than an hour behind Hillary. Like Hillary said, there are still two days to go and anything can happen, but Amber's chances of catching up are about as statistically certain as you can get. She's totally fine with it. After Ryan and her father give her a jacket and a couple of hugs, she hangs around and chats with everyone at the finish. She tarries longer than anyone else yet. In past years, she and the crew would have been gone in 60 seconds. She's largely missed the fun around the finish lines. Not this time. She says the weather conditions are "not bad," but she may be working on a different scale from others. She raced in the new Ironman event at Lake Tahoe this year. There, organizers almost canceled the swim due to ice on the water and snowfall the day before. The race went ahead with the swim, but it was so cold that more than a few athletes left their wet suits on during the bike leg to stay warm. Her father, Dave, worried about her a couple of times. Cowman was there—banditing, as usual—but he didn't go in the water. Rosy outlooks aside, it's a pretty difficult day. A couple of athletes pick up serious road rash as they wipe out turning through rain-slick intersections. Even with multiple layers on and pedaling a bike at full tilt, the chill cuts everyone to the bone. On Curtis Tyler's allegorical journey around the island, everyone arrives at the trial of wind and rain. So far, just about everyone has decided to share in his perspective on it.

The stream of participants keeps pace with the passage of time. Chris Draper crosses the line on his freshly repaired bike four minutes after Amber. There's another arrival four minutes after him. The trend reveals an unsettling incongruity: if they keep finishing at this rate, the last second will tick off the clock long before the last athlete makes it. After Maciel Venuza rides home at 10:46:30, more than half an hour passes before Roland Patzina makes it. With only 40 minutes left in the day, there are 13 people still out there fighting toward the line. Five more athletes make it ahead of the 11:40 mark; Dene is among them. Her father leaned out the passenger window of the van as they went by at one point and told her to hurry. She pushed with all her might during the last few miles. Now there are eight to go. Steve King begins to discuss the time remaining on the clock and reading the names of those still out on the course. It's getting tense. Two more at 11:51. Six to go. Eleven hours, 59 minutes, and just a few seconds to go. A crew vehicle drives in and a bike headlight appears through the mist and trees. Everyone shouts and tells the rider to hurry. Kathleen Wood guns it and hits the line in 11:59:59. There are five people still out on the course. They're officially DNF.

Lucy Ryan is devastated. She is one unforgiving minute behind Kathleen. It would have been more merciful if she'd fallen short by an hour. At least then the explanations for the failure would be overwhelming and definitive. But a minute is a mere 60 seconds. You can almost break it down to the equivalent number of grains of sand in an hourglass and put them under a microscope. An athlete can spend a lifetime trying to reconstruct the accumulation of disappointment, but it's an exercise in futility. Some try anyway. Lucy won't do that, but she does sit and cry under one of the tents. She talks about how the rain felt like razorblades against her skin and how the wind made it so difficult to push ahead. She talks about how she knew it was going to be bad after the swim, but she really thought it was going to be okay. She talks about how it hurts, inside and out. Her legs are sore. Her heart is broken. Going on tomorrow is not something she can think about right now. All she can process is the grief.

Duncan Cairns got into his crew vehicle and rode to the line before the clock ran out. He knew from his position on the course that it was impossible. Now he's at the finish, cheering on a few of the last athletes to make it under the cutoff. He's a class act, but his frustration and anger well up between arrivals. This was not how he saw the day going. Stacey Shand just takes it for what it is. This isn't her first bad day at a race and it won't be her last. She still had fun. Bill Conner abandons his effort and goes straight to KMC without stopping at the line. There's no telling what he's going through. Everyone reacts differently.

Five DNFs on the first day is neither unprecedented nor typical. There were six last year. Two the year before. None in the two years prior to that. It varies with the crop of athletes and the conditions on the day, but this was an undeniably tough year. The volunteers can't catch a break either. The rain and wind pick up right as they start breaking down the finish line and tent. With a storm front bearing down on Oahu to the north and conditions here pitching around according to the whims of the volcano god, there's no telling what the next morning will bring.

chapter seventeen

Gratitude and Toxicity on the Red Road

"Don't give up at halftime. Concentrate on winning the second half."

—Bear Bryant

DAY TWO. All but one of the 36 athletes who started the race in Kona show up to the top of the volcano for the 170.1-mile bike leg. Antonio Nascimento wakes up with flulike symptoms. He physically can't go on. The previous day's DNFs decide to continue. There are plenty of reasons—the amount of training and money spent to get here not least among them—but it's still difficult to press forward knowing it's not for an official finish. Christian Isakson rallied overnight. He's still having trouble keeping down food, but there's plenty of fight left in him. He calls his coach back in the States for some advice and gets a bare-knuckle strategy: "You didn't go out there to hold anything back. Attack them on the bike today. Maybe you can gain some time back on them. Even if you don't, you'll force them to go at your pace, maybe shake things up for the next day on the run. Make it hard on everybody, including yourself." It's the same plan he followed in Canada. No reason to change things now.

Tim Sheeper, Miro Kregar, and Alexandre Ribeiro will ride on their experience. Tim is familiar with the route and his own body, and he has the lead. He'll have to make use of all those advantages if he wants to stay ahead of two men who ride this course by rote and are used to overtaking their quarries on this day. Hillary Biscay doesn't have to do anything spectacular.

In a way, she doesn't want to try. To her, it's still all about keeping things under control and not letting the island beat her. But from first to last, there's still a palpable sense of apprehension and weariness. Each day of the Ultraman Hawaii journey brings a challenge that marks an allegorical milestone in Curtis Tyler's life. The first day is full of overwhelming odds, failure, and despair, culminating in that painful choice in the wind and rain to quit or continue on a new path. The second day is about fear—of both the known and unknown.

Everyone gathers in the KMC chow hall at 5:00 AM. The course officials and volunteers are ebullient, despite being up past midnight joking and retelling old stories of racer antics over beers. They must be pulling their energy out of the air. The athletes and crews are a little more pensive, like someone about to skydive for the second time. Breakfast is typical military-chow-hall fare, served buffet style. There are a few local fruits and vegetables, but the majority is grease pit and Uncle Ben's.

Perhaps that makes it easier for everyone to clear out by 5:30 and begin final preparations. Everyone must be at the start line by 6:15. Support crews take a side road off the main highway and then walk their athletes and bikes down. It seems as if they intentionally wait until the last second to go to the line. Only half a dozen athletes are there before 6:10. Sheryl shouts up the hill and everyone comes scurrying from the warmth of the vehicles into the predawn chill. The athletes line up two by two, in the order they finished the previous day, facing south on the side of Highway 11. Traffic is not particularly heavy at this hour. Still, Sheryl fusses at them constantly to stay off the road until it's time to start. Not a single car's headlights appear on the road without her announcing it to everyone. The cop in her is out in full force this morning. Safety first.

Meanwhile, the athletes have bigger things on their minds. They gaze intensely down the road they're about to set off upon. From the start, the route plunges down the northern slope of the volcano at a negative 4 percent grade for nearly 20 miles, making for an eye-watering descent approaching 50 mph. At that speed even the best cyclists become acutely aware of just how narrow their tire patch is. The wind and road grit play havoc with control. It starts to feel as if you're steering a bobsled on stilts. It's an almost perfectly straight shot down a well-paved road, but the previous evening's rains make it frighteningly slippery. Not everyone will go as fast as gravity will allow. It doesn't matter how good you are, asphalt treats all skin the same. But due to its length, those who don't take the slope at full speed can lose up to 20 minutes to those who do, which can be an insurmountable deficit. Few courses in racing pose the question as sharply as the start of this day: *How bad do you want it?*

Really bad, judging by the way several of the riders take off once the gathered crowd of supporters makes the final countdown. The pack eases off from the start line, but in no time at all, Newton's laws take control of the acceleration. Race rules are modified from the top of the volcano to the end of the descent near the town of Keaau. No drafting penalties are issued to keep athletes from burning up their brakes or causing wrecks with unexpected decelerations. They can worry about spreading out again once they no longer have to concentrate on not dying. In short order, Alex, Miro, Christian, Tim Sheeper, Kurt Madden, and Hillary break to the front of the pack, with a couple of others among them.

They begin pulling off their arm warmers and Windbreakers once they get near the bottom of the volcano and the road begins to level off. The low temperatures combined with the wind effect of high speed adds an extra degree of difficulty to controlling a bike with frostbitten fingers and shivering arms, but once they get back to sea level it warms up almost instantly. They could be in for a long, hot day.

From Keeau the route turns out to the southeast tip of the island along Route 130 toward the town of Pahoa, where the road forks either on an almost due southerly route through Keauohana Forest Reserve or straight east to the southeast corner of the island. The athletes take the southern route, going all the way to the end of Route 130 to the ruins of the town of Kalapana, which was wiped out by some of the aforementioned volcanic additions in 1986.

These flows did not come directly from the top of Kilauea. The volcano has two major "rift zones" radiating out from its primary cone. The southeast comprised of 10 minor craters. These generated heavy flows throughout the 1980s and '90s, reshaping the land and turning Kalapana from an area of housing developments into a geologic tourist attraction. Few people live there today. On satellite imagery, the regions appear as harsh grey-brown scabs interrupting the jade sprawl running from north to south along the east coast of the island. Up close, it's much more beautiful—glistening onyx tendrils of lava frozen in time, like an incomprehensible black ocean that stopped itself just to be marveled upon. To the athletes, it's a landmark denoting their entry to another equally enchanting portion of the Ultraman course. They turn onto Route 137, affectionately known as the Red Road.

It's not literally red, but it used to be. Before asphalt became abundant and accessible enough to overlay on the route, local construction crews incorporated red cinder gravel. It was the perfect accent to an altogether surreal landscape. Though there are homes along the 15-mile route, it's predominantly an unspoiled paradise of ancient jungle that intermittently gives way to majestic coastline views. What few buildings there are follow no discernible convention. One house looks like it was designed for a Silicon Valley tycoon. Another looks plucked right out of a Japanese cartoon. There's even a hotel modeled after a medieval castle.

Equally curious are the occasional roadside cemeteries that crop up with eerie suddenness as you ride down the path. They are quaint plots with no more than half a dozen headstones and barely enough room for a single vehicle to park beside them. Just beyond the point where the athletes turn off and head back inland is the site of an ancient navigational *heiau*—an arrangement of stone pillars used by Hawaiian sailors in centuries past—that was buried by a lava flow.

It's such a narrow road that support crews aren't allowed to track their athletes through here. They get one last chance to aid their cyclists just before the turn at Kalapana, and then the riders are on their own. Other than the bike mechanics on the race staff and a course official, their only company is the jungle and the sea breeze. Between the solitude and the otherworldly landscape, you can almost feel the air buzz with something mystical. When athletes talk about falling in love with the island and how its natural beauty is a primary motivator to return year after year, it's likely that this is where their love affair began. You don't have to go far to realize you're not in Kona anymore. This is a part of Hawaii few Ironman athletes ever venture far enough to see. Maybe they should. It's far removed from the lost cities and native bones that Scott Tinley wrote about.

Christian Isakson is the first to make it to Kalapana. Even after a 13-mile climb between Keaau and Pahoa through the rift zone, he still averages 27 mph for the first quarter of the day. He leads Sheeper and Ribeiro by 45 seconds getting onto the Red Road. Hillary comes in about five minutes later, with Amber trailing by only two minutes. If the gaps appear small, it's because after only 45 miles everyone is still relatively fresh. The group won't really begin breaking apart until the prior day's fatigue starts cracking legs. That won't take long; gravity has done them all the favors it's going to do for the day. The next 130 miles will be nearly all uphill, culminating in the second scare of the day, the final nerve-wracking climb up the Kohala Mountains. It's there every year, and a few athletes always spend a significant portion of their day wondering what the conditions near the summit will hand them.

Today the men don't have time to think about that. They've got another, much less predictable scare on their hands. Christian Isakson hits the turn at Kalapana and looks over his shoulder. He sees Ribeiro, behind him, reach for a water bottle. Instinct tells him this is it, and he makes the jump to light speed. Ribeiro and Sheeper scramble to recover around the corner. Miro Kregar sees them and gets the advantage of adjusting accordingly to do things a bit smoother. He stokes the fire and, just like that, the race is on, full throttle. Christian's opening gambit produces the result he wanted. Alex is completely taken by surprise that the rookie who he lectured at registration has gone off the front. Everyone is going faster than they want to. All Christian has to do to close the deal is hang on for the next 130 miles.

It's a shame, really. With their heads down and in the game, the top contenders don't get a chance to take in the grandeur and wonder of the road this year. As if the scene couldn't get more bizarre, their own personal narrator announces the attack live. Steve King stands on a small patch of grass between the road and the lava, announcing the play-by-play to a nearly deserted area. Except for his wife, Jean, and a couple of course officials there to make sure no one makes a wrong turn at the intersection leading toward "town," he's very nearly shouting to the wilderness. It seems an odd place for such a renowned commentator and accomplished athlete in his own right to be standing. Yet his presence in this spot is the best explanation of how one can lead such a prodigious life of accomplishment. He is uniquely talented as an announcer due to his extraordinary insight into each individual athlete's journey, gained through his own travels through time, space, and endurance.

King was born the son of a machinist and a bank clerk in London in 1948. "My parents didn't have money, but they had energy for doing things. We emphasized enjoying our lives with each other. Being poor made me focus on the present, not the future," he says. Despite their humble means, his parents insisted on paying the steep tuition for boarding school so that Steve would have the best chance at a better life. With money for little else besides school, Steve was unable to partake in many social functions or go home as frequently as the other students. He developed a friendship with one of the better-financed boys, and together they either found ways to scrape together the cash for the occasional outing or to enjoy themselves without it. For a man who says he has many acquaintances but few friends, this relationship would become one of the most meaningful and influential in his life.

After finishing boarding school, King went on to Hornchurch College in Essex, England, where he studied business. He received his general certificate of education in 1965, whereupon he began work at a brokerage firm in London. Though he did well, the work just wasn't for him. He developed a wanderlust. His grandmother died before he came to any decision. She'd helped to raise him, and her death untied an especially important mooring in his life. Bound to leave England, he applied for a job with the Bermuda Police Service in 1972, but was compelled to turn down his acceptance when his friend from boarding school contacted him to ask for help. The man's wife had deserted him, leaving him to care for his young child alone. Steve didn't hesitate. Instead of making a completely fresh start in a foreign land, he began a more gradual transition onto a road less traveled and more uncertain. His friend recovered from his misfortune by the end of the year and Steve began looking for his next personal endeavor. In 1973, he and a companion "hit the hippie trail" with no other aim than to discover where it would take them.

It ultimately took them to Yugoslavia, where their drifting was abruptly halted by a car crash. He returned to England, where he linked up with a new travel partner through an advertisement in the paper. This time he headed west, to Canada. Over the course of nine months they gradually worked their way across the North American continent until they wound up in Penticton.

Hitting town next to broke, King took up work as a bellman for a local hotel so he could save for the next leg of the journey. It was there that he met Jean Dowding. They developed a liking for each other and she soon decided the new hire was trustworthy enough and offered him a tour of the local area. He took a photo of her on that first outing and mailed it home to his mother; he suspected early on that it would be important for her to know about this new woman in his life. That suspicion gradually bloomed into adoration during the next nine months. After saying good-bye to her one early morning in 1976 while closing up at the club, Steve found himself unable to fall asleep. He'd saved up enough money to continue his journey, but felt too personally invested in his relationship with Jean to leave. So he did the only reasonable thing he could think of. He got up and walked the 16 miles to her house. He made it by 6:00 in the morning to awake her with a proposition. Steve asked her if she would join him for the next three years as he continued wandering the earth. It was no easy decision for her. Jean had an entire life built in Penticton. Still, she felt certain she was meant to go with him. So she made the necessary arrangements and embarked on adventure with Steve.

From Penticton they traveled back east across Canada, then to London to meet Steve's family. They stayed there a year to get finances together for the next leg of their journey. Steve finally got a taste of the police work he'd been interested in years before, working as a private detective. Afterward, they traveled to Iran, Pakistan, Afghanistan, India, Nepal, Thailand, Malaysia, Singapore, Indonesia, Australia, New Zealand, Fiji, and Hawaii.

Though their itinerary may sound like the outline of a survival epic, there were no traumatic encounters with fundamentalist terrorists or terrifying crossings of the Himalayas. The real challenges of their sojourn were rather more mundane and often comical. "We only argued on three occasions," Steve remembers. "She was a smoker, and I was terrified of the thought that she might get cancer. There was also the expense of it. Most of the time we only had $60 to our name, and she'd say that she needed to get smokes. It was frustrating to see the money go to that. I kept pestering her about it until finally she threatened to leave me. So I stopped ragging about it and she eventually quit on her own."

The other perennial obstacle they faced was the issue of marriage—or, to be more precise, a marriage license. Each country had its own catch-22 when it came to the requirements for matrimony. Bali mandated a Hindu service, which meant they'd have to convert. Singapore wanted them to attend a family-planning class beforehand, which was too long and seemed a bit absurd given that Jean already had three children by a previous marriage and didn't want more. Try as they might, they didn't find a supportive environment until nearly their journey's end. The day they arrived in Australia, Steve went for a run shortly after they secured a lease on an apartment. Just around the corner from their new quarters he discovered an Anglican church. He made arrangements straight away. They were wed in late November 1977. The ceremony was attended by friends they'd made during their journeys. Like Ultraman, it was an intimate ceremony with international connections—a tribute to the belief held by many in the ultra community that it really is a small world after all.

The hippie trail isn't as well worn as it used to be, Steve thinks. He wishes more people would venture out onto it. It's not lost upon him that many in the modern twenty-something crowd leaves college carrying heavy loan debts and feeling held down by a depressing economic climate. "It is more difficult today, but we just didn't feel so encumbered by things like finance back then," he says. "People didn't obsess as much over their future like now. There was a greater acceptance of the urge to explore. More people today feel trapped, so to speak, and they're really not. But it's that feeling that limits them from doing the things that really make them happy. And we all pay a little bit for that, because who knows how we'd benefit from what they'd learn?" It's part of why he feels so obligated to encourage these Ultraman athletes. There are precious few of them.

The Kings returned to Canada in 1978, ready to settle down. Before leaving England, Steve had enjoyed a brief but highly successful career as a race-walker and had run on a regular basis during their travels. He felt an urge to get back into a community of people with whom he could share his passion. It didn't take him long to see that all their hiking and running had paid dividends in his competitive absence. Instead of going back to race-walking, he decided to commit to running races. He placed fourth at the US 50-Mile Championships in 1979 and ran the fastest marathon of his life in 1981. Over the next nine years, he won four amateur marathons (two of which were the precursor marathon to the Hawaiian Ironman), finished the Western States 100-mile race, took second in the Canadian 50-mile championships and finished sixth overall at the Canadian International Ultra Triathlon, the precursor to Ironman Canada.

Yet the most important manifestation of his passion for racing—both for him and the sport—was in what he did after he crossed the finish line. He founded Penticton's running club, called the Penticton Pounders, in 1981 and regularly organized their local events. Typically reaching the end of the course before anyone else, he wanted to do something to encourage everyone else. He would immediately pick up a bullhorn and begin announcing for the race as if it were on live television or radio. People loved it and encouraged him to make a more serious effort at it. In the late 1980s his began organizing different running, swimming, and triathlon events. He also started receiving requests to fill announcing duties at other races.

New directions presented themselves to Steve in his work life as well. After attaining his Canadian citizenship, he went to work as a child-care worker at the Penticton Community Resources Society. He developed such a sense of belonging in the occupation and obligation to help people in need that he continued his education in the field, leading to his certification as a clinical counselor in 1989. Afterward, he changed jobs to work at the Pathways Addictions Center of Penticton as an addictions counselor, specializing in working with children and families.

His résumé now includes appearances at more than 100 different races around the world. He placed second at Ultraman Canada in 1994, and has announced it every year since. He has held the microphone at three different Ironman races, including the world championships in Hawaii; several half-Iron distance races; three editions of the World Triathlon Championships; nine different international championship events in skiing, cycling, and triathlon; the 1999 Pan American Games; and the US Olympic Triathlon Trials.

For his personal achievements and contributions to endurance sports in Canada and around the world, Steve was inducted into the British Columbia Athletics Hall of Fame in 2012. Steve Brown created the Steve King 100km Classic in his honor. And while Penticton athletes still raced under the Ironman banner, those who regularly participated in the event strongly preferred to see Steve at the finish line instead of Mike Reilly, who has hosted the Ironman World Championships for a decade and is known as "the Voice of Ironman." When the event became Challenge Penticton, Steve became its official announcer. In 2002, longtime Ironman aficionado and triathlon writer Dan Empfield wrote an op-ed piece titled "Steve King, Where Are You When We Need You?" In it, he proclaimed that King was the best broadcast commentator in all of triathlon.

Not that it matters to Steve. Instead of the products, he focuses on the process of loving what you do and doing what you love. The chronology of Steve's life is the dot-to-dot of moments. The magic happens in the spaces in between, the decision to dance the scenic route instead of walking a straight line. His work, his racing, his announcing, his marriage—all of it is the practice of a mantra. "The word 'enthusiasm' comes from the Latin for 'to be with your god,'" he says. "I have a friend that is really into tattoos. He has them all over his body. We got to talking about it one time, why some people have tattoos and others don't. He finally explained it to me: 'Either the tattoo gods call you, or they don't.'" Steve has lived his life heeding whatever the gods call out to him. He is neither rich nor famous, but wealth and fame are just two dots in the constellation of life.

Steve's god demands more than talking into a microphone or watching endurance sports. His enthusiasm is for acknowledging each and every athlete, as well as their attendant ambitions. It is the same intangible force that bade him to help his friend, to stop badgering Jean about her smoking, and to become an addictions counselor that forged the corresponding spirit within him so beloved by all. His god is an inexplicable fascination with and a compassion for people.

Steve has even built an altar to his god, albeit by accident. Located in a downstairs room of his house, the filing cabinet edifice took its sole craftsman decades to erect through the painstaking art of handwritten notes. In each drawer are hundreds of pages containing tidbits and trivia about an untold number of athletes. Before each race, Steve researches the participants—where they come from, how many races they've done in the past, and their best or last finishing times. He even takes special care to get the correct pronunciation of their names. After the races are over, he keeps the notes and files them away. It's his monument to the race experience—his, theirs, and what they share. He refers back to a well-known proverb to characterize the principal commandment of his enthusiasm: "It is not the quarry but the chase, not the trophy but the race."

"It's not about your finishing time," he explains. "It's about the time you have *getting* your time. Getting to see these people do these events and be part of it is an incredible privilege, and a responsibility. They really go through something to get to the finish, and I'm a small part of that. I love to hear people's stories, and it's good to tell a little bit about it to everyone else, because it's bound up in their journey and growth."

Yet for his assertion that times don't matter, Steve's records on athletes are meticulous in their years, days, hours, minutes, and seconds. He can rattle off statistics on professional marathon runners and cyclists faster than Google. "The race experience is the most important thing, but that doesn't mean the finishing time is meaningless," he says. "It certainly matters to *you* if you're running the race.

"The times can tell you something about a person's experience. Take, for instance, the 1984 Ultraman Hawaii. Woody Woodruff, then Valerie Silk's husband, was running neck-and-neck with Jim Freim. [Woodruff is] on the run course and sees a friend on the side of the road cheering him on, and he stops to give her a kiss. And when he finally finishes the run, he finds out that he's finished the race in second place by five seconds. It's the closest finish in Ultraman history, and he literally lost by a kiss! That's just absolutely an incredible story, and it's right there in the times."

Interestingly, Steve gets the date wrong; it was actually the 1986 Ultraman. Still, some numbers matter more than others. The most important factor is how relevant they are to what the story means, and the meaning that counts most is that which the athlete feels. For as much of his life that he's spent talking and as many people who have heard his voice, he has dedicated a substantially larger portion of his life to listening. "As a clinical addiction counselor, you specialize in dealing with traumatic experiences," he says. "In many cases, I'm the first person to hear some of these people's stories. It's an incredible honor to be trusted with that. I just marvel at their courage. There are people like that in racing, too. Of all the stories I hear among Ironman and Ultraman athletes, I think the military men are some of the most interesting. When you think about it, they go through some of the most extreme circumstances in war. They see things that are simply beyond the pale. And yet they remain so stoic. They're able to push those feelings back, often because they have to. But then they cross the finish line and you see this outpouring of emotion. There are tears and hugs. It's an emotional and spiritual upheaval."

Like all athletes, his clearest jewels of wisdom were the most difficult for him to mine. They are precious stones of revelation gained at the expense of regrets. Between all the start and finish lines he's run through in his life, it's the lines he's crossed within himself that allow him that deeper understanding of the athletes he encounters. Even without the volumes of names and numbers he's written, Steve knows many athletes better than they know themselves because he understands the spirit that compels them onward. "There are angels and devils within," he says, all chasing each other in orbits around an athlete's heart, trying to upset it like children tapping a spinning top. No matter how many races they take part in or what distances they cover, endurance athletes might stop running but they are never at rest. It's not enough to go the farthest or be the fastest at particular races. Those are just fixed dots. The clock keeps running, the path keeps extending, the gods keep barking. The dance beat never stops. The key to living with yourself is figuring out how to sit and just tap your feet once in a while.

"The most enjoyable race I ever had was my slowest. It was meaningful because we shared the experience," Steve remembers. He compares that memory to less happy moments in his life. At the 1989 Western States 100-miler, he came to the first support crew rendezvous point to find they'd lost the rice pudding he'd prepared and had been craving for several miles. It immediately crushed his spirits. He lashed out at his crew and Jean.

"I've always thought of running as a battle of sorts," he explains. "It's a challenge that gives you the chance to go out and be a warrior. I mean, it's certainly not real war and I would never compare myself to a soldier, but there is a very real struggle to it. It's not mano a mano like boxing. It demands that you find a way to overcome yourself. You have to find a way to be grateful for the struggle, grateful to the universe, to succeed. But more than not finishing, I was especially ashamed of the way I treated Jean and the crew. I was just this horrible, raging asshole. The people I've always looked up to most in life were gentlemen, and I aspire to do that. And the most important part of being a gentleman is to be a *gentle man*. I failed to do that that day."

It's one of a few instances in his life when he let what he calls "the asshole within" get the better of him. It's the name he gives to the darker side of passion, something that possesses people like Cory Foulk and consumes people like Cowman. It manifests itself in different ways, and he's seen a few other varieties of it in his own life. There was Jean's sister's wedding, which he skipped to go to a race. Steve wasn't familiar with her family and decided to let Jean go solo while he took the start line at a marathon he'd been looking forward to. "I knew as soon as I stepped up to the start line that I'd blown it. I thought to myself, *You idiot*. After all she'd done for me in life and all the races she'd been to with me, and I didn't support her when she asked me to. I've kept in mind how important that is ever since. That was not one of my shining moments," he admits.

He's learned to maintain equilibrium between his own angels and demons through the practice of grace. "Grace is the state of gratefulness," he says. As a man who has successfully battled his own devils and helped others to overcome the demons of addiction, he believes you can only arrive at that sense of authenticity if you chase it with gratitude. As he likes to say, "There can be no toxicity with gratitude."

The frontrunners on the Red Road today are more focused on chasing Christian Isakson with a vengeance when they emerge from the solitary stretch and link back up with their crews. Miro surges in hot pursuit, while Tim Sheeper and Alexandre Ribeiro allow Christian to gently run out a bit more line. This is more a function of what's on their minds than in their legs. Miro is down on both Tim and Alex, and he's always lost time to Alex on the second day. He can't afford to do that again if he wants to reverse his fortunes. His best shot is to join with Isakson's cause and force Alex to either yield time or burn out his legs. One way or another, he's got to put a dent in his friend and rival's armor ahead of the final battle in the lava fields.

Tim and Alex settle on a strategy of patience. They know they have to be in for the long haul today, and after 60 miles they're only now getting to the hard part. Tim has a time cushion on his side and Christian is still a rookie, albeit a fast one. It's possible he'll catch up to Christian again if he just holds to his plan. Now is not the time to panic. Better to keep an eye on Alex, who doesn't appear too excited about the breakaway. His weapon has always been the run, and right now he's well within striking distance of Tim. His gap on Christian is enormous by comparison. Christian would have to put on a phenomenal day today and still lay on a lightning-fast run to be a real threat. The only variable in the equation is Miro, but there's nothing Alex can do about that. The rookie and the challenger gamble hard. The champ gambles smart, and they all throw a few more chips onto the pile. Now it's just a matter of what hand fate deals them.

Not too far behind them there's another group of riders making a valiant effort. Kurt Madden is hanging on well, and Jochen Dembeck and Chris Draper are right with him. Also in the mix are Gary Wang and Hillary Biscay. She's slowly inching away from Amber again. It's obvious that Amber is way off her own pace. Last year she averaged nearly 21 mph for the whole course, good enough to finish seventh overall and only 18 minutes behind Miro. Today she's not even within sight of him. But not being able to see him also means she doesn't *have* to keep sight of him. More than the others, she's able to take in the beauty of the Red Road. This isn't the first time she's been here this trip. She and Ryan came out one morning to watch the sunrise the week before. Maybe another defending champion would be enraged at his or her body by now. In 2005 and 2007, two-time Ironman World Champion Normann Stadler had total meltdowns due to mechanical failures and stomach issues while on the bike. His tantrums made his ignominious exits as well known as his triumphs. The NBC broadcasts showed him cursing mightily and, in 2007, throwing his bike off the road onto the lava rocks. Amber chooses Steve King's gratitude over toxicity. So many obstacles nearly prevented her from even being here. You don't regret accepting a gift like this.

The Red Road behind them, the competitors ride about seven and a half miles back east to Pahoa on Route 132, then double back on Route 130 to Keaau. They're back on the Belt Road just north of Hilo. Now it gets painful. The terrain pitches up and down wildly as it stretches along the coast through Papaikou, Pepeekeo, and Honomu. Deep, narrow gorges cut inland like varicose veins. Bridges span the rivers spilling out to the sea, but not before dipping down the ravine walls like a roller coaster. It goes on like that for 35 miles to Paauilo before the road bends inland to Waimea. From there, it's just a long, consistent climb to the finish, rising 3,500 feet over 27 miles. The landscape changes from jungle to grassland as the road strays farther from the coast. Approaching Waimea you almost can't even tell you're in Hawaii anymore; it looks more like a hilly part of Wyoming. The hillsides are peppered with cattle. The Parker Ranch there is one of the oldest and largest cattle operations in the United States.

The coastal rifts take their tolls on the athletes in more ways than one. The steep climbs out of each one bite into the quads, generating lactic acid. They also slow them down, allowing the sun to catch up to them in its overhead arc. The temperature in Hilo is already approaching a high of 85 degrees when Christian and Miro zoom into town at 10:00 AM. The heat kicks up the wind, which blows in scattered directions as they go through the ravines. It's not consistent enough to really hold them back, but it taxes them to continuously adjust. Their mental wheelhouses shrink as fatigue sets in. The constant drumbeat of pain, hunger, and fatigue reverberating in their heads disrupts any process more complicated than eating and drinking while turning the cranks. Their faces arrange in a gallery of gritted teeth and stoic resignation. They occasionally stand up on the pedals to get some relief from the pain; all it does is shift it to different places. At least that's something.

Christian's gamble is incrementally paying off. While Miro is less than 30 seconds behind him, their gap on Ribeiro has widened to five minutes. Sheeper is less than a minute farther back. As an added bonus, they've made a clean getaway from the rest of the field. They're nearly 10 miles ahead of Kurt Madden and maybe four or five ahead of Jochen Dembeck, who finished just ahead of Christian yesterday. Christian can vault up in the standings by two spots and put himself in a good place for the run tomorrow, if he keeps this up. If.

The *if* gets bigger as they begin the slog up Waimea. Christian grits his teeth and bows his head over the handlebars, as if in prayer. Maybe it's surrender. His own body begins catching up to him. Yesterday's stomach protests have broken out into a full-scale revolution. He pukes and eats, pukes and eats. His support crew parks alongside the road to give him another resupply. Christian's son Ian runs alongside to make the on-the-go exchange. He slows down to get a fresh bottle and Miro suddenly leaps out of his saddle and makes a pass. Rhonda watches with a troubled look. Someone asks him how he's doing, and all he manages is a pained groan and something about no longer feeling like he can eat. He's still got 60 miles to go, and he'll have to find a way to eat something before the end. But if he's already in this state, things are bound to get worse. Yesterday was the worst he ever spent on the road. How much more can he withstand, and what are the consequences going to be when it hits that point?

Rhonda puts her hands to her mouth and takes a long moment for herself. Presently, Alex and Tim Sheeper appear down the road. They're out of their comfort zone, but they're not losing time anymore. The breakaway is over and the hunt begins. Rhonda recovers and gets back in the van before Alex and Tim get to them. By the time Christian's family catches up, he's surged forward and retaken the lead from Miro. His head is bowed again, but he hasn't surrendered.

Further back, Hillary passes through Hilo with a broad smile on her face. Forget about the race; she's having a great day on the bike. It's not coming to her easily, but she's getting food down, the legs are cooperating, and she's in seventh place overall. She hears the drumbeat of pain as clearly as Isakson, but in contrast to 2010, she can still bob her head in time with it. She laughs, waves, and talks to the other athletes, race volunteers, and her support crew every time she passes them. Coming up one hill she asks how everyone is doing. It's not over by a long shot, but this is the departure point for her. She's not racing the past anymore—it's behind her, and it can't catch up.

Chris Draper and James Player are also plenty happy with the way things are progressing. They arrived to the top of the volcano yesterday in 9:49 and 10:19, respectively. The swim was the biggest challenge for both of them. But Draper loves the bike and Player is a top-flight runner. They both came to the event knowing the first day would be their slowest. And today it's just nice to actually get to the part where they're going faster. Making shorter work of this day means more time to eat and sleep before the double marathon. Those are happy thoughts.

But it's not all sunshine and cheer. Draper took a spill going around a corner earlier in the day, as did Gary Wang. Road rash is the last addition anyone wants to put on the list of things to deal with on this day, but they carry on. Elsewhere, athletes are starting to pick up penalties for rules infractions. A few run stop signs when they think no one is looking. A couple persistently stray off the shoulder and into traffic. Some are not happy with the officials' calls. This will most likely leave Sheryl to have long, unpleasant conversations with athletes at the finish line in which she has to explain over and over that she's not going to overturn the decisions of her officials when she didn't see the incident herself.

The course officials do seem to have their fangs out this year more than last, and even their own accounts of handing out penalties to athletes make them sound abrasive. Peter Bourne, who's spent much of his volunteer time at the race as head referee and once served as USA Triathlon's regional director, expresses reservations about their conduct. "Being an official is about more than giving penalties," he explains. "You can't just say, 'That's the rule.' You have to interpret the situation and the rule that applies to it. Sure, running a stop sign is a black-and-white thing, but few other situations are. You have to judge on a case-by-case basis. Did the guy mean to do it? Did he break the rule in the interest of safety? Ultimately, the rule is just the letter of the law. The official's job is to uphold its spirit." Spirit is itself a highly interpretive thing. Ultraman is a unique type of race, and Jane and Sheryl are especially emphatic about that founding spirit. Still, the athletes all received the same rules briefing at the prerace breakfast that was given last year, with the same conclusion: *This is your warning.*

Christian and Miro chug onward to the wind-whipped prairies outside of Waimea. The tall grass blanketing the hills moves harmonically with the wind, creating the appearance of great golden waves washing over the earth. The cattle and horses on either side of the road barely take notice, even when the support crews pull to the shoulder and disembark. Christian's crew stops on a particularly steep portion of the course. Crews typically try to perform handoffs on an uphill section because the athlete is naturally going slow enough to do things and they don't have to hit the brakes in a place that would otherwise afford them free speed. Christian's agony is evident as he comes up the rise. The course has peeled off his veneer of toughness. His legs keep fighting, but from the waist up he appears limp. His face is drawn and he has trouble responding to his crew as they ask him questions. Pain and exhaustion are slowly beating him down into his lower brain.

Miro comes by a few moments later. Vern Sekafetz, the bike support director, has pulled over slightly behind Christian's crew, where he's waiting for the other athletes to come by in case they have any mechanical issues. Miro looks over at Vern. "Is he hurting?"

"Yeah."

And like that, Miro pounces. The acceleration is frightening. After nearly 140 miles at the pace he's been going, it's a miracle his calves don't seize up in cramps from the explosive effort. He sprints right past Christian over the crest and keeps pouring it on. Cyclists call this "burning a match." Wisdom gained from more than 100 years of professional bike racing says that a rider only has so many of these high-speed efforts in him. The exact number is unknown, and it depends on the conditions and length of the race, but it's always a small supply. So when you burn one you've got to make it count. If it's going to count anywhere, it's here. Christian has proven that he's a serious competitor in this race. Miro might need every minute against this guy on the run tomorrow. He needs to pass him so authoritatively that it knocks the fight out of him. It's another gamble, and you never know how these play out. The statisticians can't factor this kind of thing in algorithms. Heart-rate monitors and bike computers would sound off more alarm bells than Apollo 13. Big Data still hasn't figured out how to account for big moments—the slam dunks and home runs that turn underdogs into pack leaders. The only transducer for that is a veteran athlete's intuition, and Miro senses the moment. When he goes by Christian this time, there's no counterattack. Christian surrenders the lead to salvage the battle against his body.

The decisiveness of the moment raises the question of what exactly was the decisive moment: Miro's attack, or Vern's reply to the question? Was it wrong to ask? Was it right to answer? There's no such thing as a level playing field, and the bigger it gets the harder it becomes to flatten out the bumps. Miro could still hit every stoplight in Waimea and get caught by all three men behind him. Or he could get caught behind a tour bus going over the Kohalas. It's all a matter of chance. Chance puts you in a particular place at a particular time. You can never know if it's the right or wrong place, or if you do the right or wrong thing in it. You just do what the moment demands and figure that, whether you've created a divot or hill on the field, it balances out with whatever else your competition has faced throughout the day.

Alex and Tim start gaining. Christian grunts and strains against the bike, but his pursuers are reinvigorated at the sight of their target. Leaders and chasers parry and thrust across an incomprehensible psychological seesaw. You always go faster when the person you're chasing is within sight. Indeed, the best way to dull an athlete's pain is to show them a competitor who's hurting more. Conversely, it's hard to maintain your best effort when the sight in the rearview mirror keeps whispering in your ear that it's all for naught. This is why they struggle so fiercely over the lead with one more day to go. Being in front is about much more than just being in front.

Tim and Alex catch Christian on the other side of Waimea. It's the second and final source of fear for the day: a six-and-a-half-mile stretch of road that climbs more than 1,000 feet along winding, narrow roads. The Kohala Mountains. The pitch is only half an athlete's trouble. At some 750,000 years old, Kohala is the oldest of Hawaii's five volcanoes. It is also the biggest determinant of local weather on the northern end of the island. Though the prevailing trade winds run consistently from west to east, the mountains' precipitous slopes and snarling ravines create wildly unpredictable conditions. The athletes ride north on the windward side of Kohala's plateau. Here, the winds carrying moisture off the ocean meet with convection currents and turbulence to create a meteorological Frankenstein. The conditions depend on the day and the hour, but no one ever knows. Peter Bourne went hypothermic trying to get over the mountain in one of the early years. In 2011, the winds held steady at nearly 45 mph. Suzy Degazon tried walking over the top, but she could barely keep hold of her bike in the deafening 55 mph gusts. She ultimately abandoned the race altogether instead of risking it all. But then there are years like 2012, when the weather is perfectly tranquil.

It's blessedly tame this year. The only thing threatening Miro's finish is the cluster of riders behind him, but it looks like he'll take the pot on Christian's gamble. After he makes the top of the climb, it's a 12-mile descent to the finish. But that doesn't mean the work is over. It's only half as long as the one that started the morning, but it's steeper, and the road has more twists and cracks in the pavement. As the sun sets in the west, the shadows through the dense roadside trees assault a cyclist's vision with a disco-ball effect. Martin Raymond has suffered from vertigo because of it before. But even the clouds cooperate today, shielding the sun's rays.

Actually, the weather's relative cooperation depends on your point of view. Alex has commented before that one of his major advantages in Hawaii is the heat. Coming from Brazil, he's never tried to compete in Canada for fear of the cold. It was snowing in Portland when Christian left. It would have been nice if the temperature had dropped a bit more. He's just not catching any breaks today. Instead, Alex catches him halfway up the climb. The mountain road is narrow and there are few places with enough shoulder for support crew vehicles to pull off. Everyone shares as they can and when they can't they support each other's athletes. But what Christian needs now more than anything is near-constant encouragement. Every turn of the pedals is a battle to find the few sinews of muscle that will still respond to the mind's whip crack. He doesn't talk. He doesn't reach down for his water bottle. The constant trumpet of pain has crumbled his walls. Pedal and suffer. That's all he can manage. He spends the final descent vomiting a couple of times. It's worth it, though. He crosses the line in 8:05, still three minutes ahead of Tim Sheeper and just 11 minutes behind Ribeiro. The surprise is that Alex actually gets the fastest time of the day. Miro makes it across the line five minutes earlier, but he loses six after he's assessed a penalty from earlier in the day. It's his first of the race.

Christian watches as Tim crosses the line with a smile on his face. "He doesn't look like he's hurting. I can't tell if that's a mask or not," he observes from a patch of grass beside the parking lot of Kamehameha Park in Hawi. He didn't see that Miro and Alex were all grins crossing the line as well. Nor did he see that they both immediately collapsed into chairs as soon as their crews got them off their bikes. Were they happy to hear the times Steve King announced as they crossed the line, or just overjoyed at the sound of his voice signaling the ordeal was over? It's a blank the course will have to fill in tomorrow.

Alex has taken a seat in a camping chair just behind the portable canopy tent sheltering Steve's sound equipment and athlete data sheets, along with all the food and David Cobb's small workstation for managing the timing system. Miro comes over and chats with him for a few minutes before ambling off toward the massage station. When he's caught his breath, Christian makes his way over to congratulate his rival and hero. Alex offers his own admiration first. "You rode amazing today. I was completely surprised. If you stay with this, you will win this race someday. I'm convinced of this." Christian is so stunned that all he can manage is to say thank you and express how much it means to him to hear that.

Chris Draper rounds out the top five finishers of the day in 8:17. The patch job on the carbon frame of his bicycle has endured all the punishment the island roads could dish out. Jochen Dembeck is just a few minutes behind him. And then comes Hillary. Maik and Marilyn cheer like crazy as she rolls in. She goes through a lot of emotions—relief, pride, hope, gratitude. There are still 52.4 miles to go to the end of the Ultraman World Championships, but Hillary Biscay has already won her race against history.

She's also closing in on mathematical probability for the women's race. Amber arrives about 45 minutes after Hillary. The cumulative time gap between them now is nearly two hours. It would take forces of nature to close it. But it's evident Amber is okay with that. At one point she picked up a flat tire while Ryan and David got stuck behind a tour bus in traffic. It kept her off the course for 20 minutes. At that point, she decided to spend the rest of the ride sightseeing. Going faster to catch up wouldn't make any difference and would only take her to the end that much more quickly. This was her last ride here for the foreseeable future. It has been a most unexpected and quite unpredictable journey, and she never could have predicted the fulfillment it would bring her. Time was of the essence on her last three trips. This year was about the essence of time—the difference between counting every moment and living each one to the fullest. She was alone and heartbroken the first time she came here and broke the record. Competition and physical pain were things she could focus on to help block out the heartache and fill the holes in her life. Now her heart is full. She's a little slower and a lot happier. Today wasn't about catching anyone or making up for lost time; it was about being with the people who really matter and making the most of the time she has. In a word, it was about gratitude.

At the front end of the parking lot, Sheryl deals with two Brazilian athletes upset about getting penalties during the final descent off Kohala. It's often difficult to maintain spacing at those kinds of speeds, but the officials tagged both of them in this case for riding side by side and slaloming across the double yellow line on quite a few turns. Their frustration and arguments are about par for the course for South American athletes. People in cities like Rio de Janeiro have an entirely different concept of what constitutes safe driving. Most road signs are considered suggestions for how to negotiate with oncoming traffic, not hard-and-fast rules. The two men believe they've been law-abiding citizens. There's a bit of a language barrier and things get a little heated. Sheryl tries to calm the pair down with little effect until Alex's friend Jose Poinciano intervenes. He gives the two men an earful and they back down once they've been sufficiently educated.

Into all of this wanders Cory Foulk. He's bandited the course for a second day, though he's wearing a helmet and knee-length bike shorts this time. Both his shorts and jersey are all white. Coupled with this deep tan and perpetual, unflinching smile, he looks like an older version of Caesar Flickerman, the master of ceremonies in *The Hunger Games*. He smiles at everyone as they give him a mix of waves and wary looks. No one knows what to make of him here. He's not unwelcome, but the way he's trying to openly thumb his nose at the race staff makes everyone uncomfortable. After making some awkward conversation with a few folks, he stands off to the side and muses on how things have changed.

"Look at all this," he says, the smile still on his face. "It used to be so simple. Now it's huge. All this stuff. It's just like Ironman." He gestures toward the finish line. The aluminum archway is at most 12 feet high, and maybe wide enough for five people to walk under it, shoulder to shoulder. Next to it are the two canopy tents, occupying less space than most household living rooms. Underneath, Steve King keeps announcing to the maybe 20 to 30 people around the parking lot while Dave tabulates the overall results updates for the 31 athletes still in the race. There's no light show. No network TV cameras. No giant checks. Nothing indicating an event that's even remotely like Ironman. But Cory sees the world through a different lens. He's talked about this before. In an email earlier in 2013, he accused ultra race events like the Western States 100 of being "circle races" with "a cadre of PR people who year after year race the same event in an effort to achieve a PR   bragging rights at the next Twitter fest if you know what I mean. They would never show up to an event that didn't publish the results online."

He gets angry at times that the sport isn't the way it used to be. It's almost as if, like Cowman's horns, his insistence on wearing the Speedos and eschewing helmet rules are the uniform of his rebellion against change, and not necessarily against the race. He clearly acknowledges that the conduct of the race is a reflection of the culture that participates in it. He's upset that the people here in 2013 aren't the same as those who were here in 1996. He talks about those who claim to be "anti-Ironman and yet show up here for Ultraman with their tri bikes and black skin suits and [gel] packs and Oakleys. They bring what they hate with them because they *are* the corporate, sales-driven side of triathlon. It is them that make the event, not the race director.

"Back when I started, we did not use swim goggles, sunglasses were a rarity, waterproof sunscreen didn't exist, PowerBars didn't exist, there were no waterproof watches or heart-rate monitors, and you had a choice between one kind of Nike or one kind of Adidas running shoe that you used for the bike and run both. We all looked different. Many had beards. Speedos were good because they dried fast and were comfortable. Only cyclists shaved their legs. No one had swim caps or coaches or anything else. We drank soft drinks and ate peanut butter and jelly sandwiches.

"Importantly, no one knew we were anything except another person all year long. We were just accountants, fishermen, surfers, business owners, lawyers, or sales clerks who were having fun outside on our days off. Ultraman is not that complicated, and when it starts being framed like that to attract more of those who prefer being framed like that—a 'journey' for complicated people who are far too complicated to find god in a sunset, no they need to travel the lengths and breadths ad nauseum—then it loses a lot of the simple beauty that it held to begin with. The honesty is gone.

"I had a spiritual awakening during Ultraman 1997. I can tell you that. A moment of true clarity. But I wasn't seeking that, and I absolutely doubt I would find it today in the complexity of the event and the complexity of people's quests in the event. There needs to be a blank canvas for the true painting to appear on. When it is cluttered by power meters and aero wheels and every third person is seeking that healing message of spirit they have been told so much about, it turns into a 1930s-era revival out on the Texas prairies, the only thing missing is the tent."

The world has moved on but for some reason Cory can't, not even when he acknowledges that that's what an athlete should do. "For an athlete to ask that the events change to reflect the roots, that is itself the problem. The athletes are asking for someone to do the work, to change them. Because they are the ones who make it feel like it does. It is not up to the event to create me. It is up to me to shape the event as an athlete, period. Who I am is what the event is about." Earlier in the week he was a guy who accepted that he didn't qualify and came out to help in the spirit of aloha. Today he's about as toxic as he can get. But adrift in the bile he spews is one undeniable nugget of truth. For better or worse, Ultraman *has* changed. It ain't what it used to be.

Hillary Biscay faces a different dilemma of gratitude on the opposite end of the lot. She has done well, and she will likely be the women's champion tomorrow. She could lay off, win easy, and mitigate damage to her body that will otherwise keep her out of prize-money racing. But that wouldn't be her best effort, which is what she came here to make. She talks it over with Chris Draper for a long while. They met when she came here to race in 2010 and bonded over their love of the vegetarian lifestyle. Draper is also an endurance athletics coach and is on the way to his fourth straight finish here since that 2010 race. He's consistently run faster each year, cutting about 10 minutes off his time to a quite respectable 7:40. Even after the consultation she's still unsure about what to do. She decides to sleep on it and make up her mind in the morning. It's not about how fast anymore. It's about how safe, how smart, and how sincere.

There are no more DNFs today. The fates willing, there won't be any tomorrow, either. After the finish line is torn down and the trucks packed again, the race staff and volunteers repair to the Kohala Village Inn for well-needed showers and then join for dinner at a local restaurant called Bamboo. It's a tradition Jane, Sheryl, and Dave have kept going for years. The bar serves the best mixed drinks on the island, in Sheryl's opinion, and the traditional pork dishes are phenomenal. But what Jane loves most are the desserts. They're all so good that it's impossible to decide what to order. Hence the culminating tradition of this night: everyone at the table orders a different confectionary delight. If there aren't enough people to cover the entire menu, Jane just orders extra. Everything gets delivered at once, and then the ceremonial sugar-rushing begins. Everyone takes one bite of the dish before them and then passes it to the person on their left. The process repeats until it's all gone. It's more than sharing; it's an exercise in community. They're all here: Jane, Sheryl, Dave, Steve Brown, Steve and Jean King, and now Tony Horton. They are the ones shaping Ultraman now. Who they are is what the event will be. And despite whatever differences there have been among them this year, what they are right now is a community of gratitude.

chapter eighteen

A Dark Place Under the Sun

"The last three or four reps is what makes the muscle grow. This area of pain divides the champion from someone else who is not a champion. That's what most people lack: having the guts to go on and just say they'll go through the pain no matter what happens."

—Arnold Schwarzenegger

IT'S STILL DARK AT 5:00 AM when everyone gathers in the lobby of the Kohala Village Inn on the third and final day. Smiles still abound on athletes and crews, but their eyes are bleary and the crow's feet creeping from their corners more prominent. Everyone is a little rougher around the edges. It's good to be here, but it will be *really* good to be at the finish line. Tim Sheeper leads the race by 16 minutes over Alexandre Ribeiro. Miro Kregar is 15 minutes behind Alex. Christian Isakson trails Miro by another 18 minutes. For her part, Hillary Biscay has settled on reaching the finish line in 7:30. There are just 52.4 miles left to go. Even at this early hour, the temperature is already close to 75 degrees, with a predicted high of 90 before noon. Worse, the lava fields at midday work like a skillet under a spotlight. It will get close to 100 out there.

The numbers are just the skeleton of the thing, though. They can only hint at the complex workings of its greater anatomy. The nature of this beast defies statistics. There is no metric for fatigue, no scientifically objective measurement for pain. Even if you could numerically quantify them and rank-order the athletes' physical and mental states on an absolute scale, it would still give no prediction of how they'll do today. The overriding question is how they'll deal with it. It goes way beyond something as simplistic as "mind over matter." It's about the gradual depletion of all of one's intangible resources. Up to this point, everyone has endured, coped, suffered. The very definition of those words communicate a certain toleration of discomfort in the face of its continuation. For many of them today, the pain will become *intolerable*. The definitions of the first two days don't compare. The lava fields require a vocabulary completely different from anything else in the Ultraman experience. The athletes keep going, but whatever they're doing, it's not coping. This isn't an endurance race anymore. It's an expedition for a moment of truth.

Gary Wang has spent 109 hours, 29 minutes, and 24 seconds on this stretch of road in the course of his annual meditative retreats. That's a lot of time to reflect on what this is all about. He's distilled it to a potently spare metaphor. "By the third day, the suffering gets to you. There's a sense of nakedness on the run. There's no place to hide," he says. It's as if the island itself has enacted a scorched-earth strategy in a last stand against the athletes. They'll barely exit the forested areas around Hawi before the sun begins shedding light on the island's west coast. After that, the temperatures will rise mercilessly. The western side of the island is dominated by the lava. For 52 miles, there's no shelter from the sun or wind. Nor are there any obstructions to the view of the lonely black thread stretching out before them through the endless desolation. The road never seems to end. It just vanishes into the "vog," the mix of clouds and volcanic smoke that float down the mountain slopes slightly in front of the horizon. The landscape offers no milestones to call small victories. The only reference point to set their sights on is that delirious nothing-haze on the horizon, and even that constantly taunts them in its distance. There's nothing to latch onto out here except for whatever you've still got left inside. If you don't know what that is, you'll find out really fast.

Presently the hotel lobby begins to clear out. People grab their last cup of coffee or donut on the go and make their way to the crew vehicles. It's a short drive to the start line, a nondescript clearing on the side of Route 270 just south of town. The route instructions given to athletes advise them to look for a streetlight. Once there, ⎯ instructs the athletes to join hands in a circle, ar⎯ to form an outer ring around them. Kerri Tobir⎯ directions, and a silence falls over the group as ⎯ of the assembly. She speaks a few solemn word⎯ specific deity. People here come from a broad ⎯ anything, she beseeches the collective spirit of Ultraman. She asks that everyone be safe and that they find joy in what the day offers them.

When it's over, the athletes cross the road and prepare to run. They don't have long to wait. The crowd shouts out their final 10-second countdown, and off they go. It starts with a bang, though a predictable one. Miro and Alex set off at a blistering pace. It would have happened regardless of where Tim Sheeper stood on time. They do this every year, daring all who are close enough to vie for the win to chase them outside their comfort zone and tempt fate and physiology. Alex and Miro have run together five times here, and they've been the first two across the start line every time. Tim led Alex by 33 minutes in the cumulative standings when they started the run in 2007. By the time he crossed the finish, Alex had pulled ahead by 13 minutes. If Tim wants to hang on, he's got to chase them. He decides to go. No sense in finishing third again. You only live once.

Hillary Biscay gets swept up in the excitement of the moment. One of her favorite things to do in training is to run marathons on the treadmill, and she feels pretty good in the opening miles, so she picks up the tempo and goes alongside Jochen Dembeck. She's not sure if this is a wise decision, but he encourages her to come along. Off they go at a pace that doesn't make her comfortable or confident, which is exactly how she likes it. Her plan to run 7:30 was audacious enough to win with pride, but reasonable enough to avoid risking mishap. It made perfect sense, and that was sort of the problem. Nothing about her journey to this point—leaving the PhD program, taking her athletic talents to a sport with so many more liabilities than rewards, risking her body, reputation, and career to come here twice—has ever made sense. But you can never live the dream unless you brave the possibility of living nightmares. *This is crazy*, she thinks to herself, then holds alongside Dembeck.

...eably absent from the early sprint is Christian Isakson. He settles ...n eight-minute-per-mile pace as the top three men scamper off into ...darkness. He's not done gambling. He's just betting in the opposite ...irection. Alex and Miro's strategy is to run to the absolute limit and let the winner be decided by who cracks last. That's what Christian is counting on. Eventually, one or even two of them will drop off. If they're hobbled enough, and if he can keep up this pace, odds are that he'll pick them back up late in the race. He can't beat Alex and Miro head-to-head out here, but he can still reach for a top-four finish.

The sky bursts into a parade of color less than 30 minutes after the start. The last vestiges of evening tanzanite are consumed by dawn's fiery oranges and yellows, which in turn melt to pastels in the sun-soaked daytime sky. It all seems to happen so much faster because the volcano shields the sun's rise over the Pacific horizon. Someone preoccupied by things like keeping pace and withstanding the pain of aching joints might miss it entirely. But nobody misses what comes next. The heat comes on strong once the sun emerges from behind the mountain. By 7:00 AM it's almost 80 degrees.

Some of the people here, such as Gary Wang, Stacey Shand, and James Player, come from a running background and love this day of the race more than the others. Others hate it. Regardless of their personal preferences, physiological research definitively bears out that this is the most punishing part of the weekend. Racers burn as many or more calories per unit of time as they do during cycling, but the stress on their joints is tremendously higher. They sustain forces in excess of twice their body weight each step of the way. Muscles fatigue. Ligaments strain. Cartilage wears.

Those are just a few of the consequences of the day's stresses. There are also cumulative effects of the previous two days. While weight-bearing exercise has been shown to improve bone density, athletes who regularly train at these distances actually deplete their bodies of calcium and can experience symptoms of osteoporosis if they don't get adequate rest. Of more immediate concern are their nutritional and hormonal levels. After two days of prolonged, intense exercise, their metabolisms are raging. They continue to lose weight despite their best efforts to eat. The first place the body turns to is fat, but there's precious little on many of the top athletes. So the physiology goes into panic mode and initiates a process called gluconeogenesis, in which it starts drawing protein from muscles for use as fuel. It's the anatomical equivalent of pulling the insulation out of the walls to keep the fireplace going.

Most of the metabolic processes in the human body are regulated by the hypothalamus, which pulls the necessary strings by way of the network of hormone-producing organs and glands throughout the body. Most people are familiar with that group of hormones known as endorphins, which famously bless athletes with a "runner's high." But just like Dr. Jekyll's potion, it has a darker flip side, known as cortisol. Produced in the adrenal gland in response to physical stress, cortisol assists the body's biochemistry in turning different compounds into usable energy. It typically washes out soon after the body resumes a resting state. But when an athlete keeps going it creates a state of chronic stress. The cortisol continues pumping into the bloodstream. Side effects include damage to the immune system and reduced cognition. Even the adrenal glands themselves can burn out from being so overworked. It can take weeks for athletes to fully recover. During that time, they live in a constant state of fatigue. Even walking up a flight of stairs can be exhausting. It can be hard to feel excited or happy, just because the hormones associated with those feelings are gone. Few of the athletes are able make such a detailed appraisal of their condition. Many of them use a simpler diagnosis: they feel like dog shit.

The most prominent physical limitation today is the heat. It's just plain math. Take a person of a known body mass, have him run at a certain speed at a specific temperature, and he will generate heat faster than it can escape the body. It wasn't so much of a problem for athletes on the bike because the wind blowing over them as a result of their speed was enough to keep their bodies at equilibrium regardless of how hard they pushed. Relying on sweat alone is a highly inefficient way to stay cool. The heat accelerates muscle degradation and begins wreaking havoc on the organs. Different people react to it in different ways. Determining how well the human body can acclimate to the heat remains a challenge to medical research. It's a certainty that if you push hard enough and long enough, you'll pass out of heat exhaustion—or worse. But science can't begin to guess when a person hits that point. That's a betting man's territory.

Alex and Miro run onward. Though Tim is putting up a fight, he loses ground to them quickly. They're ahead of him by more than four minutes after as many miles. At this rate, he'll lose the lead well before they make the first marathon point. That will leave it between Miro and Alex. Even though he's outrun Alex most times on this course, it's dubious whether Miro could erase a 15-minute deficit. It would be close. But any chances he has are spoiled in a single, unfortunate moment. One of his support crewmembers, a journalist from his home country of Slovenia there to document his athletic career, is spotted by one of the officials while leaning out the rear window of the crew's minivan, taking photos. The official deems it as hazardous driving, a punishable offense according to race rules. The punishment for crew infractions always falls on the athlete, and Miro gets hit with another penalty. It costs him 12 minutes. The official pulls up on his motorcycle, stops him, and gives him the news. And that's when Miro knows. Suddenly he's 27 minutes behind Alex. He's fast, but not that fast. It's over. He's lost.

Events beyond our control can make bad sports of the best of us. Before Achilles' heel there was Achilles' despair. Closer to home for Miro is the story of fellow Slovenian ultra-distance athlete Jure Robic. In 2009, Robic was going for his fifth victory in the Race Across America when his crew received a second time penalty late in the race that made it all but impossible for him to beat challenger Danny Wyss of Switzerland. He had incurred his first time penalty even before the race began, for what race officials deemed unsportsmanlike conduct. Infuriated by the officials, Robic abandoned the race less than 100 miles from the finish rather than settling for second place.

Most reasonably athletic people can power through a marathon or a 100-mile bike ride on competitive fire alone. The ultra-distance demands something more. There's always that moment of truth, and it necessarily strikes in the darkest hour. To survive it, you need a light to shine on the things inside you that brought you to this place. Some people thought that the fire in Robic went out in 2009. He swore he'd never compete in RAAM again. But they were wrong. He returned in 2010 to win his fifth race. The fire can never die in athletes like Miro, Alex, Hillary, or Amber. But sometimes the light goes out. After the official leaves him, Miro takes off and catches up to Alex. There's no time to argue. Tim Sheeper is just 10 minutes behind. For his seventh and likely last time, Miro runs for something less than first place. Or maybe it's something more.

Only Miro can see it. The crew inside the van gets lost, perhaps out of despair. At first they're confused. The realizations hit them in waves. After coming to terms with the penalty, it takes a few moments before Grega works out the ramifications. "He's not going to win," he says. Erin Stephens is overwhelmed by what she later remembers as the loudest silence she's ever heard: "It sent us to a dark place as we let it sink in. The next time I got out to give him a water bottle I could hardly look at him. I felt so ashamed. But he didn't skip a beat. He just kept taking the bottles and saying 'thank you.'"

Early on in the weekend they adopted the slogan "Miro, our hero." They even wrote it on one of the side windows of the van in washable paint. Now in his darkest moment, he's the one who shines the light for them. It's the total opposite of what you'd expect of a moment like this. But what is a hero if not one who defies convention? He and Alex are motoring away from Tim Sheeper now. They're 13 minutes ahead at the 11-mile mark. Alex will have the overall race lead by the first half marathon. All Miro can do is his best. All his crew can do is hope for a miracle and maybe redemption.

Hillary and Jochen make good time together. She's starting to think this wasn't a bad idea after all. It's nice to have company. There aren't many opportunities for conversation throughout the weekend due to the no-draft rules during the bike phases. James Player has overtaken them, but other than that they're far ahead of the main group, which is already stringing out as the miles magnify the differences in their individual pacing. But now Jochen decides to make a small confession. "You know, when we reach the marathon point, this will be the farthest I've run all year."

It's not an uncommon practice. There are few genuine all-around triathletes in the world. There are specialists even among professional competitors. The signature of most champions is typically either a crushing bike or run performance. The original debate that inspired Ironman—over which sport produces the superior athlete—arose from the belief that sheer physicality trumps technical skill when you race in such unique disciplines. That may be even more true when things are blown up to Ultraman-level proportions. Hillary excels on the swim and run. Gary Wang, on the other hand, hardly bikes or swims at all in the course of a year. He relies on muscle memory and the fitness he builds while running to carry him through the other disciplines. Amber never spends much time swimming until the weeks leading up to Ultraman. Even Ribeiro's training primarily focuses on running. In a way, few if any of these people are triathletes in the conventional sense. More accurately, they're endurance adventurers. It's not the triathlon they come for so much as the ultra.

Be that as it may, Hillary finds the limit of her enthusiasm for taking chances. *Oh, hell no*, she thinks to herself. *We are* not *doing this.* Go too far into the realm of uncertainty, and you suddenly find yourself at a point where disaster becomes more certain. She backs off the pace a bit as they go through the half marathon point. Sure enough, after a few more miles Jochen starts to feel the burn. Now it's Hillary urging him on. After a few more minutes, it's Hillary running alone. It gets lonely again and she realizes that she'll likely spend the rest of the day on her own, save for the short spells when Maik or Marilyn hop out of the van to pace her for a bit. But then comes a familiar voice.

"I'm running eights. Tuck in behind me!"

It's Christian Isakson. His gamble is starting to pay off. As Jochen and others fall off their pace, Christian keeps chugging along steadily. Hillary's spirits pick up again and she latches onto him like a shadow. If they run eight-minute splits for the rest of the day, they'll finish in just under seven hours. It's slightly less audacious than what Jochen had been shooting for, so why not? Off she goes again.

Other strategies are playing out ahead of them. Tim Sheeper continues to run as fast as he can despite visible discomfort, but the lead belongs to Alex now. Everything is going according to the champion's plan. Then something happens at Kawaihae Hill, approximately 17 miles from the start. Miro knows this spot. Alex always accelerates here and pushes to the top. It makes things just a little uncomfortable for him, so to compensate he decides to hit the gas just a little early to give himself a cushion going over. Once they hit the downhill slope, he'll be able to even it out. But Alex never goes in front of him. And he never catches back up going down. Miro doesn't dare look back. He's confident Alex will sort it out; he'll never let him run out ahead this early. Then Miro's crew van slows momentarily as it goes by him. Erin shouts from the window, confirming that the improbable has happened: "You're 200 meters in front!"

Alexandre Ribeiro is coming undone. The comparative lack of training and Isakson's attack from the previous day have taken their tolls. It's still early, though, and the lead is only 200 meters. The odds are slim. Historically, Miro's fastest time on this course is 6:14; Alex's worst day clocked in at 6:59. A 45-minute spread would absorb the current 27-minute gap and still give him the win by 18 minutes. It would be the kind of miracle his crew has been hoping for. Of course, Miro doesn't know these numbers or have the time to perform the calculations. All he's got to go on is his gut. And his gut says it's now or never. *So go, already.*

He surges ahead, taking his crew's surging spirits with him. Erin and Grega can't believe what they see. A mile beyond the hill it looks like he'll add to his lead. He's going to need all the help he can get, and they resolve to give it to him. Grega starts getting out of the van and running alongside Miro at intervals. Each runner is allowed one pacer. Between decades of experience and his GPS runner's watch, Miro hardly needs help with keeping his speed constant. To him, the pacer has a different value. As a Boston Marathon finisher and Olympic hopeful, Erin knows this all too well. "You constantly fight these battles in your head," she explains. "People don't realize their impact cheering you [fights] these demons." Even knowing that, she debates whether she should get out and support Miro. They don't know each other all that well, and a recent knee injury still nags at her. She gets out for a turn, not knowing how it will go. "If I only run for a mile, it will still help," she tells herself.

Miro passes the marathon point nine minutes ahead of Alex. Christian is the next to arrive. He hits the midpoint in 3:25 and appears to be gathering steam. He's running alone now. He started feeling a rhythm around the 20-mile mark and surged onward. Hillary chose not to follow, but she's still close. Things are finally going his way. 26.2 down, 26.2 to go.

He makes it another eight-tenths of a mile before things go bad.

His wife, Rhonda, noticed something change in him at mile 23, though he didn't feel it. He feels it now. It's not bad. Something is just...off. A hint of things to come that tastes ominously like things that have happened before. He stops to change into dry socks and shoes in order to avoid blisters. In addition to everything else they go through, it's not uncommon for athletes to lose large swathes of skin and a couple of toenails in the course of these runs. Joe Lennox, a friend from the Portland Fire Department who's come with his wife to help crew, tries to encourage him by telling him he's running in third and that Alex is in trouble. "Just keep moving forward. Stick with the plan and you'll get 'em," he encourages. Christian believes him, but he only gets another mile down the course before he stops to change back to his original shoes. His feet begin swelling too much for the new ones. Rhonda sees more warning signs and she knows. Christian's final test of faith is at hand. The question is 24 miles down a road through hell. It's time to answer like a man.

Tim Sheeper crosses the marathon point in fourth place and in visible discomfort. He stops at his crew vehicle just beyond Steve King's makeshift station to change his shoes when James Player cruises by. Milton de Sousa of Brazil isn't far behind. It's the specialist phenomenon at work. Guys who have been farther in the back the last couple of days come to the fore once they're in their natural habitat. Player and de Sousa began the day in 14th and ninth place, respectively. At the pace they're running, they'll catch Isakson and possibly even Ribeiro. The final overall standings could change dramatically.

Things disintegrate rapidly for Christian. He begins puking again. Everything comes out, and nothing that goes down will stay there. He's frying in the sun and running on empty. Ian retreats to the van and begins crying. He thought he'd seen his father suffer to the utmost yesterday, but this tops everything. Rhonda becomes worried. Christian is forced to take frequent breaks to walk. He slows down, drinks some fluid, and pukes it up. He runs a little while and then repeats the process. He can't keep doing this. Not for 22 miles. It will destroy him.

And then something changes. Christian's team of five becomes his metaphorical sixth man. Joe and Dorothy start taking turns running with him, and there's always someone by his side now. They talk to him constantly, telling him how proud they are of him, how much they love him. The van pulls over nearly every 100 yards. Rhonda gets out every time and locks eyes with Christian. He has something—maybe the most important thing—to run toward now. Her love and determination have planted small victories in this purgatory where none will grow. She yells at him repeatedly, "Do not quit!" Ian gets out and runs alongside him at intervals as well. The soft-spoken 13-year-old, with tears in his eyes, turns into Burgess Meredith from the *Rocky* movies. Rhonda slaps him hard on the butt every time he runs by. It helps keep him alert.

Another team rallies around its athlete farther up the road. Miro keeps widening the gap, but Alex is still in control. The defending champ doesn't have to be very fast, just fast enough. Miro, on the other hand, has to make every step count. His crew gives him every ounce of encouragement possible. There's another long hill at about mile 35, with a nondescript pullout marked by a blue road sign that reads SCENIC POINT. Without that and the median of yellow lines painted on the road, you might not even notice it. But Miro knows. It signals 17 miles to go—almost three-quarters of the way. Farther back, Alex comes to a complete stop. He's developed a cramp in his thigh that he can no longer ignore. Jose works to wrap an ice pack on it with a bandage. Alex spends a minute or two walking before he tries to run again. Meanwhile, Miro's crew drives back to check the distance. They return with an update, and he knows. *He's doing it. He's winning the Ultraman.* He just has to keep it up for another 16 miles. Grega ends a round of pacing and Erin gets out to take another turn. Miro looks at her as she comes alongside. "Are you tired?" he asks her.

"I'm running for you. I'm not tired." The knee cooperates, but she'd still be out here even if it didn't. Most people don't get to experience something like this many times in their life. Before the day is over, she'll run 18 miles.

Alex stays ahead of the rest of his pursuers going past Scenic Point, but these are his last moments in second place. Hillary, James Player, and Milton de Sousa gain fast on Christian, and they're upon him soon after. He doesn't know exactly how far ahead Miro is, but he doesn't need to. It's far enough. He knows his friend. He won't retire as champion. Alex's parting shot to Kona will be the most difficult run of his career.

From the lookout at Scenic Point, a straggled line of figures appear one by one over the crest of the previous hill. Down they go, and then up the long, gradual slope. It's not terribly steep, but in their state it feels like a mountain and it just seems to go on forever. Christian is the first to come into view, his crew van creeping along in front of him maybe 50 yards at a time. Hillary, Player, and de Sousa follow. It's not even a matter of time anymore; they've caught him. He slows to a walk less than 50 yards from the overlook parking. His van is waiting on him. He almost makes it.

Joe and Ian bail out and start the pit crew routine, preparing a variety of liquids in case he asks for something at the last minute. When athletes are in this state, there's no telling what they'll want or how they'll react to anything. When she was in the throes of digestive distress in 2010, Hillary asked Maik for orange juice. He drove 10 or 15 miles to a convenience store to find some. By the time he brought it back and gave it to her, things had worsened. She took one swallow of it and threw it on the ground in disgust.

Dorothy has adjusted the tone of her encouragement per Christian's request. "Just be quiet please," he says. The sound of her footsteps alongside his is comforting, but anything more is sensory overload. Physical pain has extraordinary and mysterious effects on people. It can bring them to a point where encouragement provides the opposite of its intended effect. Lucy Ryan's crew knows not to try the silly costumes and raucous applause that Dene and Amber's crews have this weekend. "God, I fucking hate it when they cheer," she said when recalling a waypoint she passed during the run in Canada. Michael Brown is the same way. "It's just so fucking hot out there, and I'm in a lot of pain, and I can't deal with anything else. Just don't even talk to me."

They don't start out that way. They're as enthusiastic at the beginning of the run as Christian or Alex. It's the course that does it. "I just go into this dark place," says Lucy. The transition looks like something from an old black-and-white werewolf movie. Michael Brown hit the half-marathon point at Ultraman Canada all smiles. Then he started breathing heavier on a hill shortly afterward. His speech became more staccato and less frequent. Just before the midpoint, the disgruntled driver of a pickup truck whizzed by a little too close for comfort and blared his horn. Michael flew into a tirade of obscenities. He spent the next 15 minutes occasionally muttering additions to a manifesto against rude drivers. He finally got over it, but for the rest of the day he only spoke to ask for nutrition or liquids. He didn't smile again until he got to the finish line.

No one who knows them would recognize the surly, snarling versions of Lucy or Michael—or any of the athletes for that matter. The ceaseless agony of moving forward coupled with the knowledge that they are not nearly as close as they want to be puts a fierce edge on despondence. Maybe the past few days have made them a little rough around the edges, but today the environment peels them like an onion. This is what it takes for some people. For Miro, the truth is something you have to find by shining your inner light through the darkest hour. For Christian, Alex, Lucy, and several others on the Queen K, it's something buried within a dark place, out here under the relentless sun.

Christian asks for water as he and Dorothy approach the van. He staggers as she runs ahead to grab a bottle for him. He barely has time to say "Uh oh" before he doubles over and vomits. Yellow-colored water flows out of him with eerie silence and hits the rocks by the road with a gentle splash. He tries to recover, but doubles back over as if someone hit him on the back of the head with a rock. More fluid empties out of him. He vomits a third time. Then he dry heaves. He figures that's got to be it. Time to drink again. Then suffer.

Hillary runs by him while this is happening. She's emerging from her own rough patch that started back at Kawaihae Hill. "I hate that hill. Even on the bike during Ironman, it's demoralizing. I went into a valley there," she says, referring to her emotional state. "I felt like death, just like in 2010. And I thought, *Oh, shit. Not again.*" She holds off on calling anyone in her crew to pace her, though. "You just wait as long as you can. You don't want to use that help until you absolutely need it." Yet fear of repeating the 2010 experience doesn't sink in. It's been a great two days. If things stay bad for the rest of the day, that's just how the ball bounces. She's prepared to run a "terrible pace" and accept whatever may come. There's nothing to do but continue putting one foot in front of the other and try to look past the impending miles of pain. She doesn't look at her GPS watch either. Ironically, the things meant to assist you turn into psychological imps when things go bad. "My watch died around mile 30, I think. But I didn't look at it most of the day. You don't want to compound problems by looking at it. You use it to control your pace when you're feeling good, but you stop when things go to hell. I mean, when it's bad, you look at yourself and say, 'This is all I can do,' so what's the point of looking at the watch? The suffering only gets magnified when you're not going fast."

But she's well out of the emotional valley by the time she summits Scenic Point. Things turned around for her at the marathon split. She began to catch sight of Christian again a few miles back, and watches him unravel as she comes up the hill. She sees him double over on the side of the road before she realizes who it is, then figures it out when she gets a closer look at the crew van. *Oh my God*, she thinks. She offers him encouragement and a smile. She even manages a little humor as she passes the race volunteers ahead. "This is harder than it looks on paper," she says. She may be the happiest person on the course right now. That's fair. After all, she may have had the longest, darkest road to get here. She's also chasing history again. If she can catch Alex, she'll become only the second woman in Ultraman history to place second in the double marathon—a feat that hasn't been accomplished since Ardis Bow did it in 1985. It hurts, but not in the same way or as badly as it did in 2010. She's not running to the finish, she's floating. Now that she's out of her valley, the rest of the day will be a personal victory lap.

The miles keep falling away. Miro isn't running the fastest race of his life, but his lead on Alex and the others is big enough that Steve King has to book it to the finish line to prepare. No one at the three-quarters point is quite sure if Miro's got it, but they're all talking excitedly. It's up to him. Jane has to go, as well. She found out earlier in the day that the florist she found on Wednesday fell through on their agreement to make leis for the arriving athletes. She has to go to the airport, where the lei stand there has been owned by the same family for years. She knows they won't let her down.

Alex has never finished lower than second place on the run here. It's always been his specialty, the weapon with which he's secured his six titles. Today the weapon fails him. Hillary overtakes him just before the three-quarter point. James Player and Milton de Sousa aren't far behind. The lack of training this year has caught up to Alex. Maybe it seems unfair that an athlete of his caliber can't rely more on the fitness he spent decades building to stay ahead of the others, but what it really shows is just how tough the competition in this sport has become. Instead of racing Ultraman Hawaii this year, Dave Matheson chose to do Ironman Florida in early November. He finished the race in 9:08:56—faster than some of the pro men. Both he and Craig Percival are already planning future runs in Hawaii. Whoever wants to keep up with them will have to be in top shape—and there are plenty of people out there who do want to keep up with them. If anything, the field is growing. And Alex has played no small part in that growth. The consequence of having such an inspirational career is that you inspire other people to follow in your footsteps. The thing about sports idols is that people dream of becoming like them, and competition is the highest form of flattery. This is either an uncharacteristic finish or the passing of a torch. It depends on whether you believe Alex is finishing a run of 52.4 miles or 30 years.

Miro is also preparing to end a lengthy run at the Old Kona Airport. The music is pumping and a crowd of maybe 50 people has gathered. Even the mayor of Kona stops by. Despite the fact that it's been around for years, he'd never heard about Ultraman before reading about it in the Saturday sports section of *West Hawaii Today*. He tells Jane that he'd like to know if there's anything he can do to help her. She smiles and says there's probably one or two items she'd appreciate getting assistance with. They agree to talk later. At the moment, Jane has to break away to prepare to fulfill more official duties of her own.

Miro is in the final stretch. Erin and the rest of the crew have gone back into the van and driven ahead to await his arrival. He doesn't sprint down the runway. He doesn't whoop and holler as he comes down the chute to the line. He smiles. He holds his fists in the air. He takes his hug and lei from Jane, celebrates with the crowd for a few minutes, then walks over to the picnic shelters in the park. It's a pretty muted reception for a new world champion. Then again, everything still hangs in the balance. He's not the champion yet. Alex still has 27 minutes to get in before Steve King can properly anoint Miro the winner.

Miro is still sitting at the park bench when the clock runs out. He's not even waiting for it when Steve King begins making the announcement, but suddenly he hears his name and the words "new world champion," followed by the cheers of the crowd. Everyone is looking his way. He rises slightly from the park bench and waves to the crowd, and then sits down just as quickly. He's still too tired—and too modest—for anything more. He resumes the conversation he was having right where he left off. When the gravity of the situation soaks in, his first reaction sounds more like a confession than a declaration. "Finally. This is 30 years of my triathlon career. I can finish with this win. I am happy now. I was three times second place, two times third place, fourth place, fifth place. I prepared this year. I trained a lot. I've wanted this for 14 years."

Christian Isakson has to stop to empty his stomach again at mile 46. His stomach wrenches so horrendously that he goes to his hands and knees right there on the road. He doesn't even care about the searing temperatures of the asphalt as he puts his forehead on the pavement. That's it for him. He answers his God like a man, and his answer is to surrender. He has followed his experience, his plan, his coach's advice, and the voice of his family and friends. It's brought him this far, but he can go no further. With no juice left in him, he asks a higher power for a loan. "Please Lord, give me the strength."

Sometimes, God answers back. "Get up Christian! Let's go! You can pray while you run but we are not stopping again!" It is neither God nor Rhonda, but Dorothy Lennox, one of his friends from Portland who came to crew. Her slight, 5'3", 110-pound frame suddenly assumes the imposing demeanor of a marine drill sergeant. He only has six miles to go. He could walk and still finish. She encourages him to jog. "Move it!"

The second finisher of the day gets what she came three years and 320 miles to achieve. Steve King doesn't need to wait to tell the world that Hillary is the women's world champion; that's been pretty evident for a while. Less obvious is the cause of her joyful tears as she crosses the line. The win feels great, but the important thing is that she's won the race against herself. She ran seven minutes faster today than she had initially planned, finishing in 7:23:55, improving on her 2010 run by 31 minutes. Despite the currents and weather holding her back on the first day, her overall time is 10 minutes better than her first effort. The only thing left for her to beat out there was Amber Monforte's course record, but that was never part of the plan. Beating someone else rarely helps you get even with yourself.

James Player arrives seven minutes later. His wife and five daughters get out of the van and jog across the finish line with him. They've been his support crew all weekend. Milton de Sousa comes in just three minutes later. His run boosts him from ninth to sixth place in the final overall standings. Player moves from 14th to ninth. Then, 10 minutes after de Sousa celebrates the end of a successful race, Alexandre Ribeiro appears at the end of the runway.

If you were just showing up and didn't have the benefit of Steve King calling it, you'd never know that Alex had such a hard day. He doesn't look much different from how he did last year. If he's slower or limping, you can't tell. If he's faking it to put on one last good show for the crowd, you can't tell that either. There's no sign of the miles of ache and injury he's endured today. He still looks invincible. Maybe he is. The clock reads 7:43:31 when he crosses the line to meet Jane for the last time. At 48 years old, he's finishing two back-to-back marathons at a pace only slightly slower than the time it takes for an average man half his age to finish one. He moves through the crowd, thanking everyone for coming out and wishing him well. Miro ambles over on legs turned to rubber to embrace his friend. Alex shakes his hand and congratulates him on his win. They don't spend much time standing around. Jose is there to usher him to the park benches.

There's an uneasy lull in the celebration. The next one in should be Christian Isakson. If it's not him, then it's possible Dorothy hasn't been able to keep him going on. And if he's stopped his crew may not be able to bring him back from the dead for a third time. Fifteen restless minutes later, the answer reveals itself at the end of the airstrip.

There are moments in sports that simply defy explanation. Space and time unravel and the equations of the known universe fail to balance. Some call them miracles. Others call them acts of God. One of Christian Isakson's favorite refrains is, "I am nothing." In the short autobiography on his website, he writes, "It would be a waste of time to write all about me when it's more about 'them.' The ones I race for, and those who keep me going. The 'them' is actually what makes me-*me*." He points to his family, his friends, the causes he supports, and, most of all, God. That mantra has never been so fully demonstrated as during his final, agonizing moments coming down the runway. He wasn't even sure if he'd make it until the last two miles. Suffering can stretch 5,280 feet into light years. He staggers down the flight line like a marionette with a few broken strings, tears streaming down his face. He's gone, physically and mentally. The question he felt God asking him this weekend was if he was prepared to give up every part of himself for his faith. He answered it like a man of faith. Christian Isakson has reduced himself to nothing. He isn't the one forcing one foot in front of the other, God is. There's no other explanation.

It's a rare occasion when Jane isn't the first person to hug an athlete upon his finish, but she recognizes the moments when she sees them.

Having made His appearance, God leaves Christian to deal with the painful aftermath. Rhonda and the rest of the crew come forward to catch him. He doesn't have to keep going, and they don't have to make him anymore. Joe and Rhonda each take an arm and hold him up. Christian shuffles two steps over to Jane and receives his lei. He sobs uncontrollably into her shoulder as she pats him on the back. Then Rhonda and Joe take him over to the outdoor shower and turn on the water. He slumps to his hands and knees and just lies there as the salt and grime rinse off him.

Amber Monforte finishes later in the afternoon, a little more than 90 minutes after Hillary. Once again, she crosses the line with Ryan and her father on either side. They join hands high over their heads. She is their champion, and they're her heroes. Everyone who has come before her today—Miro, Hillary, Alex—has demonstrated the same sentiment, but Amber underscores it somehow. Winning is nice, but it really isn't as important as how you play the game. There's the argument out there that whoever says that has never won, but Amber tramples that rhetoric as she walks the walk across the line toward Jane.

This year's race boasts the most past champions who have ever participated in an Ultraman, tying the number who were here in 2010. Miro has won in spectacularly unlikely fashion. Hillary has conquered all her doubts and regrets. Amber and Alex have bid farewells that define the character of Ultraman as much as their own. All of them have put their hearts and souls into the effort and caused themselves no small amount of damage in the process. Champagne showers and water coolers kicked across the locker room would be understandable—if they cared enough to do so. The thing is that they don't care. It's not about that for them. It never was.

An hour after crossing the line, Christian Isakson has bounced back from nothingness. He's limping around slowly, with Ian's help. He comes around the picnic shelter closest to the finish line, where Alex, Miro, Tim Sheeper, and several others are sitting with their crews. They're all exchanging stories about the last few days. Freed from the requirement to be totally focused on their own pain and performance, they finally get to hear the greater scope of how the race unfolded around them. Everyone is smiling, but the weariness in their eyes gives them the appearance of having just been through a natural disaster—reveling in the camaraderie of the shared experience but also relieved that it's over.

Christian is comparatively quiet. He's in a daze, trying to gather his own sense of the last few hours, let alone the entire journey. The game face that's been carved onto him for the last three days has eroded, replaced by a troubled look, as though he's aware that something is wrong but can't figure out exactly what. Alex reaches out from behind him and puts a consoling hand on his shoulder. Christian has discovered a place that few people can find and fewer still go. It's incomprehensible to all except those who have been there, and it has driven more than one athlete crazy trying to map its shores or describe its landscape. Alex knows it well; you can see it in his eyes. He doesn't say much to Christian. He doesn't have to. It's enough to know that he understands. They have a much different relationship now than they did upon that first meeting at the Kona Sheraton. The rookie isn't a rookie anymore. He's much more than just another finisher, too. Alex sees something much greater in Christian. Something from that uncharted badland that's now their common ground.

Its potential for greatness may only be matched by its consequences. Jose Poinciano ushers Alex toward the crew vehicle in due course. He's mothering him again, but Alex's grin is gone this time. He's hurt enough now that he's ready and willing to get back to a room where they can tend to his body. Nine runs in 11 years. Six wins. Three decades of Ironman. He doesn't feel old that often, but today is one of those times. Jose knows it, and he's happy that this is Alex's last Ultraman. For 30 years he's been at Alex's side. He talks about the retirement with the same matter-of-fact angst. "I'm glad this is it for him," Jose says. "I told him, if he came back again I would not come. It's time. He needs to retire. This is too much. It's all been too much.

"Did you know that the first time he won this race he carried the Brazilian flag across the finish? And the triathlon magazines in Brazil wrote a 200-word column about him! He should have been on the cover! After all he's won and given to the sport, no one ever gave him any help. He coaches and trains and races around the world, and do they recognize him? No! It's shameful. Everything is about soccer, soccer, soccer in Brazil.

"And the running and athletics committees are corrupt. I didn't know how much better it could be until I came to run a marathon in the United

States for the first time. That's when I knew I would leave Brazil and never go back. I wish he had, too. I told him, 'You've got to stop doing this. You've got kids. You can't keep doing this for people if they're not going to help you. Think of yourself for once. It's time.'"

Alex admits as much in the moments before Jose comes to whisk him away. Surrounded by friends and admirers, he casts a thoughtful gaze out to the sun as it closes on the ocean horizon and grows distant. "I'm tired now," he says.

The words are magic. Suddenly everyone else disappears, and Alexandre Ribeiro has it all to himself one last time—the finish line, the virgin beach, the amber sky, the park bench, the parking lot at the end of the world. He's been coming here for 29 years, but maybe never again. Everyone has to go sometime. Valerie Silk. Scott Tinley. Curtis Tyler. Cowman. Amber Monforte. Even Jane Bockus, eternal as she appears. Why not him? Why not now? One answer is as good as another, because the questions aren't really that important. The only one that really matters to him is the same one that all the others have had to answer. This has become such a big part of his life. Can he find a way to be happy when he's no longer part of it?

He can. Because somewhere along the way he found the secret to being happy. "The life is very simple," he says. "I don't need the money. I have the ocean, the mountain. People work for money. I work for my life. I'm happy every day. When I wake up at 6:00, I say, 'Hey, kids. Watch the sun. See the birds.' It's so simple. People say, 'No, I need the big car, the boat.' I say, 'For what?' Look at my bike. It's 10 years old. It's good enough. I have my legs.

"I talk to clients every day. One of them came in one day looking sad, and I asked him what was wrong. He said, 'My life is terrible. I keep working for a nice house and it never comes.' I pointed out to the ocean and told him, 'Look. That's free.' I named my children Kaillani, Kaipo, and Maila—three Hawaiian names. Ocean celestial, Sweetheart, Skin Brown. It's perfect."

After a day of people seeking their own personal moments of truth, Alex provides the all-encompassing, absolute truth. It is the essence coursing through all these people as they run through the lava fields of Hawaii. Alex ends his journey here. Christian is just getting started. Amber pauses for a moment on her path. The way ahead isn't clear to Hillary—yet. But they are no different from each other, or any of the other 32 people who began the race this weekend—or Jane, Sheryl, Dave, Steve Brown, or Tony Horton. It's only on the last day that Ultraman stops looking like an endurance race. The lava fields peel back the layers of the event itself just as they peel the athletes. And when it's finally stripped bare you see it for what it really is: the journey of love that Curtis Tyler meant it to be.

That's what everyone here knows and what drives them. When you're in love with something, you don't ask how far you have to go. You go as far as you have to. The distance is different for everyone. Everyone runs his or her own race, and you can never lose so long as you don't lose the love. Love asked for a lot of miles out of Alexandre Ribeiro and Miro Kregar. It holds a lot of miles in store for Christian, Amber, and Hillary. It's asked a lot of Jane Bockus and Steve Brown, and it will probably do the same of Sheryl and Dave Cobb. But they all say the same thing: it's worth every inch.

chapter nineteen

The Difference

"I had pro offers from the Detroit Lions and Green Bay Packers, who were pretty hard up for linemen in those days. If I had gone into professional football the name Gerry Ford might have been a household word today."

—Gerald Ford

AMBER PERFORMS ONE FINAL test of endurance after the finish. Eventually, Miro, Hillary, and Alex retire for the day. But Amber sticks around. In past years she's always moved quickly from the finish line to an ice bath and then a hotel room on the first two days. But she always sticks around until the end of the last day. It's her one chance to celebrate everyone else, and this year it's her last opportunity to be part of the Ultraman experience.

Dene Sturm doesn't give up. From the beginning, she knew this part of the race would be all mental. She's not a fast runner, but she can finish as long as she can withstand the punishment. Smiling helps. And that's what she does for 11 hours and 20 minutes, right to the line. Then she bursts into tears of joy. Maybe there's no explanation for how such a physically brutal experience could become the achievement of a person's dream. Or maybe it's one that only people like Dene can understand.

There are just four men left on the course after her. Lars Heurich cuts it close with an 11:57:03 finish, but Jason Nixon takes the cake. He doesn't make it onto the airfield for almost another minute, leaving himself only 120 seconds to cover a quarter-mile. The crowd screams wildly for him to hurry, but it looks as if he's got nothing left. The clock just keeps running out, and he never picks up speed. Even Steve King abandons his signature detached pleasantness and pleads desperately with Jason to hurry. Finally he can take no more. "For goodness sake! Someone get out there and help him or he's not going to make it!"

For all that Jane Bockus and Valerie Silk have in common in the way they have loved and protected their races over time, there are a few subtle differences between them. Things like minor rules. Take crawling, for instance. It's illegal in Ultraman. Had Julie Moss crawled the last 50 yards in Jane's race as she did in Ironman, she would have been given a penalty and listed as a DNF for missing the cutoff. On the other hand, Valerie necessarily had to restrict outside aid after Ironman got too big for support crews. Other than taking some Gatorade and a PowerBar at the aid stations from official volunteers, Ironman was a strictly individual effort. But here, a little helping hand is still allowed. As Jason shuffles onto the green mat of the finish chute with just seconds left, a human wave surges out from the crowd and engulfs him. They grab him by the arms and shove him in the back with such force that he nearly falls over, but it does the trick. He's an official finisher in 11:59:59. A defining moment in a man's life turns on one little rule.

That's how it's different here. That's what Ironman would be like today if it hadn't been for the television coverage and the prize money and everything that came after. Ironman became a big thing. Ultraman stayed small but embraced bigger things.

And just like that, just like every year, it's over. Bill Armer and the crew of volunteers begin gathering up the green AstroTurf mat and French barricades that make the finish chute as the crowd congratulates Jason. The rest comes down in less than 20 minutes. Once it's all packed into the trucks there's no indication it was ever there. The only thing resembling a closing ceremony is the ad hoc parade of cars that forms as everyone drives back down the runway to get on the main road.

And just like that, all's quiet at the parking lot at the end of the world.

chapter twenty

Happily Ever After

"Baseball is drama with an endless run and an ever-changing cast."

—*Joe Garagiola*

MONDAY EVENING IS THE POSTRACE BANQUET. The volunteers, athletes, crews, and families gather together one last time. Each finisher will receive a plaque—those who made all the cutoffs get one in the shape of the island and the DNFs get a rectangular one—and they all get to tell their story. There are a couple of special guests this year. Vito Bialla came to crew for Keith Bergh. Curtis Tyler normally travels on Thanksgiving, but not this year; he gives a short speech after Jane introduces him. It's a memorable moment, not because of anything he says, but for all that can't be said that gets communicated anyway. Hardly anyone in the room knows what Curtis did for Ultraman, except for Jane and Kurt Madden and a few others who actually saw him do it. No one knows all the details of his life story and how it inspired him to bring Ultraman into becoming what it is. But everyone understands it. You can see it in the way they made their own journeys around the island this weekend. You can hear it in the way they tell their stories.

It was magical that Curtis found in Jane Bockus a person who would keep faith in his idea of the journey and turn it into a legacy 30 years and going. And though it's been a tough year, Sheryl and Dave have proven they've got what it takes to keep the legacy alive. The look in Christian Isakson's eyes as he watches Alexandre Ribeiro step to the podium and speak reverently about how Kurt Madden inspired him 30 years ago says that there's plenty of magic to come. Maybe it's already at work.

Hillary reconsiders her previous vow never to do this again after getting it right this time. She's the world champ, after all. There's a title to defend. But more than that, there's a journey to take, people to come back and see, and something else about Ultraman that pulls her back. Statistically, she has fewer days in Ironman ahead of her than she does behind her, but she's still very young for this sport. Maybe this is her new calling.

She gets a phone call from one of her sponsors earlier in the day. Word has spread via social media that she's won. She's surprised to get a congratulatory call so soon. She's even more surprised when they tell her how they want to express their encouragement. "We will comp your entire trip for this. Just send us the invoice when you get home," they tell her. She's blown away. It will be a while before it really starts to sink in, when sponsors and people promoting her upcoming appearances start putting her new title on their signs, but Hillary has accomplished something few people in the world ever do. She's a world champion. Forget about prize money, televised coverage, magazine covers, or anything else.

"For sure, this is something I'll always have," she says, "and few people ever get to call themselves a world champion. I don't see mine as on the same level as the Ironman World Championship. They're different. But this is definitely one of the top accomplishments of my life. It's up there with my win at Ironman Wisconsin. And the difference isn't whether it's Ironman or not. It's that I had to work really hard to win that race in the last mile. In some ways, the 2010 race stands out more to me. I had to give everything I had for that." For her, there's something more important to take away from a race than a trophy. For as good as she is at running against the same clock as everyone else, she's learned even more about how to live according to her own expectations.

Amber announces that she's taking a break from ultra endurance racing for a while. She and Ryan are going to explore other parts of the world, and find new ways to test their endurance. It's time for them to actually do things together rather than for him to chase her around in a van. Climbing Mount Kilimanjaro is on their list. They've also talked about racing the Tour Divide, a 2,700-mile mountain bike race from Canada to Mexico, along the Rocky Mountains. There are no support crews allowed in that race. Participants carry their own gear, so Amber and Ryan can do it together. Like Ultraman, there's no prize money for the winner, no media coverage, and very few participants. On its website, the organizers describe it as less of a race than an adventure.

People come, people go. Ultraman is a stage, and the athletes merely actors. Everyone is the protagonist of their own story arc, but at some point they all go their own way. For some that means a return to Ironman. For others it means venturing further out into the undiscovered country of endurance, where the next improbable contest awaits. But every one of them will always have a place here, where the magic and the journey continue without end, and the stories keep getting told year after year. Sometimes the heroes of forgotten years can return for special guest appearances, like Curtis and Kurt Madden did today. But even if they don't, the collective spirit that all of them are part of will keep their memory forever.

What's On Your Mind?

THE RECKONING WAS INEVITABLE.

The Ohana Loa Board meeting as Steve Brown and Jane envisioned it never happens. With all the postrace activities, pleasantries, and cleanup to attend to, there just isn't time. Instead, the group settles for a lunch meeting with Tony Horton so they can iron out a few details and finish some necessary business to move forward with the Australian event. A lot is left unsaid and unresolved. On December 4, Sheryl posts an update to the Ultraman Facebook group page from the official Ohana Loa account: "Ohana Loa, Inc. is excited to announce the expansion of our Ultraman Ohana to the Land Down Under. The first Ultraman Australia will be held in Noosa in May 2015."

The Ultraman community reacts with great enthusiasm, and comments on the post suggest the race will sell out as soon as registration opens. Then on May 8, 2014, Juan Craveri makes another kind of race announcement— one that draws comments of a starkly different nature. He discovers a website for an event called Ultraman Europe, which states that its inaugural race will take place in Mallorca, Spain, in September 2015. The page has no further information or links, but it bears what appears to be the official petroglyph-man logo of Ultraman, as owned by Ohana Loa. He posts the link to the website on the Ultraman Facebook group and asks if it's official. An hour after it goes up, David Cobb responds in the comments: "WTF????? This event has NOT been cleared with the Ohana Loa Board. This is the first I have heard of it and I do NOT consider it official in any way until all the Ohana Loa Board members vote on whether to allow such an event. This announcement is premature at best, and completely without approval!"

Eighteen minutes later, Steve Brown makes an extraordinarily rare use of social media by posting his own comment:

> Hi Everyone, While this announcement is slightly premature we are working closely with the group in Mallorca to bring you Ultraman Europe in September of 2015. We felt it was time to bring an official Ultraman back to Europe to replace the former Ultraman UK. We will make a more formal announcement shortly with more detail once the rest of the Board has been briefed and consulted. As David mentioned this announcement was premature but I guess that is the new world of Social Media. Steve.

Dave and Sheryl are utterly shocked. After everything they've been through in the last year, they thought they'd established at least an uneasy stability within the Ohana Loa board. Sheryl talks to Jane later in the day to confirm if her worst fears are true. They are. Over the last several months, Steve has pushed Jane hard in private conversations about a group in Europe interested in putting on the Mallorca race. It started with simple permission to explore possibilities. But Jane is the fairy godmother who can't say no. Soon enough Steve cajoled her into giving the organizers vast authority to start logistical planning. Worst of all, neither Jane nor Steve ever mentioned anything to Dave or Sheryl.

Feeling betrayed and powerless, Sheryl resigns from the Ohana Loa Board. Dave does the same the next day. They'll stay on as directors of the Hawaii race, but they remove themselves from all decisions regarding the operations of the Ultraman series. The complications of such rapid expansion deteriorate the principles of Ultraman at the least and at worst run completely counter to them. As hard as it is to tell Jane she won't stand by her anymore, Sheryl believes it's more important now than ever before to stand by principles. Suddenly, Jane is without her right hand, and Ultraman is without an heir apparent. Feeling torn like never before over these events, both women reach out for counsel from the same man: Curtis Tyler.

Weeks of soul searching, legal consultations, and a board meeting or two ensue. Thirty years spent making Ultraman what it is come down to this. Some people think that Jane has been doing it too long and is too tired to make the hard choices necessary to preserve the race. Even Sheryl doubts that Ultra Mom can put the brakes on Steve at this point. But Jane has stood with principle over people before. She nearly walked away from Ultraman in 2000 when Vito Bialla changed things too much. She knows how to put her foot down and when to do it. This is one of those times, and that's exactly what she does. Jane dissolves the Ohana Loa Board entirely. In its rush to branch out, Ultraman has gotten too far away from its roots. If the race is going to survive, it has to get back to them.

The year 2013 was one of unprecedented upheaval in Ultraman, and for all they've built together the cost has been high. The UMUK controversy remains unresolved. Simon Smith says he'll call the 2015 race UCUK, for "Ultra-Challenge United Kingdom," but it's still UMUK for 2014. Jane has an even worse debacle on her hands. Somehow, Ohana Loa has come to pursue all those material things Alexandre Ribeiro said don't matter and will only make a person unhappy. And Jane is most certainly unhappy. This is not what she wanted—for herself or for the sport. This was never what it was supposed to be about. And if this is what it is going to be about, she wants no part of it. There's only one thing to do.

In late June, she tells those closest to her of her decision. The European organizers can come to Ultraman Canada in July to make their proposal to the new board of directors of Ohana Loa. The new board members will be Jane, Curtis Tyler, Peter Bourne, Sheryl, and Dave. But not Steve Brown. He loves the event and he's been passionately dedicated to it for years, but loving something requires you to be satisfied with the way it is. He's made it clear over the last couple of years that he's not satisfied. He has always worried about the future of Ultraman, but he's forgotten that the whole purpose of Ultraman is to stay true to the past. The changes he's tried to make and the way he's gone about them look and feel a lot like Ironman, the big thing that forgot how to embrace the bigger things and abandoned its own history. Jane refuses to let him influence Ultraman that way any longer. Steve responds to the decision after the 2014 edition of Ultraman Canada. On September 30, he issues a press release announcing that starting in 2015 his race will no longer be associated with Ultraman. He renames it Ultra Canada 515. The website and race logo have been completely redesigned. After more than 20 years of friendship with Jane, he doesn't even give her a call or send her an email to tell her beforehand. She finds out the same way as everyone else.

What happens next is anyone's guess. Consuela and Trung Lively will most likely keep theirs an Ultraman event. Tony Horton is locked into a contract with Ultraman for one year. After that, he could form a series with Steve's race in Canada. And Steve still has his partners interested in creating the race in Europe. For as much rough water Jane and her friends have been through in the last year, the storm clouds remain stretched to the horizon. But she's still at the wheel. Instead of stepping completely away from the conflict like Valerie Silk did, Jane decides to stick it out. For how long is anyone's guess, but when she eventually does leave, the race is once again in secure hands. Love endures. The race will go on.

Papyrus, You Little Bastard

IN THE END, there are only so many stories you can tell. Some people—too many—have to be left out. The hardest choices I had to make in putting this book together were in deciding whose stories to tell. I picked those that I thought were most representative of the entire group, but there's still one left to tell.

I spent countless hours talking to dozens of people during the 2013 Ultraman season. I began the process of documenting Ultraman as a journalist—objective and detached. It seemed as if that would be easy enough. After all, the group seemed small and insular. But the more I learned, the more they shared with me. The more I understood of them, the more they welcomed me. It wasn't until Darwin Holt told me outright during an interview that it occurred to me, too: "You're part of this, Jim." I'm forced to agree. Besides, being such an authoritative figure within the Ultraman community, he won't accept any argument. And I do consider him a friend.

I'm friends with many in the Ultraman community now. Like most of them, the physical distance between us forces us to use Facebook to remain in contact with each other. We chat, share photos, and exchange news on the Ultraman page. But there is nothing I like more (and I always hit the "Like" button to show it) than to see Adam Peruta's newest addition to his photo album titled "Papyrus, you little bastard." Adam is a professor of media and marketing at Syracuse University. Among his pet peeves are poorly designed fonts in advertising. To make the point with his students, he created the photo album showing the use of Papyrus in popular advertisements.

I met Adam during the 2012 Ultraman World Championships We sat by each other at the awards banquet. He kept checking his phone during the ceremony. I asked him what he was so anxious to see. He told me that a photographer was covering the race for Slowtwitch.com, and that each day he posted a daily update of the race with photos of the athletes. "I'm never going to be that fast, and maybe it's narcissistic. But dammit, just once I want to say that I made it into the Slowtwitch photo gallery." We had a long discussion about narcissistic and intrinsic impulses in Ultraman athletes, the importance of news coverage to a race's success, and how social media influences our perceptions of self and society. We became friends.

Adam never made it into the Slowtwitch gallery. In the end, there isn't enough room for everyone in the photos either. Adam's story is bigger than the little bit I've told, but there just aren't the pages for the rest. But what is here—and perhaps more importantly what *isn't*—says something about Ultraman just as important as what Hillary or Amber or Alex or Christian have contributed. At every turn in this wonderfully, unbelievably true story full of good people doing amazing things, there were scores of others just as inspiring who were squeezed outside the margins of the printed page. Their stories are mesmerizing, tragic, humorous, and inspiring. I can't tell them all, but I'll never forget them. I don't want the reader to forget that either. That's why I typed all the chapter titles in Papyrus. I never forgot Adam. Though you never saw him, he was always there, in every chapter. That little bastard is my little story about Adam. And, like every other story in this book, it represents much greater things.